"The Marv Tolman science activity books were always a hit with teachers and were valuable for use with my science method course students."

—Dr. Donald R. Daugs, professor emeritus, Utah State University

"I love the Hands-On Science books by Marv Tolman. They sit right next to my desk within easy reach. The lesson plans are teacher friendly and student friendly. The books are put together in such a way that it is easy to find any subject. From Kindergarten to 6th grade the lessons are set up for all students to use. I know, I have used them in all grades and my students love to be involved in science. I highly recommend these books for any teacher whether you struggle with science or are an expert in the field."

—Marilyn Bulkley, fifth grade teacher, Garfield School District, Panguitch, Utah

"Our sixth-, seventh-, and eighth-grade students have literally worn out our copies of Dr. Tolman's Hands-On Activities. We have two copies of each activity book and students select them for their concise instructions, excellent diagrams, and easy-to-find materials. Even though the title indicates grades K-6, students and teachers in seventh and eighth grades found the activities very helpful in classroom demonstrations and as a beginning point for science fair problems. I loved the way that the activities are divided into the three different disciplines: physical, earth, and life. It was fast and easy to locate just what you needed using the table of contents organization. There was always an activity for whatever concept my students were learning. Our school will need to purchase the newly revised activity books."

—Rosalee Riddle, science teacher, Red Hills Middle School, Richfield, Utah and science curriculum coordinator, Sevier School District, Richfield, Utah

"I began working with Marv Tolman ten years ago. I was new to the world of elementary teaching. I had heard of a workshop that helped teachers simplify, and pinpoint science concepts that could be taught repeatedly through hands-on, basic application. That workshop was the first of many and I still—ten years later-use the concepts to teach my students. The basic and simple mechanics of science that are incorporated into these lessons reach the gifted and struggling learner and can be adapted and adjusted to time and to the needs of students' individual levels and learning styles."

—Marcie H. Judd, fourth grade teacher, Valley Elementary School, Kanab School District., Kanab, Utah.

"Many elementary teachers lack science background knowledge. The Hands-On Science Activities series provides teachers with both background knowledge and engaging methods to help all students learn science concepts. Marv explains them using simple, clear, and concise language that equips teachers to teach with confidence. These books have increased both the accuracy and the quality of science education."

—Julie Cook, Title I Literacy Coordinator and former kindergarten teacher, Logan City School District, Logan, Utah.

Jossey-Bass Teacher

Jossey-Bass Teacher provides K–12 teachers with essential knowledge and tools to create a positive and lifelong impact on student learning. Trusted and experienced educational mentors offer practical classroom-tested and theory-based teaching resources for improving teaching practice in a broad range of grade levels and subject areas. From one educator to another, we want to be your first source to make every day your best day in teaching. *Jossey-Bass Teacher* resources serve two types of informational needs—essential knowledge and essential tools.

Essential knowledge resources provide the foundation, strategies, and methods from which teachers may design curriculum and instruction to challenge and excite their students. Connecting theory to practice, essential knowledge books rely on a solid research base and time-tested methods, offering the best ideas and guidance from many of the most experienced and well-respected experts in the field.

Essential tools save teachers time and effort by offering proven, ready-to-use materials for in-class use. Our publications include activities, assessments, exercises, instruments, games, ready reference, and more. They enhance an entire course of study, a weekly lesson, or a daily plan. These essential tools provide insightful, practical, and comprehensive materials on topics that matter most to K–12 teachers.

Hands-On Earth Science Activities for Grades K–6

Second Edition

Marvin N. Tolman, Ed.D.

JOSSEY-BASS
A Wiley Imprint
www.josseybass.com

Published by Jossey-Bass
A Wiley Imprint
989 Market Street, San Francisco, CA 94103-1741   www.josseybass.com

Jossey-Bass books and products are available through most bookstores. To contact Jossey-Bass directly call our Customer Care Department within the U.S. at 800-956-7739, outside the U.S. at 317-572-3986, or fax 317-572-4002.

Jossey-Bass also publishes its books in a variety of electronic formats. Some content that appears in print may not be available in electronic books.

ISBN-13: 978-0-7879-7866-2
ISBN-10: 0-7879-7866-3

Printed in the United States of America
SECOND EDITION
PB Printing   10 9 8 7 6 5 4 3 2 1

*I dedicate this book to
the late Dr. James O. Morton, my mentor, dear friend, and
coauthor of* **The Science Curriculum Activities Library,**
from which the current series evolved.

Acknowledgments

Mentioning the names of all individuals who contributed to *The Science Problem-Solving Curriculum Library* would require an additional volume. The author is greatly indebted to the following:

- Teachers and students of all levels.
- School districts throughout the United States who cooperated by supporting and evaluating ideas and methods used in this book.
- The late Dr. James O. Morton, my mentor, dear friend, and co-author of *The Science Curriculum Activities Library,* from which the current series evolved.
- Dr. Garry R. Hardy, my teaching partner for many years, for his constant encouragement and creative ideas.
- Finally, my angel Judy, for without her love, support, encouragement, patience, and acceptance, these books could never have been completed.

Contents

Section One: Air

Section Two: Water

Section Three: Weather

Section Four: The Earth

Contents

Section Five: Ecology

Section Six: Above the Earth

Section Seven: Beyond the Earth

About the Author

Dr. Marvin N. Tolman trained as an educator at Utah State University and began his career as a teaching principal in rural southeastern Utah. The next eleven years were spent teaching grades one through six in schools of San Juan and Utah Counties and earning graduate degrees.

Currently professor of elementary education, Dr. Tolman has been teaching graduate and undergraduate science methods courses at Brigham Young University since 1975. He has served as a consultant to school districts, taught workshops in many parts of the United States, and published numerous articles in professional journals. With Dr. James O. Morton, Dr. Tolman wrote the three-book series of elementary science activities called *The Science Curriculum Activities Library*, published in 1986.

Dr. Tolman now lives with his wife, Judy, in Spanish Fork, Utah, where they have raised five children.

About the Library

The Science Problem-Solving Curriculum Library evolved from an earlier series by the same author, with Dr. James O. Morton as coauthor: *The Science Curriculum Activities Library.* The majority of the activities herein were also in the earlier publication, and the successful activity format has been retained. Many activities have been revised, and several new activities have been added. A significant feature of this series, which was not in the original, is a section called "For Problem Solvers," included in most of the activities. This section provides ideas for further investigation and related activities for students who are motivated to extend their study beyond the procedural steps of a given activity. We hope that most students will pursue at least some of these extensions and benefit from them.

The Science Problem-Solving Curriculum Library provides teachers with hundreds of science activities that give students hands-on experience related to many science topics. To be used in conjunction with whatever texts and references you have, the Library includes three books, each providing activities that explore a different field. The books are individually titled as follows:

- *Hands-On Life Science Activities for Grades K–6*
- *Hands-On Physical Science Activities for Grades K–6*
- *Hands-On Earth Science Activities for Grades K–6*

More than ever before, children of today grow up in a world impacted by science and technology. A basic understanding of nature and an appreciation for the world around them are gifts too valuable to deny these precious young people, who will be the problem solvers of tomorrow. In addition, a strong science program with a discovery/inquiry approach can enrich the development of mathematics, reading, social studies, and other areas of the curriculum. The activities in the Library develop these skills. Most activities call for thoughtful responses, with questions that encourage analyzing, synthesizing, and inferring, instead of simply answering yes or no.

There is not a clear division between the life, physical, and earth sciences; each of these general areas of study overlaps the other two. This is especially true for the earth sciences. Ecology deals with the interrelationship of organisms and their environment, with content from the biological, physical, and earth sciences. Geology also requires knowledge in all of the basic scientific fields. In general, earth science is interdisciplinary.

Development of thinking and reasoning skills, in addition to learning basic content information, are the main goals of the activities outlined herein. Learning how to learn, and how to apply the various tools of learning, are more useful in a person's life than is the acquisition of large numbers of scientific facts. Students are encouraged to explore, invent, and create as they develop skills with the processes of science. The learning of scientific facts is a by-product of this effort, and increased insight and retention associated with facts learned are virtually assured.

How to Use This Book

This book consists of more than 160 easy-to-use, hands-on activities in the following areas of earth sciences:

- Air
- Water
- Weather
- The Earth
- Ecology
- Above the Earth
- Beyond the Earth

Use in the Classroom

The activities herein are designed as discovery activities that students can usually perform quite independently. The teacher is encouraged to provide students (usually in small groups) with the materials listed and a copy of the activity from the beginning through the "Procedure." The section titled "Teacher Information" is not intended for student use, but rather to assist the teacher with discussion following the hands-on activity, as students share their observations. (Be sure to cover this section before copying.) Discussion of conceptual information prior to completing the hands-on activity can interfere with the discovery process.

Correlation with National Standards

The National Research Council produced the *National Science Education Standards.* Published in 1996 by the National Academy of Sciences, this document has become the standard by which many sets of state and local science standards have been developed since that time. The document is available from the National Academy Press, 2101 Constitution Avenue, NW, Box 285, Washington, DC 10055. It is also available online by searching for National Science Education Standards.

For grades K–12 there are seven Standards, identified as Standards A–G. Within each grade-level cluster (K–4, 5–8, 9–12) general sub-parts are identified.

Content Standard A: Science as Inquiry

Content Standard B: Physical Science

Content Standard C: Life Science

Content Standard D: Earth and Space Science

Content Standard E: Science and Technology

Content Standard F: Science in Personal and Social Perspectives

Content Standard G: History and Nature of Science

This book is one of a series of three books that focus separately on the Life, Earth, and Physical Sciences. Following is a list of the Content Standards to which the set of three books relate for Levels K–4 and 5–8 of the National Science Education Standards. Collectively, the Standards identified for correlation purposes are Standards A, B, C, D, and F. These Standards and their sub-parts are listed below. In the Standards document, the sub-parts are in a bulleted list. They are numbered here to facilitate referencing them individually within this book. The appropriate Standards and sub-parts are repeated in each section of all three books to provide a section-by-section correlation with the National Standards. This information is found on the page immediately preceding the first activity of each section in each book. Since the activities are designed for inquiry, you will note that Content Standard A is included in all sections of each book.

K–4 Content Standard A: Science as Inquiry
As a result of activities in grades K–4, all students should develop:

1. Abilities necessary to do scientific inquiry
2. Understanding about scientific inquiry

K–4 Content Standard B: Physical Science
As a result of activities in grades K–4, all students should develop understanding of

1. Properties of objects and materials
2. Position and motion of objects
3. Light, heat, electricity, and magnetism

K–4 Content Standard C: Life Science

As a result of activities in grades K–4, all students should develop understanding of

1. The characteristics of organisms
2. Life cycles of organisms
3. Organisms and environments

K–4 Content Standard D: Earth and Space Science

As a result of activities in grades K–4, all students should develop understanding of

1. Properties of earth materials
2. Objects in the sky
3. Changes in earth and sky

K–4 Content Standard F: Science in Personal and Social Perspectives

As a result of activities in grades K–4, all students should develop understanding of

1. Personal health
2. Characteristics and changes in populations
3. Types of resources
4. Changes in environments
5. Science and technology in local challenges

5–8 Content Standard A: Science as Inquiry

As a result of activities in grades 5–8, all students should develop:

1. Abilities necessary to do scientific inquiry
2. Understanding about scientific inquiry

5–8 Content Standard B: Physical Science

As a result of activities in grades 5–8, all students should develop understanding of

1. Properties and changes of properties in matter
2. Motions and forces
3. Transfer of energy

5–8 Content Standard C: Life Science

As a result of activities in grades 5–8, all students should develop understanding of

1. Structures and function in living systems
2. Reproduction and heredity
3. Regulation and behavior
4. Populations and ecosystems
5. Diversity and adaptations of organisms

5–8 Content Standard D: Earth and Space Science

As a result of activities in grades 5–8, all students should develop understanding of

1. Structure of the earth system
2. Earth's history
3. Earth in the solar system

5–8 Content Standard F: Science in Personal and Social Perspectives

As a result of activities in grades 5–8, all students should develop understanding of

1. Personal health
2. Populations, resources, and environments
3. Natural hazards
4. Risks and benefits
5. Science and technology in society

Teacher Qualifications

Two important qualities of the elementary teacher as a scientist are (1) commitment to helping students acquire learning skills and (2) recognition of the value of science and its implications in the life and learning of the child.

You do not need to be a scientist to conduct an effective and exciting science program at the elementary level. Interest, creativity, enthusiasm, and willingness to become involved and try something new are the qualifications the teacher of elementary science needs most. Your expertise will grow, and your "comfort zone" will expand as you teach, and as you find opportunities to expand your knowledge in the topics you teach. If you haven't yet really tried teaching hands-on science, you will find it to be a lot like eating peanuts—you can't eat just one. Try it. The excitement and enthusiasm you see in your students will bring you back to it again and again.

Early Grades

Many of these concrete activities are easily adaptable for children in the early grades. Although the activity instructions ("Procedures") are written for the student who can read and follow the steps, that does not preclude teachers of the lower grades from using the activities with their students. With oral instructions and slight modifications, many of these activities can be used with kindergarten, first-grade, and second-grade students. In some activities, steps that involve procedures that go beyond the level of the child can simply be omitted and yet offer the child an experience that plants the seed for a concept that will germinate and grow later on.

Teachers of the early grades will probably choose to bypass many of the "For Problem Solvers" sections. That's okay. The "For Problem Solvers" sections are provided for those who are especially motivated and want to go further. Use the basic activities for which procedural steps are written and enjoy worthwhile learning experiences together with your young students.

Capitalize on Interest

These materials are both nongraded and nonsequential. Areas of greatest interest and need can be emphasized. As you gain experience with using the activities, your skill in guiding students toward appropriate discoveries and insights will increase.

Organizing for an Activity–Centered Approach

Current trends encourage teachers to use an activity-based program, supplemented by the use of textbooks and many other reference materials, including those available on the Internet. The activities herein encourage hands-on discovery, which enhances the development of valuable learning skills through direct experience. Opportunities abound for students to work together, and such collaboration is encouraged throughout.

One of the advantages of this approach is the elimination of the need for all students to have the same book at the same time, freeing a substantial portion of the textbook money for purchasing a variety of materials and references, including other textbooks, trade books, audio- and videotapes, video discs, models, and other visuals. References should be acquired that lend themselves developmentally to a variety of approaches, subject-matter emphases, and levels of reading difficulty.

Grabbers

The sequence of activities within the sections of this book is flexible and may be adjusted according to interest, availability of materials, time of year, or other factors. Many of the activities in each section can be used independently as *grabbers,* to capture student interest. Used this way, they can help to achieve several specific objectives:

- To assist in identifying student interests and selecting topics for study.
- To provide a wide variety of interesting and exciting hands-on activities from many areas of science. As students investigate activities that are of particular interest, they will likely be motivated to try additional related activities in the same section of the book.
- To introduce teachers and students to the discovery/inquiry approach.
- To be used for those occasions when only a short period of time is available and a high-interest independent activity is needed.

Unique Features

The following points should be kept in mind while using this book:

1. Most of these activities can be used with several grade levels, with little adaptation.
2. The student is the central figure when using the discovery/inquiry approach to hands-on learning.

3. The main goals are problem solving and the development of critical-thinking skills. The learning of content is a spin-off, but it is possibly learned with greater insight and meaning than if it were the main objective.

4. It attempts to prepare teachers for inquiry-based instruction and to sharpen their guidance and questioning techniques.

5. Most materials needed for the activities are readily available in the school or at home.

6. Activities are intended to be open and flexible and to encourage the extension of skills through the use of as many outside resources as possible: (a) The use of parents, aides, and resource people of all kinds is recommended throughout; (b) the library, media center, and other school resources, as well as classroom reading centers related to the areas of study, are essential in the effective teaching and learning of science; and (c) educational television, videos, and Internet resources can greatly enrich the science program.

7. With the exception of the activities labeled "teacher demonstration" or "whole-class activity," students are encouraged to work individually, in pairs, or in small groups. In most cases the teacher gathers and organizes the materials, arranges the learning setting, and serves as a resource person. In many instances, the materials listed and the procedural steps are all students will need in order to perform the activities.

8. Information is given in "To the Teacher" at the beginning of each section and in "Teacher Information" at the end of each activity to help you develop your content background and your questioning and guidance skills, in cases where such help is needed.

Integrating

Students do more than just science as they become involved in science inquiry activities. Such experiences are loaded with applications of math, reading, and language arts. They often involve social studies, art, music, and physical education as well. This is true of activities throughout this book. Meaningful application and reinforcement of skills learned throughout the curriculum are embedded in the child's science experiences. These connections are noted within the individual activities, as described under "Format of Activities."

Format of Activities

Each activity in this book includes the following information:

- *Activity Number:* Activities are numbered sequentially within each section for easy reference. Each activity has a two-part number to identify the section and the sequence of the activity within the section.

- *Activity Title:* The title of each activity is in the form of a question that can be answered by completing the activity. Each question requires more than a simple yes or no answer.

- *Special Instructions:* Some activities are intended to be used as teacher demonstrations or whole-group activities, or they require close supervision for safety reasons, so these special instructions are noted.

- *Take Home and Do with Family and Friends:* Many activities could be used by the student at home, providing enjoyment and learning for others in the family. Such experiences can work wonders in the life of the child, as he or she teaches others what has been learned at school. The result is often a greater depth of learning on the part of the child, as well as a boost to his or her self-esteem and self-confidence. An activity is marked as "Take home and do with family and friends" if it meets all of the following criteria:

  (1) It uses only materials that are common around the home.
  (2) It has a high chance of arousing interest on the part of the child.
  (3) It is safe for a child to do independently, that is, it uses no flame, hot plate, or very hot water.

  Of course, other activities could be used at the discretion of parents.

- *Materials:* Each activity lists the materials needed. The materials are easily acquired. In some cases special instructions or sources are suggested.

- *Procedure:* The procedural steps are written to the student, in easy-to-understand language. To avoid interfering with the discovery process, no conceptual information is given in this section.

- *For Problem Solvers:* Most activities include this section, which suggests additional investigations or activities for students who are motivated to extend their study beyond the activity specified in the procedural steps.

- *Teacher Information:* Suggested teaching tips and background information are given. This information supplements that provided in "To the Teacher" at the beginning of each section. This section is not intended for student use, but rather to assist the teacher with discussion following the hands-on activity, as students share their observations. Discussion of conceptual information prior to completing the hands-on activity can interfere with the discovery process.
- *Integrating:* Other curricular areas from which students will likely use skills as they complete the activity are recognized here.
- *Science Process Skills:* This is a list of the science process skills likely involved in doing the activity.

Use of Metric Measures

Most measures used are given in metric units, followed by units in the English system in parentheses. This is done to encourage use of the metric system.

Word Search Puzzles

The final activity of each section is a "Word Search," intended for fun and for encouraging vocabulary development. Each Word Search includes an answer key and a challenge for students to create word search puzzles of their own, with a form provided for ease of use.

Assessment and Evaluation

The activities in this book should effectively supplement and enrich your science curriculum. While a comprehensive testing system is not provided, a small collection of questions, titled "Do You Recall?" is included at the end of each section. The "Do You Recall" questions could be used as short quizzes or added to other assessments such as pretests or post-tests. These may include true/false, multiple-choice, and short-answer questions. No performance assessment items are included. Each list of questions is followed by an answer key, which identifies the related learning activities as well as providing answers to the questions.

Grade Level

The activities in this book are intended to be nongraded. Many activities in each section can be easily adapted for use with young children, while other activities provide challenge for the more talented in the intermediate grades.

Scientific Investigation

Scientists sometimes seem to flip-flop with theories that support a particular health remedy or behavior, then refute it, or alter their position on an established scientific theory. If we understand why that happens, we are less likely to be annoyed with it. It isn't because they are an indecisive lot, but because they are doing what scientists do. If we know of a certain drug that shows promise of helping us with a serious health problem, but is undergoing extended testing prior to approval for public use, we become impatient with the system. If it is marketed without sufficient proof of safety and we suffer ill side effects, we bring a class-action lawsuit against those who marketed it with insufficient testing.

The Tentative Nature of Scientific Knowledge

Scientific knowledge is, by its very nature, tentative and subject to scrutiny and change. It results from empirical evidence, but the interpretation of that evidence is often unavoidably influenced by human observation, inference, and judgment. To be respected by the scientific community, evidence must usually be verified by multiple scientists.

Occasionally, a long-held theory is shown to be flawed and, in light of new information, must be altered or abandoned. In 1633 Galileo was punished and imprisoned for defying the commonly held "truth" that the earth is the center of the universe and that all celestial bodies revolve around it.

If we criticize change that is based on the best current information, we make light of a process that deserves, instead, to be applauded, and we show our ignorance regarding the scientific way of learning. If we understand and encourage the continuous cyclical process of acquiring new information, we will not be frustrated when later on the "new" theory is also adjusted in light of newer data and revised perspectives.

We are bombarded with so-called "scientifically proven" health remedies that are at odds with each other. Two conflicting theories can both be wrong, but they cannot both be right. In such cases, we must wonder why more data were not collected before certain claims were made, and we question the motive that inspired the marketing of the product.

Taking a Less Formal Approach

In our efforts to spawn lifelong learners, we need to capture the general concept that science is an ongoing search for observable and reproducible evidence. Current thinking is leading us away from the once-held rigid sequence of memorized steps of the scientific method. We are, instead, encouraged to think of scientific investigation as a logical process of acquiring information and solving problems, applicable and useful in virtually every area of study and every walk of life.

In the face of a dilemma brought about by a question or problem, we need to first examine the information currently available. If this is insufficient, we pursue possible ways to acquire additional information (data) and to determine the accuracy of the new data. Having done that, we are better informed and thus better prepared to provide an answer to the question or a solution to the problem.

When Mother comes home from shopping and finds milk spilled on the kitchen floor, the problem is immediately apparent. Her mind quickly surveys current information by considering who has probably been in the house and, based on past behavior, age of children, and other information that would indicate who is most likely responsible for the mess. It may be that the child she first suspected is at scout camp and was nowhere around on that day. Mom quickly adjusts her thinking, considers other ideas, and forms a tentative conclusion (hypothesis). As she seeks out the young suspect for clean-up patrol, she might consider alibis, the stories of witnesses, and other new information, all of which contribute to a final conclusion. Her systematic approach might result in evidence that it was Dad, in a hurry to get to work on time!

Although this example does not involve clear-cut scientific experimentation, it does use a systematic procedure for acquiring information and/or arriving at a solution to an everyday problem, which is the very point being made. The procedure is very simple:

1. Examine information currently available regarding the question or problem at hand.
2. Determine the most logical conclusion (hypothesis) from the information already known.
3. Devise a way to test the accuracy of the hypothesis.

The scientific method, in some form, applies to many situations in everyday life, even if it is not commonly recognized as a scientific approach. If students are trained in the use of a logical, simple, systematic way to gather information and solve problems, they will be better equipped to meet life's inevitable dilemmas.

Now let's go back to the drug company that challenges our patience with extended testing delays. The whole process began with a question raised about the possible effectiveness of a particular formula in dealing with a specific health problem or class of problems. Interested scientists likely examined all of the information they could find about the possible effects of the separate ingredients and of this particular mixture of ingredients. They posed their best tentative conclusion (hypothesis), based on the available information. They then devised ways to test the substance for its effectiveness in the intended application, and perhaps other related applications, and the potential side effects. From their new data, they either concluded that their earlier tentative conclusion (hypothesis) was right, or they adjusted it and did more testing and examination of information (data) acquired. They likely will not allow the substance to be marketed as a solution to the targeted health problem until they are quite certain the substance has been adequately proven to be effective and safe—that their hypothesis was right. Even if you and I are impatient with the lengthy process and the substance shows promise of reducing suffering and saving lives, we won't see it on the market until it has been conclusively proven. Even then, the new formula could later be shown to be inadequate or to have unforeseen harmful side effects, and now it backfires. Those who tested, approved, and marketed the new drug are facing the wrath of those who used it—perhaps many of the same people who criticized them earlier for taking so long in the approval process.

Broad Application

Your students may use this approach in a variety of subject areas. For example, in the science classroom they might apply it as they experiment with the effect of light on plant growth or the effect of vinegar on baking soda and other powders. Perhaps they will find ways to check their hypothesis regarding the direction of the earth's rotation and do numerous other scientific explorations.

In another setting, they might study diacritical markings and their uses in unlocking word pronunciations, making logical conclusions or predictions based on information at hand. Testing such predictions becomes a learning experience as students read and study further, compare known words, ask an expert (perhaps the teacher), and so forth.

Your students might also enjoy the challenge of identifying elements of scientific investigation in a mystery story. When introduced to a variety of experiences in applying a basic approach to problem solving, they will recognize its universal application and down-to-earth logic, and chances are they will use it with confidence throughout their lives.

Application in This Book

Good habits of scientific investigation are encouraged in this book in the following ways:

1. Students are encouraged to work together in completing the activities, collaborating and learning from each other as they go along.

2. The form "Science Investigation Journaling Notes" is provided to help students record what they do and what they observe, as they practice scientific behavior in their study of science. It will serve as a template that can be applied in numerous problem-solving situations.

3. To help students make the transition into the use of journaling notes to record what they do and observe, the "Science Investigation Journaling Notes" form is reproduced within a few activities of the book. In each of these cases, the activity number is referenced in the heading, and part 1, the "Question," is provided on the form. In addition, the procedural steps guide the student in making appropriate connections and filling out the form as they complete the activity. This help is provided with the following activities:

    Section 2 (Water): Activities 8 and 19.

    Section 4 (Earth): Activity 15.

4. Help is also provided for making the next step in the transition—designing an investigation and completing the form independently. The following activities suggest, in "For Problem Solvers" and/or at the beginning of the "Procedural Steps," that students get copies of the "Science Investigation Journaling Notes" from the teacher and use them as they design and complete their own science investigation from the ideas provided:

    Section 2 (Water): Activities 1, 9, 17, and 22.

    Section 3 (Weather): Activities 5, 6, 7, and 10.

    Section 4 (Earth): Activities 9, 21, and 34.

    Section 5 (Ecology): Activities 13 and 22.

    Section 6 (Above the Earth): Activities 6 and 7.

5. We hope that copies of the following "Science Investigation Journaling Notes" form will be made available for students to use as needed, and that students will prepare journaling notes as they complete these and many other science investigations from this book and from other sources, including those devised by the students themselves.

Science Investigation
Journaling Notes

1. Question:

_____

_____

2. What we already know: _____

_____

_____

3. Hypothesis: _____

_____

_____

4. Materials needed: _____

_____

_____

5. Procedure: _____

_____

_____

6. Observations/New information: _____

_____

_____

7. Conclusion: _____

_____

_____

Final Note: Let's Collaborate, and Learn Together

Discovering the excitement of science and developing new techniques for critical thinking and problem solving are major goals of elementary science. The activities in this book are written with the intent that students work together in a collaborative way in the learning process. The discovery/inquiry approach, for which these activities are written, also must emphasize verbal responses and discussion. *It is important that students experience many hands-on activities* in the learning of science *and that they talk about what they do.* Working in collaborative groups facilitates this. Each child should have many opportunities to describe observations and to explain what he or she did and why. With the exception of recording observations, these activities usually do not require extensive writing, but that, too, is a skill that can be enriched through interest and involvement in science.

There is an ancient Chinese saying: "A journey of a thousand miles begins with a single step." May these ideas and activities help to provide that first step—or the appropriate next step—for all who use this book and are traveling the road of lifelong learning and discovery.

Marvin N. Tolman

Correlation with National Standards Grid

Grades K–4	Section	Pages
A. Science as Inquiry		
1. Abilities necessary to do scientific inquiry	Air	1–67
2. Understanding about scientific inquiry	Water	69–128
	Weather	129–192
	Earth	193–284
	Ecology	285–351
	Above the Earth	353–411
	Beyond the Earth	413–464

B. Physical Science
1. Properties of objects and materials
2. Position and motion of objects
3. Light, heat, electricity, and magnetism

C. Life Science
1. Characteristics of organisms
2. Life cycles of organisms
3. Organisms and environments

D. Earth and Space Science		
1. Properties of earth materials	Air	1–67
2. Objects in the sky	Water	69–128
3. Changes in earth and sky	Weather	129–192
	Earth	193–284
	Ecology	285–351
	Above the Earth	353–411
	Beyond the Earth	413–464

E. Science in Personal and Social Perspectives		
1. Personal health	Ecology	285–351
2. Characteristics and changes in populations		
3. Types of resources		
4. Changes in environments		
5. Science and technology in local challenges		

Grades 5–8	Section	Pages
A. Science as Inquiry		
1. Abilities necessary to do scientific inquiry	Air	1–67
2. Understanding about scientific inquiry	Water	69–128
	Weather	129–192
	Earth	193–284
	Ecology	285–351
	Above the Earth	353–411
	Beyond the Earth	413–464

B. Physical Science
    1. Properties of objects and materials
    2. Position and motion of objects
    3. Light, heat, electricity, and magnetism

C. Life Science
    1. Characteristics of organisms
    2. Life cycles of organisms
    3. Organisms and environments

D. Earth and Space Science		
1. Properties of earth materials	Air	1–67
2. Objects in the sky	Water	69–128
3. Changes in earth and sky	Weather	129–192
	Earth	193–284
	Ecology	285–351
	Above the Earth	353–411
	Beyond the Earth	413–464

E. Science in Personal and Social Perspectives		
1. Personal health	Ecology	285–351
2. Characteristics and changes in populations		
3. Types of resources		
4. Changes in environments		
5. Science and technology in local challenges		

Key to Icons

 Whole class

 Group/Partner

 Home

 Individual student

 Younger/Less advanced

 Older/More advanced

Listing of Activities by Topic

Air

Topic	Activities
Air Can Be Compressed	1.6, 1.7
Air Can Hold Moisture	1.30
Air Expands and Contracts	1.6, 1.7, 1.9, 1.10, 1.15, 1.16, 1.23, 1.24, 1.25, 1.26, 1.27
Air Has Weight	1.3, 1.4
Air Pressure	1.4, 1.5, 1.6, 1.7, 1.8, 1.9, 1.10, 1.11, 1.12, 1.13, 1.14, 1.15, 1.16, 1.17, 1.31
Air Takes Up Space	1.1, 1.2
Bernoulli's Principle	1.18, 1.19, 1.20, 1.21, 1.22
Warm Air Rises	1.24, 1.28

Water

Topic	Activities
Absorbency	2.19, 2.20
Buoyancy	2.1, 2.17, 2.21
Effect of Heat on Water	2.6, 2.18, 2.19, 2.23, 2.25
Effect of Salt Water	2.16, 2.17, 2.22
Effect of Water on Light	2.12, 2.13, 2.14, 2.15
Evaporation and Condensation	2.2, 2.3, 2.4, 2.5
Ocean Currents	2.24, 2.25
States of Matter	2.2, 2.3, 2.19
Surface Tension	2.8, 2.9, 2.10, 2.11
Water Pressure	2.7

Weather

Measuring the Atmosphere

The Earth

Ecology

Ecosystem Interactions

Topic	Activities
Energy	5.4
Home as an Ecosystem	5.7
People	5.5, 5.6
Pollution	5.13, 5.14
Recycling	5.21
School as an Ecosystem	5.8, 5.9, 5.10
Simple Communities	5.1, 5.2
Simple Ecosystems	5.3
Waste Disposal	5.11, 5.14, 5.23
Wise Consumer	5.18

Above the Earth

Topic	Activities
Action/Reaction	6.13, 6.14, 6.15, 6.16, 6.17
Glider Designing	6.4, 6.5, 6.6, 6.7, 6.8
Gravity	6.19, 6.22, 6.23, 6.24
History of Flight	6.1
Inertia	6.20, 6.21, 6.22, 6.23
Rockets	6.17, 6.18
Shape Affects Lift and Movement	6.2, 6.3, 6.4, 6.5, 6.6, 6.7, 6.8, 6.9, 6.10, 6.11, 6.12
Weightlessness	6.24

Beyond the Earth

Topic	Activities
Earth as a Planet	7.1
Earth Movements	7.2, 7.3, 7.4, 7.5
Eclipses	7.13
Moon	7.7, 7.8, 7.9, 7.10, 7.11, 7.12
Satellites	7.6, 7.7
Solar System	7.14, 7.15, 7.16, 7.17, 7.18
Sundial	7.4

Air

To the Teacher

A fundamental understanding of air is important to further studies in such areas as weather, air flight, plants and animals, and pollution. Although children live in an ocean of air, they often have difficulty realizing it really exists.

Air is a vital natural resource. Until recent decades, many people thought the earth's supply of air was so vast that it could not be significantly affected by the actions of living creatures. We now know that this precious resource is vulnerable to the pollutants that are put into the atmosphere every day by humans. We also know that the quality of life for all inhabitants of this planet depends on the way humans care for the huge, yet fragile supply of air that surrounds it.

Air is colorless, odorless, and tasteless. Although it is invisible, it is real, it takes up space, it has weight, and it is held to the earth by gravity. Air pressure, or atmospheric pressure, presses on all surfaces and in all directions. It presses upward and sideways just as hard as it presses downward; this is a characteristic of fluids. (Air is a fluid, as are all gases and liquids.)

The weight of the air at sea level exerts a pressure of about 1 kilogram per square centimeter (14.7 pounds per square inch). At higher altitudes, the pressure decreases because the amount of air above, from any given location of higher altitude, is less.

Air pressure in a sealed container can increase or decrease as certain conditions change. The pressure is caused by the air molecules inside the container striking against the walls of the container. If the pressure on the inside of the container is equal to the pressure on the outside of the container, the container is said to have zero pressure. Pressure inside the container will increase if more air is added (there are more air molecules striking the same amount of inside wall space), if the air inside the container is heated (the air molecules have increased energy and strike the wall with greater force), or if the volume of the container is decreased while the amount of air inside the container stays the same (there are more air molecules per unit of wall space). Pressure inside the container will decrease if some air is removed (there are fewer air molecules striking the same amount of inside wall space), if the air inside the container is cooled (the air molecules have less energy and strike the wall with less force), or if the volume of the container is increased but the amount of air inside remains the same (there is more wall space for the same number of air molecules).

Bernoulli's Principle states that the pressure in a fluid decreases as the speed of the fluid increases. The principle applies to air, water, or any other fluid. If air, for example, is blown across a strip of paper that is in the form of an airfoil, the paper will rise. With air rushing across the top of the paper, air pressure is reduced at that point and the paper is lifted by atmospheric pressure from beneath the paper. Airplane wings are designed with a curved top and a nearly flat bottom to force air to travel faster over the top than across the bottom, reducing the pressure on the top surface, thus providing lift from atmospheric pressure beneath the wing.

The following activities are designed as discovery activities that students can usually perform quite independently. You are encouraged to provide students (usually in small groups) with the materials listed and a copy of the activity from the beginning through the "Procedure." The section titled "Teacher Information" is not intended for student use, but rather to assist you with discussion following the hands-on activity, as students share their observations. Discussion of conceptual information prior to completing the hands-on activity can interfere with the discovery process.

Regarding the Early Grades

With verbal instructions and slight modifications, many of these activities can be used with kindergarten, first-grade, and second-grade students. In some activities, steps that involve procedures that go beyond the level

Hands-On Earth Science Activities

of the child can simply be omitted and yet offer the child an experience that plants the seed for a concept that will germinate and grow later on.

Teachers of the early grades will probably choose to bypass many of the "For Problem Solvers" sections. That's okay. These sections are provided for those who are especially motivated and want to go beyond the investigation provided by the activity outlined. Use the outlined activities, and enjoy worthwhile learning experiences together with your young students. Also consider, however, that many of the "For Problem Solvers" sections can be used appropriately with young children as group activities or as demonstrations, still giving students the advantage of an exposure to the experience and laying groundwork for connections that will be made at a later time.

Correlation with National Standards

The following elements of the National Standards are reflected in the activities of this section.

K–4   Content Standard A: Science as Inquiry
As a result of activities in grades K–4, all students should develop
   1. Abilities necessary to do scientific inquiry
   2. Understanding about scientific inquiry

K–4   Content Standard D: Earth and Space Science
As a result of activities in grades K–4, all students should develop understanding of
   1. Properties of earth materials
   2. Objects in the sky
   3. Changes in earth and sky

5–8   Content Standard A: Science as Inquiry
As a result of activities in grades 5–8, all students should develop
   1. Abilities necessary to do scientific inquiry
   2. Understanding about scientific inquiry

5–8   Content Standard D: Earth and Space Science
As a result of activities in grades 5–8, all students should develop understanding of
   1. Structure of the earth system
   2. Earth's history
   3. Earth in the solar system

Air

How Can You Test to See Whether Air Takes Up Space?

(Take home and do with family and friends.)

Materials Needed

- Eight-ounce clear plastic cup
- Facial tissue
- Deep bowl filled with water

Procedure

1. Look at the cup. What is in it?
2. Crumple a piece of the tissue and put it in the bottom of the cup.
3. Turn the cup over (be sure the tissue does not fall out) and push it, open end first, into a deep bowl of water.
4. Now remove the cup without tipping it.
5. What happened to the tissue?
6. What can you say about this?

Figure 1.1-1. Bowl of Water with Inverted Cup at Bottom

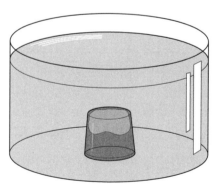

Teacher Information

When the cup is lowered mouth first into the bowl of water, the air will be trapped inside the cup and prevent water from entering the cup. Thus, the tissue will remain dry. Air is a substance, and it does take up space.

Science Process Skills

Observing, inferring

How Can You Pour Air?

Materials Needed

- Two eight-ounce plastic cups marked A and B
- Deep bowl filled with water

Procedure

1. Look at the cups marked A and B. What is in them?
2. Push cup A, mouth first, into the bowl of water.
3. Turn it on its side. What happened?
4. Push cup B to the bottom of the bowl, mouth (open end) first.
5. Put the mouth of cup A right above cup B and slowly tip cup B on its side.
6. What happened? What can you say about this?

Figure 1.2-1. Bowl of Water Containing Cup A Above Cup B

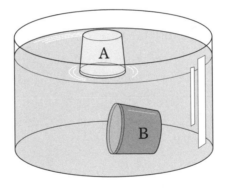

Teacher Information

When cup A is pushed into the bowl, it will contain air. When it is tipped on its side, the air will bubble out and the cup will fill with water. When cup B is pushed to the bottom and tipped on its side, and if the mouth of cup A is directly above it, the air will bubble from cup B into cup A because air is lighter than water. Students will be able to see the air travel from cup B and force the water from cup A. Water in cup A is displaced by air from cup B, demonstrating that air truly does take up space.

Science Process Skills

Observing, inferring

How Can You Tell Whether Air Has Weight?

(Take home and do with family and friends.)

Materials Needed
- Meter stick
- String
- Whiteboard eraser (or chalkboard eraser)
- Balloon

Procedure
1. Suspend a meter stick from a string tied in the middle of the meter stick.
2. Tie the eraser to one end of the meter stick with another piece of string.
3. Using a third piece of string, tie an empty balloon (not inflated) to the other end of the meter stick. Suspend the balloon 5 cm (2 in.) from the end of the meter stick.
4. Now balance the meter stick by sliding the center support string back and forth as needed.
5. Remove the balloon and inflate it. Retie the balloon in the same place (5 cm, or 2 in., from the end). Does it balance? What can you say about this?

For Problem Solvers
Find out the actual weight of air in a balloon. Compare balloons of different sizes and see how much air you can put in them, in grams. For each balloon, weigh it empty on a gram balance, estimate what it will weigh when it's full of air, then blow it up and find out. Can you think of any other way that you can weigh air?

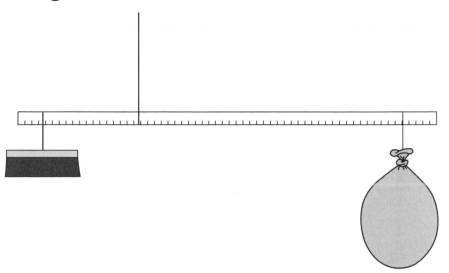

Figure 1.3-1. Eraser Balanced with Balloon

Teacher Information

When the balloon is inflated and hung on the meter stick again, it will tip the balance down, showing that air has weight. Make certain the eraser does not move while the balloon is being removed and inflated. Tape it in place if necessary.

Integrating

Math

Science Process Skills

Observing, inferring, comparing and contrasting, measuring, estimating

How Can You Feel the Weight and Pressure of Air?

(Take home and do with family and friends.)

Materials Needed

- Large, wide-mouthed, clear glass (or rigid plastic) jar
- Plastic bag
- Rubber band

Procedure

1. Push the plastic bag down inside the jar with about 5 cm (2 in.) hanging over the rim.
2. Place the rubber band around the rim of the jar, just below the threads (the plastic should be under the rubber band all the way around).
3. Reach inside the jar and gently pull the plastic upward.
4. What happened? What can you say about this?

Figure 1.4-1. Plastic Bag Hanging Inside Glass Jar

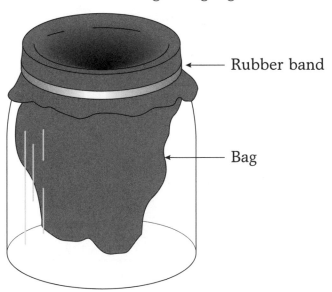

Rubber band

Bag

Hands-On Earth Science Activities

Teacher Information

When the student pulls up on the plastic bag, the space inside the bottle is increased and the air pressure is reduced. The outside air pushing down on the plastic bag will keep it from being pulled out. You can feel the weight of the air. This can be a group activity, but be sure each child has a chance to feel the pressure holding the bag inside the jar as he or she tugs lightly on the bag.

Integrating

Math

Science Process Skills

Observing, inferring

Air

What Is Another Way to Feel Air Pressure?

Materials Needed

- Two suction-cup plungers
- Water
- A partner

Procedure

1. Moisten the edges of the two plungers.
2. With the help of a partner, push the plungers together. Now try to pull them apart.
3. What happened?
4. What can you say about this?

For Problem Solvers

Suction cups are used to hold directional compasses onto automobile windshields, to mount pencil sharpeners onto desktops, to pull out car body panels in a repair shop, and for a wide variety of applications. Find as many uses for suction cups as you can and design a way to test their holding strength. Do certain applications use better suction cups? Are some brands better than others? And for all of them, what really is the force that holds them in place?

Teacher Information

When the plungers are pushed together, much of the air between them is forced out, creating a partial vacuum. The outside air pressure keeps them together. Plungers will not work on the moon, due to lack of air pressure. If there is a glass shop nearby, arrange for someone in the class to ask the shop owner about carrying large glass panels with suction cups.

Integrating

Math, social studies

Science Process Skills

Observing, inferring, measuring, identifying and controlling variables, experimenting

ACTIVITY 1.6

How Can Air Be Compressed?

(Take home and do with family and friends.)

Materials Needed

- Clear, flexible plastic bottle filled with water
- Eyedropper with a small amount of water inside

Procedure

1. Observe the eyedropper in the capped bottle.
2. Gently squeeze the bottle.
3. What happened? Can you explain why?

Figure 1.6-1. Eyedropper in Plastic Bottle Full of Water

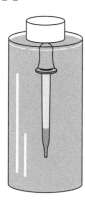

For Problem Solvers

With this activity you made a Cartesian diver. Can you make one that will go up and down by itself as the water temperature changes? What are the variables that you might want to change? Consider using a glass bottle, and be sure the lid will seal. What will happen if you begin with cold water and with the diver barely able to float, then put the bottle in the sunshine? What will happen if you begin with warm water and the diver barely able to float, then put the bottle in a refrigerator (not in a freezer)?

Try the same thing again, only using a plastic bag as the container. Be sure you seal the bag tightly and that you have no air trapped at the top of the bag above the water. Predict what will happen before you begin.

Teacher Information

This is called a Cartesian diver. Fill the plastic bottle with water. Put enough water in the eyedropper so it will just barely float in the bottle and place the dropper in the bottle, bulb end up. Put the cap on the bottle. When pressure is exerted on the bottle, water, which will not compress, is forced into the eyedropper, compressing the air and making the dropper heavier. It will sink lower in the bottle. When pressure on the bottle is released, the compressed air in the dropper will force some of the water out, and the dropper will float to the surface. If pressure on the bottle is varied, the dropper can be stopped in the middle or at any point desired.

Integrating

Language arts

Science Process Skills

Observing, inferring, measuring, predicting, identifying and controlling variables, experimenting

Hands-On Earth Science Activities

What Is Another Way Air Can Be Compressed?

(Advance teacher preparation needed)

Materials Needed

- Clear glass soda bottle
- Head from wooden match
- Water

Procedure

1. Float a head from a wooden match in a soda bottle completely full of water.

2. Use your thumb to push down on the water in the mouth of the bottle. Your thumb should completely cover the bottle's mouth.

3. What happened? What can you say about this?

Figure 1.7-1. Match Head in Soda Bottle Full of Water

Teacher Information

This is another Cartesian diver. The wood in the match head is porous—full of air spaces—so it floats on top of the water. When you use your thumb to push on the surface, water is forced into the air spaces in the match head and it will sink. When the pressure is released, the match head will float to the surface again as the compressed air in the match head forces the water out.

Note: The thumb must cover the mouth of the bottle completely. This activity is not appropriate for young children except as a demonstration, because it requires a larger and stronger hand. You will need to remove the wood right up to the head of the match, until the match head barely floats.

Science Process Skills

Observing

What Can a Card Teach You About Air?

(Take home and do with friends, over the sink, please.)

Materials Needed

- Plastic cup
- 4-inch by 6-inch index card
- Water and sink

Procedure

1. Working over a sink, fill the cup with water.
2. Put the index card over the mouth (open end) of the cup.
3. Hold the card in place with one hand, the cup in the other.
4. Turn the cup upside down and carefully remove your hand from the card.
5. Slowly turn the cup right-side up, but don't touch the card.
6. What happened?
7. What can you say about this? Discuss your ideas with your group.

Figure 1.8-1. Inverted Cup of Water Over Card

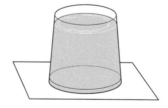

For Problem Solvers

Try this activity with cups of different sizes and find out whether size makes any difference. Try it with different materials in place of the index card. Predict what will happen with each material before you try it. Does a heavier card work as well? A sheet of paper? Try to find a very fine-mesh screen. Does that stay on the cup just the same as the card? Can you explain your results?

Teacher Information

Be sure to try this activity before using it with students. When the cup full of water is turned upside down and the hand is removed, the card will usually stay on the cup and the water will stay inside the cup. This is because the pressure of the air pushing on the card is great enough to hold the water in. When the cup is turned right-side up, the card will usually stay on the cup, showing that air pushes in all directions.

Tip: You might consider doing this activity over a bucket, a sink, or other appropriate container, just in case!

Integrating

Language arts

Science Process Skills

Observing, inferring, predicting, communicating

How Can You Crush a Gallon Can Without Touching It?

(Teacher demonstration)

Materials Needed

- Gallon can with tight fitting lid
- Hot plate
- Water
- Oven mitts

Procedure

1. Put a small amount of water ($\frac{1}{2}$ cup or so) in the can.
2. Put the can on the hot plate with the lid off and turn the hot plate on high.
3. When there is a good stream of steam coming out the spout, use oven mitts to remove the can from the hot plate.
4. Put the lid on tight, immediately after you remove the can from the hot plate. (See Figure 1.9–1.)

Figure 1.9–1. Gallon Can Being Removed from Hot Plate and Cap Ready to Be Put On

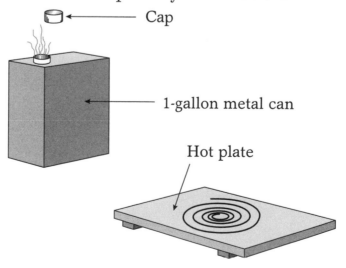

Cap

1-gallon metal can

Hot plate

5. Have students predict what will happen to the can.

6. As students observe for a few minutes, discuss what is happening and why.

Teacher Information

Caution: There are two possible hazards with this activity. First, students could get burned. Second, the can should never be left on the hot plate with the lid on, as the can will likely explode. This activity should be done only by the teacher as a demonstration.

This is one of the more popular demonstrations of the great force of air pressure. For older students, it's an excellent time to apply math skills. Have them measure the dimensions of the can and compute the air pressure (about 14.7 pounds per square inch at sea level). Their figures will probably show that there are approximately 3,000 pounds of force on the can, and they will see the effect of that pressure as the can is crushed right before their eyes. To involve 3,000 pounds of force assumes that you were successful in driving out all of the air by water vapor, and that won't happen, but it will come close enough to provide students with a lasting memory about the force of air pressure.

The overabundant supply of gallon cans at school went out with the ditto machine. Gallon cans are sometimes available, however, at paint-supply stores. Businesses that mix paint usually even have new cans that they will sell at a reasonable price. Another possible source is your local auto-body shop. These shops get some of their reducers (thinners) in gallon cans, and they throw empties away. *CAUTION:* If you use cans that have had flammable material in them, be sure to *rinse them well* before putting them on a hot plate!

Integrating

Math, language arts

Science Process Skills

Observing, inferring, measuring, predicting, communicating

How Can You Crush a Soda Can with Air Pressure?

(Teacher demonstration)

Materials Needed

- Empty soda can
- Hot plate
- Pan of water
- Oven mitts

Procedure

1. Put a small amount of water ($\frac{1}{8}$ cup or so) in the can.
2. Put the can on the hot plate and turn the hot plate on high.
3. When there is a good stream of steam coming out the spout, use oven mitts to remove the can from the hot plate.
4. Immediately turn the can upside down in the pan of water. Only the top of the can needs to enter the water. (See Figure 1.10–1.)
5. Have students hypothesize as to what happened to cause what they saw.

Figure 1.10–1. Soda Can Being Removed from Hot Plate with Pan of Water Ready

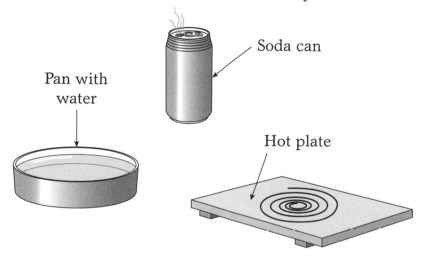

Soda can

Pan with water

Hot plate

Teacher Information

Caution: Do this activity as a demonstration, to avoid the possibility of students getting burned.

This is an excellent substitute (or addition) for the gallon-can crusher to demonstrate the force of air pressure. For older students, math skills can still be applied by computing the amount of air pressure on the surface of the can. Many people recycle aluminum cans, and they usually stomp on the cans to minimize storage space. Here's a more exciting way to crush the cans!

Integrating

Math, language arts

Science Process Skills

Observing, inferring, measuring, predicting, communicating

How Can Air Pressure Make Things Stronger?

(Take home and do with family and friends.)

Materials Needed

- Paper straws
- Potato

Procedure

1. Hold a straw near one end and try to stick the other end in a potato. What happened?
2. Place your finger over the top of the straw and stick the other end into the potato (do it fast and hard). What happened?
3. What can you say about this? Discuss your ideas with your group.

For Problem Solvers

Try this activity with a variety of straws—fat straws, skinny straws, plastic straws, and paper straws. Cut some of them shorter and try it. Can you penetrate the potato with all of the straws? If not, which ones work best? With which ones do you have to seal the opening with your finger in order to push them into the potato? Does this help you to see what difference it makes to seal the opening? Tell your teacher what you learned about straws, potatoes, and air pressure.

Teacher Information

When you try to stick the straw with both ends open in the potato, the straw will bend. When you place your finger over the upper end of the straw, the air is trapped inside and the column is strengthened. The straw will go into the potato. (Be sure to stab rapidly and hold the straw near the top during all parts of the activity.)

Figure 1.11–1. Potato with Straws Inserted

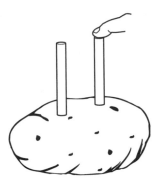

Integrating
Language arts

Science Process Skills
Observing, inferring, measuring, identifying and controlling variables, experimenting

How Can Air Help Us Drink?

Materials Needed

- Clear glass soda bottles filled with water
- Plastic or paper straws
- Modeling clay

Procedure

1. Drink some water through the straw.
2. Use clay to seal the top of the bottle all around the straw.
3. Drink some more water through the straw.
4. What happened? What can you say about this? Discuss your ideas with your group.

For Problem Solvers

Think about what really happens when you drink through a straw. You don't pull the liquid up the straw. Instead, you reduce the pressure inside the straw. See whether you can explain what really causes pressure inside the straw to be decreased. Then explain what causes the liquid to rise in the straw.

Teacher Information

In order to drink through a straw, you must have air pushing on the surface of the liquid. When the top of the bottle is sealed, any effort to get liquid to move up the straw reduces the pressure of the air above the surface of the liquid, more air cannot get in, and drinking is impossible. Soda cans have either two holes or one hole shaped in such a way that air can get in as the liquid pours out; narrow-necked bottles "gurgle" because they are not designed to let air flow in easily as liquid flows out.

Think about what you do physiologically as you drink through a straw. You seal your mouth over the straw with your mouth closed, and then open your mouth. This increases the size of the air space inside your mouth without allowing more air to come in, thus reducing the air pressure inside your mouth. Since the end of the straw is in your mouth, pressure of the air inside the straw is also reduced, and it is now less than atmospheric pressure. Atmospheric pressure on the surface of the liquid forces the liquid up the straw. You don't "suck" the liquid up the straw.

Suction is not a force; it is only a word that we use to imply a lack of air pressure. You simply reduce the pressure inside the straw. The force that moves the liquid up the straw is atmospheric pressure.

Figure 1.12-1. Soda Bottle with Straw Sealed to the Top

Integrating
Language arts

Science Process Skills
Observing, inferring, communicating

How Does Air Pressure Affect Water Flow?

(Do this over a sink or bucket.)

Materials Needed

- Gallon or quart metal can with tight-fitting lid and a hole punched into the side near the bottom
- Masking tape
- Water
- Sink or bucket

Procedure

1. There is a small hole near the bottom of the can. Find it and cover it with a piece of masking tape.
2. Fill the can with water.
3. Remove the masking tape and observe the stream of water.
4. Put the lid on the can tightly. Observe the stream of water. What happened?
5. Listen carefully as you loosen the lid. What happened?
6. What can you say about this?

For Problem Solvers

Do some research and find answers to the following questions:

1. Why is the hole in a pop-top can shaped the way it is?
2. Why do you punch a second hole in the solid lid of a juice can before you pour?
3. There are usually open plumbing pipes sticking out of the roof of your house or apartment. Why?

Teacher Information

Be sure the lid seals so the container is airtight. Without the lid, gravity will cause the water to flow in a stream from the hole. When the lid is on tight, the flow will gradually stop, even though water still remains in the can. When the lid is removed, gravity takes over and the water will flow from the hole again.

With the lid sealed, air cannot enter the can. Although the force of gravity still exerts a downward force on the water, the inside air pressure will be reduced enough that atmospheric pressure will hold the water in the can against the force of gravity, and the flow of water will stop.

Note: A rigid plastic bottle can be used in place of the metal can.

Your problem solvers will learn, through their research, that the hole in a pop-top can is designed to allow air to flow into the can while the liquid refreshment runs out, keeping the air pressure equalized. Two holes are needed in a juice can in order to allow air to flow into the can as liquid flows out, for the same reason. And a plumbing system is vented to the roof, also to allow equalization of pressure.

Integrating

Reading, language arts

Science Process Skills

Observing, inferring, researching

Hands-On Earth Science Activities

How Hard Can Air Push?

(Take home and do with family and friends.)

Materials Needed

- Clear glass soda bottle
- Balloon

Procedure

1. Put the balloon into the soda bottle, holding onto the balloon's open end.
2. Stretch the lip of the balloon over the mouth of the bottle.
3. Inflate the balloon inside the bottle.
4. What happened? Can you explain why?

Figure 1.14-1. Soda Bottle with Balloon Hanging Inside

For Problem Solvers

Try this activity with bottles of different sizes. Be sure all of them have small openings, so you can stretch the balloon over them. Can you blow the balloon up any further with some of the bottles than with others? What seems to make the difference? Try it with your friends and discuss your ideas about it.

Teacher Information

When the child blows into the balloon, the increased air pressure inside the balloon will push against the air trapped in the bottle. The pressure of the air in the bottle will increase and push harder on the balloon. The child will discover that the balloon cannot be inflated inside the bottle. Remember, the lip of the balloon must cover the mouth of the bottle and completely seal it.

Just for fun, make a small hole in the bottom of a *rigid* plastic bottle; then use this bottle for the above activity. Hold the bottle and seal the hole with your finger (students must not see this happen) as the student tries to blow up the balloon. Then carefully slide your finger from the hole and let the student try again. The student will now be able to blow up the balloon. Seal the hole again with your finger, just as the student stops blowing, and the balloon will remain inflated just from atmospheric pressure. Of course, the students still don't know about the hole in the bottom of the bottle. Let them puzzle over it and discover the hole. This is an excellent inquiry activity, and a lot of fun for all.

Integrating

Language arts

Science Process Skills

Observing, inferring, communicating, identifying and controlling variables, experimenting

How Can You Put an Egg into a Bottle?

(Teacher demonstration or supervised activity)

Materials Needed

- Hard-boiled egg, peeled
- Glass milk bottle or juice bottle, 1 liter (1 qt.) or larger
- Wooden matches

Procedure

1. Insert two wooden matches into the pointed end of the egg.
2. Holding the bottle upside down, light the matches and put the egg into the mouth of the bottle, pointed end first. Hold the egg lightly against the mouth of the bottle, but don't push! Keep the bottle upside down.
3. What happened? What can you say about this?

Figure 1.15-1. Bottle with Egg and Matches

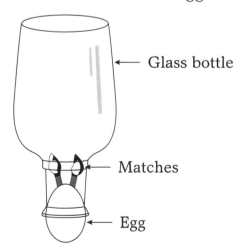

Teacher Information

The mouth of the bottle should be somewhat smaller (5 mm or $\frac{1}{4}$ in.) in diameter than the egg. If an old-style milk bottle is not available, you might find a juice bottle that will be about right if you use large eggs. Pullet eggs could be used with bottles having a smaller opening. (A pullet is a young hen, and it lays small eggs.)

The lit matches in the pointed end of the egg will heat the air inside the bottle, causing the air to expand. When this happens, warm air is forced out of the bottle (don't push the egg into the top of the bottle or the air can't get out). Soon the matches will go out and the air inside the bottle will cool and contract, leaving less pressure inside the bottle than outside the bottle. When this happens, the outside air pressure will force the egg into the bottle.

If the egg is not broken, you can get it out of the bottle by reversing the process. Hold the bottle above your head with the pointed end of the egg in the mouth of the bottle. Blow very hard into the bottle. The blowing will increase the air pressure inside the bottle and push the egg out. If the egg comes only partway out, try pouring warm water on the bottle. The air inside will expand and force the egg out.

Integrating

Math, language arts

Science Process Skills

Observing, inferring

How Can You Put a Water Balloon into a Bottle?

(Teacher demonstration)

Materials Needed

- Large bottle (with an opening of at least 4 cm [$1\frac{1}{2}$ in.])
- Balloon
- Bowl of water
- Paper towel
- Match
- Aluminum foil (or other fireproof surface)

Procedure

1. Place a sheet of aluminum foil or other fireproof surface on the table and place the bottle and the bowl of water on the foil.
2. Put water in the balloon, making a water balloon that is a bit larger than the opening of the bottle.
3. Place the water balloon in the bowl of water, just to get it wet and provide lubrication.
4. Take half a sheet of paper towel (or other paper) and twist it lengthwise so that it fits easily into the opening of the bottle, but don't drop it into the bottle yet.
5. Hold the twisted paper above the spout of the bottle, light it with the match, and drop the burning paper into the bottle. (See Figure 1.16–1.)
6. Immediately place the water balloon on the bottle, while the paper is still burning, holding the balloon lightly by the neck.
7. Discuss what happened and why they think it did that.

Air

Figure 1.16-1. Large Bottle with Water Balloon on Top and Paper Burning Inside

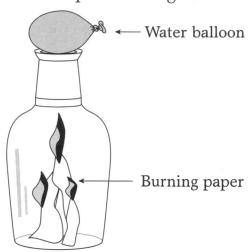

← Water balloon

← Burning paper

Teacher Information

Caution: This activity should be done only by the teacher as a demonstration, to avoid the possibility of students getting burned.

This is an excellent substitute (or addition) for the egg-in-the-bottle demonstration of air pressure, except that it doesn't provide breakfast. The water balloon has the advantage of flexible size, so most any bottle can be used.

Without disclosing conceptual information, you might want to describe the steps of the activity before lighting the paper afire and ask students to predict what will happen when you put fire in the bottle and place the water balloon on the top of the bottle.

After the balloon is in the bottle, have students hypothesize about what made the water balloon go into the bottle. Be sure they don't leave with the notion that a vacuum in the bottle "sucked" the balloon into the bottle. A vacuum is only a lack of pressure. Pressure is a force, and lack of force can't do work. The air expanded as it heated, and you probably noticed that the water balloon danced on the top of the bottle as the heating air escaped. As soon as the fire went out, the air began to cool and contract. With the water balloon sealing the spout and preventing air from reentering the bottle, air pressure inside the bottle decreased, resulting in less air pressure inside the bottle than outside the bottle. The balloon was pushed into the bottle by atmospheric pressure.

Have students hypothesize also about how you might get the water balloon out of the bottle. If you turn the bottle upside down, position the balloon over the opening to seal air from coming out of the bottle, then blow air into the bottle. The increased air pressure will force the balloon out of the bottle, just as air pressure pushed the balloon into the bottle.

Note: The operation of a vacuum cleaner is related to the process of getting the balloon into the bottle. The spinning of the fan creates reduced pressure immediately in front of the fan. Reduced pressure, however, cannot reach out and pull on the air in front of it. Rather, as the air pressure in front of the fan is reduced, more air is forced in by atmospheric pressure. This is also related to the movement of air outdoors. As the sun heats a large mass of air, the air expands. Pressure within the air mass is thereby reduced and surrounding air of greater pressure rushes in. We call it wind.

Integrating
Language arts

Science Process Skills
Observing, inferring, predicting, communicating

How Much Can You Lift by Blowing?

(Take home and do with family and friends.)

Materials Needed

- Small garbage bags, newspaper bags, or other plastic bags (at least six)
- Two tables (alike and medium sized)
- Chair

Procedure

1. Place a book on a bag and blow into the bag to see whether you can lift the book.
2. Do you think you can lift three books by blowing into the bag? Try it.
3. If you could lift three books, find something heavier and try lifting it the same way.
4. Turn one table upside down on top of the other.
5. Have several people circle the table, each one inserting his or her bag, open end out, between the two tables. (See Figure 1.17–1.)

Figure 1.17–1. Two Tables Ready to Use

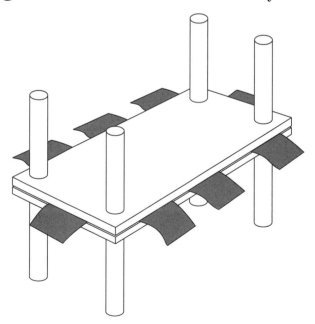

6. Have everyone blow together in the bags, on signal and in unison. Did the table rise?

7. If you were successful in raising the table by blowing into the bags, place a chair on the upside-down table and repeat steps 5 and 6.

8. Finally, put a person on the chair and do it again.

9. Discuss everyone's ideas about why they were able to lift such a lot of weight by blowing.

For Problem Solvers

Talk to someone who works in a mechanic shop and find out how much air pressure is used to lift a car on a hydraulic hoist. How can air pressure lift a car?

Find out how much air pressure is in the tires of your family car, or ask someone about theirs. Find out how much the car weighs. Discuss your information with your teacher and other class members. How can that much air pressure hold up a car?

Teacher Information

Students will be amazed at how much weight they can lift by blowing into a bag. Talk about the fact that automobiles ride on a cushion of air. A two-thousand-pound car (or more) is held up by tires that have approximately 30 pounds of air in them. This means 30 pounds per square inch of surface area. If you blow into a bag through an opening of 1 square inch, the air pressure you force into the bag can be multiplied by the number of square inches of surface area of the bag.

The total force that can be applied by a small amount of air pressure is astounding.

Integrating

Math, language arts

Science Process Skills

Observing, inferring, measuring, predicting, communicating, formulating hypotheses, researching

How Can Air Pressure Help Airplanes Fly?

Materials Needed

- Sheets of standard-sized notebook paper

Procedure

1. Hold the sheet of paper by the corners just below your lower lip.
2. Permit the paper to hang down in front of you. (See Figure 1.18–1.)
3. Blow across the top of the paper.
4. What happened? What can you say about this? Discuss your ideas with your group.

Figure 1.18–1. Student Blowing Air Over Paper

For Problem Solvers

Place two textbooks flat on the table, side by side, leaving about 10 cm (4 in.) of space between them. Put a sheet of notebook paper on top of the books. Predict what will happen if you blow into the space beneath the paper between the books. Try it. What happened to the paper?

Repeat the activity, blowing through a soda straw. Which worked better for you?

Teacher Information

When a student blows across the top of the paper, it will rise. As air moves faster, its pressure is reduced and the greater air pressure below pushes the paper up. This is called Bernoulli's Principle, and airplane wings are shaped to take advantage of it. The same principle is applied to move chemicals out of the bottle of a garden-hose sprayer.

Your problem solvers will find that, as they blow beneath the paper that is supported by two books, air pressure under the paper is reduced, following Bernoulli's Principle, and air pressure above forces the paper down between the books.

Integrating

Language arts

Science Process Skills

Observing, inferring, predicting

What Is the Relationship Between Moving Air and Its Pressure?

(Take home and do with family and friends.)
(Advance teacher preparation needed)

Materials Needed

- Two Ping-Pong balls with thread attached
- Paper and pencils
- Drinking straws

Procedure

1. Suspend two Ping-Pong balls from threads, leaving approximately 2 cm ($\frac{3}{4}$ in.) between them. (See Figure 1.19–1.)

Figure 1.19–1. Ping-Pong Balls Hanging from Thread

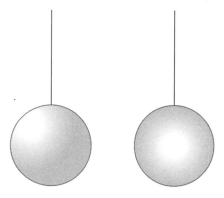

2. Predict what will happen if you blow between the balls with a drinking straw.
3. Write your prediction, then try it.
4. What happened? Was your prediction accurate? What can you say about this?

Teacher Information

Advance preparation: You will need to have a piece of thread (approximately 45 cm [18 inches]) already attached to each Ping-Pong ball. The easiest way is to thread a needle, then force the needle into one side of the ball and out the other, and tie a knot in the thread.

When air is blown between the Ping-Pong balls, they will come together because the molecules of air between the balls are moving faster, which reduces the pressure between the balls. The balls are pushed together by atmospheric pressure.

Integrating

Math, language arts

Science Process Skills

Observing, inferring, predicting

How Far Can You Blow a Ping-Pong Ball from a Funnel?

(Take home and do with family and friends.)

Materials Needed
- Standard kitchen funnels
- Ping-Pong balls

Procedure

1. Place a Ping-Pong ball in your funnel.
2. Hold your funnel at enough of an angle that the ball will stay in the funnel. (See Figure 1.20–1.)

Figure 1.20-1. Funnel at an Angle so Ball Will Stay in Place

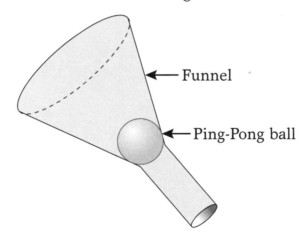

3. Predict what will happen if you blow into the small end of the funnel. How far do you think you can blow the ball across the room?
4. Try it. How far did the ball go?
5. Can you explain what happened?
6. Discuss your ideas with others.

Teacher Information

If you get three (or more) funnels and Ping-Pong balls, you can have a contest with a group of students. Of course, it's important that they haven't already tried the activity, so they will earnestly compete as you give them the signal to blow. Ask the other students in the class to predict which of the "blowers" will be able to blow the ball the farthest across the room, and notice the surprised looks on the faces of all when the balls go nowhere.

This is an application of Bernoulli's Principle. As air rushes past the ball, pressure is reduced where the air is moving fastest. Atmospheric pressure pressing in on the center of the ball is then greater than the pressure around the perimeter of the ball, where the air is moving more rapidly. The harder you blow, the tighter the ball is held in the funnel.

Try it with the funnel upside down. Hold the ball in place, and then release it after you begin to blow hard. The ball will fall after you stop blowing.

Note: Be sure to wash the funnels with soap and water before using them with other students.

Integrating

Language arts

Science Process Skills

Observing, inferring, predicting, communicating, formulating hypotheses

Why Can't the Ball Escape the Air Stream?

(Take home and do with family and friends.)

Materials Needed

- Hair dryer (with "no heat" setting)
- Ping-Pong ball

Procedure

1. Set the hair dryer on "no heat" and turn the fan on high speed.
2. With the air blowing upward, hold the ball in the air stream.
3. Carefully let go of the ball and move your hand away.
4. What happened?
5. Can you explain this?
6. With the ball still in the air stream, tilt the hair dryer back and forth slightly.
7. How can this happen? Discuss your ideas with your teacher and with your group.

Figure 1.21-1. Ping-Pong Ball Suspended in a Stream of Air

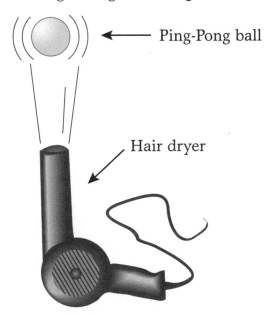

Ping-Pong ball

Hair dryer

Teacher Information

This is another application of Bernoulli's Principle. As the ball moves to the side of the air stream due to the force of gravity, the air moving past the ball on the air stream side is moving faster than the air on the other side of the ball, reducing the pressure on the air stream side, and the ball is pushed back into the air stream by atmospheric pressure. As you direct the air stream vertically, you will see the ball waver back and forth, and as you tip it at a slight angle, atmospheric pressure will support the ball.

This activity also works fine with a tank-type vacuum as the blower. Plug the hose into the rear of the tank, so that air blows out through the hose.

Integrating

Language arts

Science Process Skills

Observing, inferring, communicating, formulating hypotheses

How Can You Make an Atomizer with a Drinking Straw?

(Take home and do with family and friends.)

Materials Needed

- Drinking straw
- Small cup of water
- Scissors

Procedure

1. Cut the drinking straw almost through, with about one-third of the straw on one end of the cut and two-thirds of the straw on the other end. (See Figure 1.22–1)
2. Bend the straw at a right angle.

Figure 1.22–1. Straw Cut and Bent, Ready to Use in Cup of Water

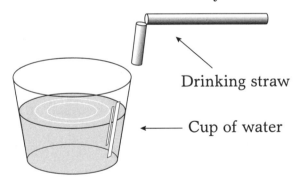

Drinking straw

Cup of water

3. Insert the short end of the straw into the water.
4. Predict what will happen if you blow on the other end of the straw.
5. Blow hard on the other end of the straw.
6. What happened? Was your prediction correct?
7. From what you have learned about Bernoulli's Principle, can you explain this?
8. Discuss your ideas with your group.

For Problem Solvers

Does the angle of the vertical straw change the way the atomizer works? Does the length of the vertical straw make any difference in how easy it is to use? Does the size of either straw matter, or the size of the cup? Think of ways to test these variables and answer them. What other variables do you wonder about? Test them, too, and share your information with your teacher and with other students.

Teacher Information

This is another application of Bernoulli's Principle. Air pressure is reduced in the vertical straw as air rushes over its opening. Atmospheric pressure is now greater than the pressure inside the straw, and the liquid is forced up the vertical tube by atmospheric pressure pushing down on the surface of the liquid in the cup.

Squeeze-bulb atomizers use this principle, as do paint sprayers and the type of weed sprayer that attaches to a garden hose. This principle has many other applications in life, including in the operation of a carburetor of a gasoline engine. Airplanes are supported in the air largely by atmospheric pressure, in another application of Bernoulli's Principle.

Incidentally, you might want to do this activity at the end of the day, or at least just before recess, because students will spray water everywhere—and they will always remember Bernoulli's Principle. Isn't that terrific! (And parents love you when you teach their children things like this!)

Integrating

Language arts, social studies

Science Process Skills

Observing, inferring, predicting, communicating, formulating hypotheses, experimenting

What Happens When Air Is Heated?

(Teacher demonstration)

Materials Needed

- Masking tape
- Meter stick
- Candle
- Match
- Chair
- Two lunch-sized paper bags

Procedure

1. Use masking tape to attach a lunch-sized paper bag, open end down, to each end of the meter stick.
2. Balance the meter stick on the back of a chair.
3. What do you think will happen if you place a lighted candle under the open end of one of the paper bags?
4. Try it, being very careful to keep the candle a safe distance from the bag.
5. What happened?
6. What can you say about this?

Figure 1.23-1. Paper Bags Balanced on Chair

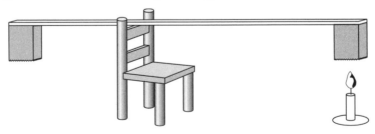

For Problem Solvers

Hot-air ballooning has become very popular. Flying safely requires a great deal of knowledge and skill, so balloon pilots must be licensed. What causes a hot-air balloon to rise into the air? Read about hot-air balloons and find out all you can about how they function. Observe the operation of one if you have the opportunity.

Teacher Information

Caution: Do this activity over a concrete surface, and take precautions that are appropriate in the use of an open flame.

As the air in the paper bag above the candle is heated, the rapid movement of air molecules causes the air to expand. As some of the air inside is forced out, the air in the bag becomes lighter and the paper bag will begin to rise. This is the same principle hot-air balloons use.

Integrating

Reading, language arts, social studies

Science Process Skills

Observing, predicting, researching

How Can You Tell That Warm Air Rises?

Materials Needed

- Lamp
- Compass
- Paper
- Thread
- Scissors

Procedure

1. With a compass, draw a circle with a 20-cm (8-in.) radius. Cut out the circle with scissors. Cut a spiral about 1 cm thick by starting on the outside of the circle and moving in to the center as you cut. Suspend your spiral by a thread attached in the center.

2. Hold the spiral over your head and blow gently. Did your spiral turn? Hold your spiral over a lamp that has been turned on. (See Figure 1.24–1.)

3. What does this tell you about warm air?

For Problem Solvers

Can you create other designs that would respond to moving air and show that warm air rises? Try it, and hang it over a lamp to see whether the lamp is heating the air.

Figure 1.24-1. Paper Spiral Held Over a Heat Lamp

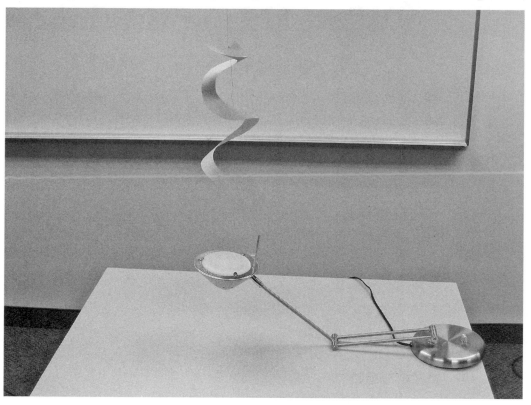

Teacher Information

When you blow on the spiral, it will turn. When you hold the spiral over the lamp, it will turn in the same manner, demonstrating that the heated air above the lamp is rising or blowing upward.

Integrating

Art

Science Process Skills

Observing, inferring

What Happens When Air Gets Warmer?

(Teacher demonstration)

Materials Needed

- Bowl
- Drinking cup
- Birthday candles
- Plastic modeling clay
- Food coloring
- Rubber bands
- Matches
- Water

Procedure

1. Put about 3 cm (1 in.) of water into the bowl. Add a drop of food coloring to the water to help you see it more clearly.

2. Put a birthday candle in the clay and stand it up in the bowl.

3. Light the candle.

4. Put the mouth of the cup over the candle and into the water all the way to the bottom of the bowl.

5. What happened? What can you say about this?

6. Repeat the same activity using two, three, and four candles at a time. Use one rubber band around the cup to mark the water level each time you add a candle.

7. Can you predict what will happen if you use five candles? Try it.

Figure 1.25-1. Bowl Containing Water and Candle with Drinking Cup Above

Teacher Information

When the cup is placed over the burning candle, the air inside will be heated and forced out. The water will prevent more air from getting in. When the candle goes out, the air inside the cup will cool and contract. There will now be less air (and air pressure) inside the cup than outside. The outside air pressure will force water up into the cup. Increasing the number of candles will produce more heat, causing more air to be forced out, and the water will rise higher.

Integrating

Math

Science Process Skills

Observing, inferring, measuring, identifying and controlling variables

How Can We Watch Air Expand and Contract?

(Teacher-supervised activity)

Materials Needed

- Glass soda bottles or heat-resistant flask
- Balloons large enough to cover bottle mouth
- Bowls of very hot (not boiling) water
- Bowls of cold water

Procedure

1. Place the mouth of the balloon over the top of the bottle. Be sure no air can escape.
2. Put the bottle in very hot (not boiling) water for a few minutes.
3. What happened?
4. *Caution:* Remove the bottle from the hot water and wait several seconds before putting it in the cold water, to prevent possible cracking of the bottle. Now place the bottle in cold water for a few minutes.
5. What happened?
6. What can you say about this? Discuss your ideas with your group.

For Problem Solvers

Take a plastic bag that zips closed. Blow air into it until the bag is tight. Predict what will happen to the bag if you put it in a refrigerator. Seal the bag and place it in a refrigerator for a few minutes. Remove the bag and see whether your prediction was right. Now put it over a heat vent or in front of an electric heater for a few minutes. Predict what will happen, and then test your prediction.

Figure 1.26-1. Bottle in Bowl of Hot Water and Balloon on Top

Teacher Information

When the bottle is placed in hot water, the air inside will expand and cause the balloon to inflate slightly. When the bottle is placed in cold water, the air will contract and the balloon will deflate.

Integrating

Language arts

Science Process Skills

Observing, inferring, predicting

How Can Bubbles Show Us That Air Expands and Contracts?

(Take home and do with family and friends.)

Materials Needed

- Bubble solution in a bowl
- Soup can, empty with one end removed
- Warm water
- Ice water

Procedure

1. Dip the open end of the soup can into the bubble solution, then remove it and notice the bubble film across the opening of the can.

2. Predict what will happen to the soap film if you dip the closed end of the can in warm water. Write your prediction, then do it and watch the bubble.

3. What happened? Can you explain why? Was your prediction accurate?

4. Dip the closed end of the can in ice water and observe. Make your prediction first.

5. What happened? Explain why you think it did that.

For Problem Solvers

Try the same thing with larger and smaller cans. See which one you can get the largest bubble from. Figure out a way to measure how far the bubble dome extends out from the edge of the can.

Remove the other end from one of the cans and dip both ends into the bubble solution. Apply heat, then cold, by soaking a cloth in the water and wrapping it around the can.

With a small can that has both ends removed, dip one end in the bubble solution, remove it, and blow on the other end. Can you make large bubbles? Small bubbles?

Cut the neck off a balloon and stretch the balloon across one end of a can that has both ends removed, forming a diaphragm. Dip the open end of the can into the bubble solution, then pinch the center of the balloon and pull out, then push in. What happens?

What other ways can you make bubbles with a can?

Teacher Information

The bubble film across the end of the can will respond to the expansion and contraction of air inside the can as the air is heated and cooled, forming a concave surface when cooled and a convex surface when heated. Your problem solvers will have fun investigating in different ways with cans and bubbles.

Integrating

Math

Science Process Skills

Observing, measuring, predicting, communicating, comparing and contrasting, identifying and controlling variables

How Does Cold Air Behave?

(Teacher demonstration)

Materials Needed

- Hemp rope or incense
- Flashlight
- Refrigerator
- Match

Procedure

1. Light a hemp rope or use incense to make smoke. Observe how the smoke behaves.
2. Put the smoking object in the freezer compartment of a refrigerator.
3. Close the refrigerator door and darken the room.
4. Open the freezer compartment door and use a flashlight to observe the smoke.
5. What happened? What can you say about this?

Teacher Information

In air at room temperature, the smoke will rise. When it mixes with cold air in the freezer compartment, it will sink with the cold air when the door is opened. Cold air contains more molecules per cubic centimeter and therefore is heavier.

Note: Be sure to blow all the smoky air out of the refrigerator at the conclusion of the demonstration. (You could use an ice chest with ice as a substitute for the refrigerator if necessary.)

Integrating

Language arts

Science Process Skills

Observing

What Happens When Warm Air and Cold Air Mix?

(Teacher-supervised activity)

Materials Needed

- Two quart-sized clear jars
- Pan of hot water
- Hemp rope or incense
- Ice cubes
- Flashlight
- Match

Procedure

1. Put one jar upright in the pan of hot water.
2. Have your teacher put smoke in the two jars.
3. Then stand the second jar upside down on the first jar with the mouths together.
4. Put several ice cubes on top of the upper jar.
5. Darken the room. Use a flashlight to observe the smoke.
6. What happened? What can you say about this?

Figure 1.29-1. One Jar Inverted on Another. Lower Jar in Pan of Hot Water.

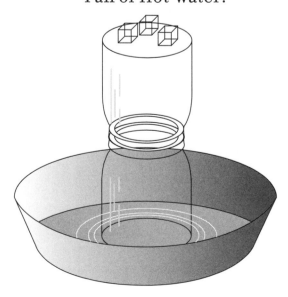

Air

Teacher Information

The air in the bottom jar will be heated and rise. When it nears the top of the second bottle, it will cool and begin to sink. Air currents will swirl in the two jars.

When you open a window to cool a room, another window should be opened above or below the first, if possible, so the air can circulate.

Integrating

Language arts

Science Process Skills

Observing

How Can You Get Water Out of the Air?

Materials Needed

- Ice cubes
- Clear bottles with lids
- Sheets of white paper
- Food coloring
- Water

Procedure

1. Put several ice cubes in the bottle and fill the bottle with water.

2. Add a few (about 3 to 6) drops of food coloring to the water and stir. Then put the lid on the bottle.

3. Place the bottle on a piece of white paper and let it stand for 30 minutes or so, checking it occasionally.

4. What happened? What can you say about this?

For Problem Solvers

Have you noticed that your bathroom mirror is clean and shiny before you run water in the shower or bathtub, but that it gets foggy as warm water runs from the faucet or showerhead? Where does the water come from that gets on the mirror? Try to explain how it happens.

Notice the outside of the windows of cars and houses on a cool summer morning. Often you will find moisture on them. Where did the moisture come from? Investigate and find out how this happened. If you live in a cold climate, you will sometimes find frost on the windows during cold weather. Where does the frost come from? Why does it form?

Teacher Information

As air cools it condenses and tends to give up moisture. As the bottle of ice water stands, the air around it will be cooled and moisture will condense on it unless the air is very dry. Food coloring and white paper are used to show that water is not passing through the bottle; if it did, the paper would become color-stained. The lid assures that the water collected on the outside of the bottle did not come over the top. The water formed on the outside will be clear.

We often use coasters under cold-drink glasses because of moisture that collects from condensation.

Integrating

Reading

Science Process Skills

Observing, inferring, communicating, using space-time relationships, identifying and controlling variables, experimenting

Hands-On Earth Science Activities

How Can a Balloon Remain Inflated with Its Mouth Open?

(Take home and do with family and friends.)

Materials Needed

- Balloon
- Rigid plastic bottle with small hole in bottom

Procedure

1. Tuck the balloon into the bottle, but hold onto the mouth of the balloon.
2. Stretch the mouth of the balloon over the mouth of the bottle, as shown in Figure 1.31–1.

Figure 1.31–1. Plastic Bottle with Balloon Hanging Inside

3. Put your finger over the hole in the bottom of the bottle, to seal the hole.
4. Try to blow up the balloon.
5. What happened? Explain why.

6. Now remove your finger from the hole in the bottom of the bottle and try again to blow up the balloon.

7. When the balloon is blown up and fills the bottle, seal the hole in the bottle again with your finger, and then remove the bottle from your mouth.

8. What happened to the balloon? Explain why it does this.

For Problem Solvers

You can have fun at home with this activity by holding the bottle for the person who is blowing up the balloon. You can hold your finger over the hole in the bottle the first time the other person tries, and he or she won't be able to blow up the balloon. The second time the person tries, secretly move your finger off the hole. Then after the balloon is blown up, quickly put your finger over the hole again and take the bottle away from the person's mouth. Let him or her wonder why the balloon is still blown up. Explain it to the person if he or she can't figure it out on his or her own.

Teacher Information

For this activity, you need a rigid plastic bottle. A small hole can be easily drilled in the bottom of the bottle with a drill or with a knife or other sharp instrument. Some juices are sold in rigid bottles, as are other materials. Two-liter soda bottles are flexible and will be crushed by atmospheric pressure, instead of the balloon remaining inflated. This still demonstrates the force of atmospheric pressure, but in a different way. With a rigid bottle, the balloon will remain inflated with the mouth of the balloon open to the atmosphere. This is a very impressive demonstration of the force of air pressure.

Integrating

Language arts

Science Process Skills

Observing, inferring, predicting, communicating, formulating hypotheses, identifying and controlling variables

Can You Solve This Air Word Search?

Try to find the following Air terms in the grid below. They could appear in horizontal (left to right), vertical (up or down), or diagonal (upward or downward) position.

air	space	displace
weight	pressure	vacuum
compress	push	atmosphere
suction	blow	expand
contract	exhale	inhale

```
M  N  B  C  W  S  V  C  X  Z  I  A
A  T  M  O  S  P  H  E  R  E  N  S
I  F  L  M  G  A  H  J  D  C  H  E
R  B  L  P  P  C  O  S  K  O  A  L
P  N  K  R  L  E  M  U  L  N  L  A
W  R  I  E  K  U  U  C  P  T  E  H
E  H  E  S  X  Y  U  T  O  R  X  X
I  T  O  S  J  P  C  I  I  A  Z  E
G  R  P  U  S  H  A  O  U  C  A  S
H  F  P  K  B  U  V  N  Y  T  Q  W
T  V  L  M  N  T  R  R  D  E  W  R
D  I  S  P  L  A  C  E  T  R  E  E
```

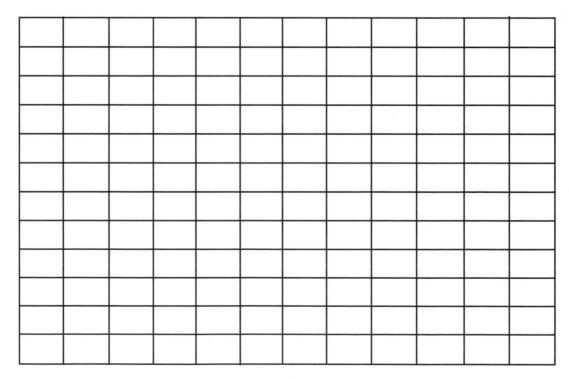

Can You Create a New Air Word Search of Your Own?

Write your Air words in the grid below. Arrange them in the grid so they appear in horizontal (left to right), vertical (up or down), or diagonal (upward or downward) position. Fill in the blank boxes with other letters. Trade your Word Search with someone else who has created one of his or her own, and see whether you can solve the new puzzle.

_____   _____   _____

_____   _____   _____

_____   _____   _____

_____   _____   _____

_____   _____   _____

Answer Key for Air Word Search

```
M  N  B  C  W  S  V  C  X  Z  I  A
A  T  M  O  S  P  H  E  R  E  N  S
I  F  L  M  G  A  H  J  D  C  H  E
R  B  L  P  P  C  O  S  K  O  A  L
P  N  K  R  L  E  M  U  L  N  L  A
W  R  I  E  K  U  U  C  P  T  E  H
E  H  E  S  X  Y  U  T  O  R  X  X
I  T  O  S  J  P  C  I  I  A  Z  E
G  R  P  U  S  H  A  O  U  C  A  S
H  F  P  K  B  U  V  N  Y  T  Q  W
T  V  L  M  N  T  R  R  D  E  W  R
D  I  S  P  L  A  C  E  T  R  E  E
```

Do You Recall?

Section One: Air

1. Is air a form of matter?

2. Does air weigh anything at all?

3. If you press a suction cup onto a table and you can't pull it off, what holds the suction to the table?

4. Imagine that you place a card on a full cup of water, turn the cup upside down, and let go of the card. If the card stays in place, keeping the water in the cup, what is holding the card on the cup?

5. An airplane wing is rounded on top and flat on the bottom. How does this help to hold the plane in the air?

6. Why does a drop in temperature often bring rain?

Answer Key for Do You Recall?

Section One: Air

Answer	Related Activities
1. Yes	1.1, 1.2
2. Yes	1.3
3. The weight of air pressing against it	1.4, 1.5
4. Air pressure	1.8–1.17
5. Air pressure is reduced on top of the wing, resulting in a lifting force under the wing	1.18–1.22
6. Cold air cannot hold as much moisture as warm air can. If there is a lot of water in the air, and the air cools, it's like squeezing a wet sponge.	1.30

Water

To the Teacher

Water is essential to all forms of life. People can live for weeks without food, but only for a short period of time without water. Because it is usually available, we often take it for granted, yet it plays an important role in almost every area of science. Even the study of nonliving materials includes the study of how water acts upon and interacts with them.

Water is the most abundant substance on the planet, yet much of the earth suffers from water shortages. Huge amounts of water are required for agriculture, for the manufacture of goods, for personal needs, and for many other purposes. Although there is a global abundance of water, getting the right amounts in the right places and in the right form is a constant challenge in many parts of the world.

Water evaporates into the air, then condenses and returns to the surface of the earth in various forms of precipitation. Called the water cycle, this process is vital to all forms of life as it recycles and redistributes this precious resource.

The following activities are designed as discovery activities that students can usually perform quite independently. You are encouraged to provide students (usually in small groups) with the materials listed and a copy of the activity from the beginning through the "Procedure." The section titled "Teacher Information" is not intended for student use, but rather to assist you with discussion following the hands-on activity, as students share their observations. Discussion of conceptual information prior to completing the hands-on activity can interfere with the discovery process.

Regarding the Early Grades

With verbal instructions and slight modifications, many of these activities can be used with kindergarten, first-grade, and second-grade students. In some activities, steps that involve procedures that go beyond the level of the child can simply be omitted and yet offer the child an experience that plants the seed for a concept that will germinate and grow later on.

Teachers of the early grades will probably choose to bypass many of the "For Problem Solvers" sections. That's okay. These sections are provided for those who are especially motivated and want to go beyond the investigation provided by the activity outlined. Use the outlined activities, and enjoy worthwhile learning experiences together with your young students. Also consider, however, that many of the "For Problem Solvers" sections can be used appropriately with young children as group activities or as demonstrations, still giving students the advantage of an exposure to the experience and laying groundwork for connections that will be made at a later time.

Correlation with National Standards

The following elements of the National Standards are reflected in the activities of this section.

K–4   Content Standard A: Science as Inquiry

As a result of activities in grades K–4, all students should develop

1. Abilities necessary to do scientific inquiry
2. Understanding about scientific inquiry

K–4   Content Standard D: Earth and Space Science

As a result of activities in grades K–4, all students should develop understanding of

1. Properties of earth materials
2. Objects in the sky
3. Changes in earth and sky

5–8   Content Standard A: Science as Inquiry

As a result of activities in grades 5–8, all students should develop

1. Abilities necessary to do scientific inquiry
2. Understanding about scientific inquiry

5–8   Content Standard D: Earth and Space Science

As a result of activities in grades 5–8, all students should develop understanding of

1. Structure of the earth system
2. Earth's history
3. Earth in the solar system

Why Do Some Things Float on Water and Others Do Not?

Materials Needed

- Gallon cans with a nail hole near the top
- Cookie sheets
- Masking tape
- Marking pens
- Two cups per small group
- Balance scales
- Small blocks of wood (need to fit easily into the cup)
- Rocks (need to fit easily into the cup)
- Variety of other objects (each must fit easily into the cup)
- Copies of "Science Investigation Journaling Notes" for all students

Procedure

1. Do the following as a Science Investigation. Obtain a blank copy of the "Science Investigation Journaling Notes." Write your name, the date, and your question at the top. Plan your investigation through step 5 of the form (Procedure) and have it approved by your teacher. Complete the Journaling Notes as you perform your investigation. When you are finished, share your project with your group and submit your Journaling Notes to your teacher if requested.

2. Fill the can with water until the water begins to flow out the nail hole.

3. When the water has stopped coming out the hole in the can, carefully move the can onto the cookie sheet. Tip the can back a bit so water will not come out the nail hole as you move the can.

4. Use the masking tape and marking pen to label one cup "A" and one "B."

5. Label one end of the balance scale "A" and the other "B" in a similar way.

6. Place the cups on the balance scale, one on each end, matching A with A and B with B, and balance the scale.

7. Check to be sure the gallon can has all the water it will hold without spilling out the nail hole.

8. Place the rock in the water, being careful not to splash, and keeping your hand out of the water. Did some water spill out the nail hole in the can?

9. Move the gallon can off the cookie sheet, being careful not to pour more water out the nail hole. The only water that is now on the cookie sheet should be the water that was forced out the nail hole when you placed the rock in the gallon can.

10. Pour the water from the cookie sheet into Cup A.

11. Remove the rock from the gallon can and place it into Cup B.

12. Place each of the cups on its end of the scale, according to the labels.

13. Cup B contains the rock, and cup A contains the water displaced by the rock. Which is heavier, Cup A or Cup B?

14. Since the scale was balanced with both cups empty, what are we really comparing, the weight of the cups or the weight of the rock and the water that was displaced (pushed out) by the rock?

15. Now fill the gallon can with water again, just as you did before, and put it back on the cookie sheet.

16. Put the block of wood in the water. Push it into the water until it is all the way in, but try to keep your hands out of the water. Hold it there until the water stops running out of the nail hole.

17. Repeat steps 9 through 12 with the block of wood, just as you did with the rock.

18. Which is heavier, the block of wood or the water that was displaced by the block of wood?

19. Complete your "Science Investigation Journaling Notes." Are you ready to explain why some things float on water and some do not? Discuss it with your group.

For Problem Solvers

Obtain another copy of the "Science Investigation Journaling Notes" and try the same investigation with several other objects of various sizes and weights. With each one, predict whether it will sink or float, try it, then compare the weight of the object with the weight of the water that was displaced by the object.

Find a small boat that will fit into the gallon can. Capture the water that spills while the boat floats and compare the weight of the boat with the weight of the water displaced by the boat. Go back to the block of wood you used in the above activity and do the same thing; compare the weight of the block of wood with the weight of the water displaced as the block of wood floated. Try several floating objects and compare your results.

Teacher Information

Students will learn much about buoyancy as they do this activity. Simply stated, an object is buoyed up by a force equal to the weight of the water displaced.

If the weight of an object is less than the weight of the water displaced by the object, the object will float on water. If the weight of an object is greater than the weight of the water displaced by the object, the object will sink. A piece of steel does not float on water; yet a ship made of steel not only floats but carries thousands of tons of cargo across the sea. The ship is shaped in such a way that it displaces an amount of water that weighs far more than does the loaded ship. If the ship is loaded so heavily that it weighs more than the water it displaces, the ship will sink. Similarly, if so many people climb into a rowboat that the boat (including its load) is heavier than the weight of the water displaced by the boat, the rowboat will sink.

If you have a rock collection that includes a sample of pumice, this is a good item to include in the above activity. Pumice is a volcanic rock that cooled very quickly after being expelled from a volcano. It is full of air holes, giving it some resemblance to a sponge. It is a rock that will float on water.

Integrating

Math, language arts

Science Process Skills

Observing, inferring, measuring, predicting, communicating, comparing and contrasting, using space-time relationships, identifying and controlling variables, experimenting

How Does Water Disappear?

Materials Needed

- Sponges
- Chalkboard
- Water
- Heavy pieces of cardboard

Procedure

1. Moisten the sponge.
2. Make a wide, damp streak on the chalkboard.
3. Observe for several minutes. What happened?
4. Make two streaks about 1 m (1 yd.) apart.
5. Use the cardboard to fan one of the streaks.
6. Compare the time it took for each to disappear.

For Problem Solvers

Measure 50 ml ($\frac{1}{4}$ cup) of water and pour it into a drinking glass. Put the same amount into a soup bowl, the same amount into a fruit jar, and the same amount into a pie plate. Put the lid on the fruit jar. Predict what will happen to the water in these containers over a three-day period. Observe these four containers each morning and afternoon for three days. Write your observations each time. Discuss your observations with others in the class.

Teacher Information

This is an initial experience with evaporation. If the sponge is just moist, the results will be faster than if it is soaking wet.

Using the cardboard as a fan will increase the rate of evaporation.

An alternate activity is to put a small amount of water—1 cm ($\frac{1}{2}$ in.)—in two small jars. Seal the lid of one and leave the other open. Observe for 24 hours.

Students should learn from this activity that water is absorbed into the air by a process called evaporation. Increasing the amount of air moving over the water (fanning) increases the rate of evaporation. The amount of moisture the air already contains (humidity) will be a factor.

Integrating
Math, language arts

Science Process Skills
Observing, inferring, measuring, predicting, communicating, comparing and contrasting, using space-time relationships, identifying and controlling variables, experimenting

What Is Condensation?

(Teacher-supervised activity)

Materials Needed

- Metal pans (or beakers)
- Water
- Heat source
- Sheet of glass or hand mirror

Procedure

1. Put about 1 cm ($\frac{1}{2}$ in.) of water in the pan.
2. Heat the water until it boils.
3. Hold the sheet of glass over the boiling water.
4. Observe the glass carefully. What do you see forming on the glass? Explain why you think this happens.

Teacher Information

As water is heated, the rate of evaporation is increased. The sheet of glass or mirror held over the escaping water vapor cools the vapor and causes it to condense into liquid form, shown by the drops of water forming on it. *Caution:* This process will be speeded up if the mirror or sheet of glass is cooled first, but this can be dangerous because of the risk of breaking the glass.

Similar evidence of condensation can be observed by placing a pitcher (or other container) of ice water on a table. Water vapor in the air is cooled by the pitcher, and drops of water form on the surface of the pitcher.

Integrating

Math, language arts

Science Process Skills

Observing, inferring, measuring, communicating

How Did the Bottle Get Wet on the Outside When the Water Is Sealed on the Inside?

(Take home and do with family and friends.)

Materials Needed

- Ice cubes
- Clear bottles with lids
- Sheets of white paper
- Food coloring
- Water

Procedure

1. Put several ice cubes in the bottle. Fill the bottle with water and put the lid on.
2. Add a drop of food coloring to the water and stir.
3. Put the bottle on a piece of white paper and let it stand for several minutes.
4. What happened? What can you say about this?

For Problem Solvers

An important variable here is weather. Try this activity on a hot, clear day; on a hot, cloudy day; on a cool, clear day; and on a cool, cloudy day. Make notes of your observations each time, especially regarding how long it took to get real results. After you have made all of your observations—this might take a month or more, depending on where you live—compare your notes. Discuss them with others who are doing the activity and teach the rest of the class what you learned.

Teacher Information

When air is cooled, it condenses and gives up moisture. As the bottle becomes cold, the air around it will be cooled and moisture will condense on it. Food coloring and the white paper are used to show that the water is not passing through the bottle; if it did, the paper would have a colored stain. The lid assures that the water collected on the outside of the bottle did not come over the top. The water formed on the outside will be clear.

We often use coasters under cold-drink glasses because of moisture that collects from condensation.

Integrating

Language arts

Science Process Skills

Observing, inferring, communicating, using space-time relationships, identifying and controlling variables, experimenting

What Is Another Way to Get Moisture Out of the Air?

(Teacher demonstration)

Materials Needed

- Large, wide-mouthed, clear glass jars
- Rubber bands (heavy duty)
- Wooden matches
- Plastic bags (bread sack or similar size)
- Water

Procedure

1. Pour enough water into the jar to cover the bottom of the jar.
2. Light a wooden match. Hold it down in the jar to make smoke.
3. Push the plastic bag down inside the jar with about 5 cm (2 in.) hanging over the rim. (Don't let the smoke escape.)
4. Secure the bag with the rubber band.
5. Reach inside and pull up sharply on the plastic bag.
6. What happened? What can you say about this? Discuss your ideas with your group.

Figure 2.5-1. Plastic Bag Hanging Inside Glass Jar

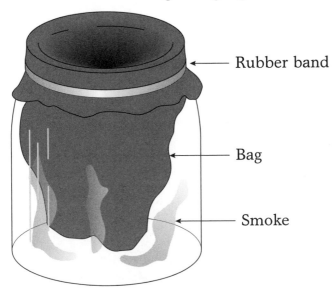

Rubber band

Bag

Smoke

Teacher Information

Adding a small amount of water to the jar provides additional moisture, and smoke provides tiny particles in the air. When you pull up sharply on the plastic bag, air pressure in the jar is reduced and the air suddenly becomes cooler. Cool air cannot hold as much moisture as warm air can, so tiny droplets of water form around the smoke particles and make a cloud. The cloud will form in the bottle for only an instant before disappearing, but you can usually make it form over and over again.

This is very similar to the way clouds form in the atmosphere. As air cools, water molecules collect around smoke and dust particles in the air. The particles are called *condensation nuclei.* Water is clear, but clouds often look dark because of the smoke and dust in them, which are providing condensation nuclei around which raindrops form.

Integrating

Language arts

Science Process Skills

Observing, inferring, communicating

How Can You Boil Water in a Paper Cup?

(Teacher demonstration)

Materials Needed

- Non-waxed paper cups (not plastic or foam)
- Candle or alcohol lamp
- Water

Procedure

1. Put about 5 cm (2 in.) of water in a paper cup.
2. Put a candle or alcohol lamp under the cup.
3. What happened? Can you think of a reason why?

For Problem Solvers

Different class members probably have cousins and friends in many parts of the country—north, south, east, and west. Write letters to people in various locations. Ask them to boil some water on the stove and tell you what temperature the water boiled at for them. Ask them to use distilled water if they can and to let you know whether they used distilled water or tap water. Ask them to include their altitude in the information they send.

Plot on a map the boiling points and altitudes for each location. Be sure to include the same information for your own location. Use both distilled water and tap water, so you have both to compare with data coming in from the different locations.

Analyze your data. Is boiling point the same for all locations? Is boiling point the same for tap water as for distilled water? What seems to have made a difference? Longitude? Latitude? Altitude? What effect, if any, does each of these variables seem to have on boiling point?

Teacher Information

Caution: Note that for safety reasons this activity is suggested as a teacher demonstration.

Soon the water will become hot enough to boil, but the paper cup will not burn. Water boils at 100 degrees Celsius (212 degrees Fahrenheit) at sea level. Paper must be much hotter to reach its kindling point. As long

Hands-On Earth Science Activities

as water remains in the cup, it will keep the paper cool enough to prevent it from burning. Remember, once water reaches its boiling point, it does not become hotter if the pressure on the surface remains the same.

If the pressure on the surface of the water is increased, the boiling point will be increased and the water can become hotter (as in a pressure cooker). If the pressure on the surface is decreased, water will boil at a lower temperature, which is why high-altitude cooking requires more time; atmospheric pressure decreases as altitude increases.

Your problem solvers will have a valuable experience in writing to people in various parts of the country and in analyzing the data they obtain. They will learn that boiling point decreases with increasing altitude. Impurities in water will be somewhat of a confounding variable, because boiling point increases with the addition of impurities, but it shouldn't be a big problem. The only way to control for impurities would be to ask everyone to use distilled water, which would likely decrease the number who respond. There will also be minor differences in thermometer accuracy, but these differences also should not be significant.

Integrating

Math, language arts, social studies

Science Process Skills

Observing, inferring, measuring, communicating, identifying and controlling variables, experimenting, researching

How Can We See Water Pressure?

Materials Needed

- Gallon cans or plastic bottles
- Nails
- Hammers

Procedure

1. Use the nail to punch three holes, equally spaced from top to bottom, in the can or plastic bottle.
2. Place the container in the sink and hold all three holes while filling it with water.
3. Release all three holes at the same time.
4. What happened? What does this tell you about the weight and pressure of water?

For Problem Solvers

Repeat this activity using containers of different diameters and different heights. Place all containers the same distance from the ground. Let your measure of water pressure be the distance of the stream from the container when it reaches the ground. What variable seems to make the difference: Diameter of the container? Height of the container? Depth of the water? All of these?

Do some research on depth of water in dams and oceans, and on the pressure of water at the bottom. When water comes through the bottom of a dam and runs through a turbine to spin a generator, what is the pressure of the water at that point? Is it the same for all dams?

What is the water pressure at the deepest part of the ocean? Could you survive there without protection? How do fish live deep in the sea? Could all fish live miles below the surface? What would happen if they came quickly to the surface?

Teacher Information

The stream of water will be greatest from the lowest hole in the can. Less will flow from the middle hole and the least from the top hole.

This demonstrates that the pressure of water increases with its depth. (This is also true of air pressure. Pressure at sea level is greater than at an altitude of a few thousand feet.)

Your problem solvers will learn that water pressure is directly affected by depth of the water. Pressure of water coming through the bottom of a dam is the same at a given depth whether there is a half mile of water backed up behind the dam or forty miles of water backed up behind the dam.

Integrating

Math, reading, social studies

Science Process Skills

Observing, inferring, measuring, predicting, communicating, comparing and contrasting, formulating hypotheses, identifying and controlling variables, experimenting, researching

Water

How Can You Make Water Pile Up on a Cup?

(Take home and do with family and friends.)

Materials Needed

- Small cups (one-ounce pill cup or other small cup)
- Eyedroppers
- Water
- Pencils
- Paper towels
- Copies of the "Science Investigation Journaling Notes" for this activity for all students

Procedure

1. As you complete this activity, keep a record of what you do, just as scientists do. Use a copy of the "Science Investigation Journaling Notes" form and write the information that is called for, including your name and the date.

2. For this activity, you will learn about how water can pile up on a cup. For item 1, the question is provided for you on the form.

3. Item 2 asks for what you already know about the question. If you have some ideas about how water can pile up on a cup, write your ideas.

4. For item 3, write a statement of how or why water piles up on a cup, according to what you already know, and that will be your hypothesis.

5. Now continue with the following instructions. Complete your Journaling Notes as you go. Steps 6 through 11 will help you with the information you need to write on the form for items 4 and 5.

6. Lay your pencil across the top of the cup. (See Figure 2.8–1.)

7. Pour water into the cup. Pour very slowly as the water level approaches the pencil. Keep pouring until the water barely touches the pencil; then stop pouring and remove the pencil.

Figure 2.8-1. Pencil on Cup

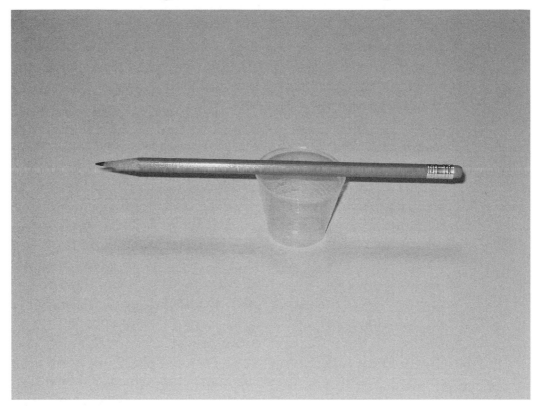

8. Look at the dropper and the full cup of water, and think about times you have used a dropper before. Think about how big a drop of water is as it comes from the dropper, but leave the dropper on the table for now.

9. Predict how many drops of water you will be able to put in the cup you just filled with water before it spills over. Write that number. If you are working with others, do not discuss your prediction until each person has written a number.

10. Now test your prediction by counting the drops as you add them to the cup. Hold the dropper quite close to the surface, so they don't splash, but far enough from the surface that the drop does not touch the surface without leaving the dropper.

11. Compare your counted number with your prediction.

12. For item 6 of your Journaling Notes, write about your observations. If you were surprised with your results, why do you think it happened that way? Write your answer on your paper.

13. Discuss your ideas with others in your group and with your teacher.

14. For item 7 of the form, think about your hypothesis (item 3) and write your explanation of how or why water piles up on a cup before it spills over.

For Problem Solvers

Try to find other cups that are a bit larger or a bit smaller than the one you used for this activity. Using just one cup at a time, fill the cup level full, using the pencil as a straight edge as before. Be sure to write your prediction before you begin adding drops. Try to improve your predicting skills as you use the different-sized cups.

Try to find 2 cups (or bottles) that are different sizes but have the same size mouth. If you fill each one level full, which one do you think you can add more water to before it spills over? Discuss your hypothesis with others, including why you think this might be. Then test your hypothesis by counting drops. You might need to test it three or four times to obtain reliable results.

Predict the number of drops of water you can put on the surface of a penny. Try it. How many drops of water can you put on a dime? A quarter? Are your prediction skills improving? Compare several pennies, writing your prediction each time. Are they always the same? Why? Compare heads with tails. What factors do you think affect the amount of water you can add without spilling over?

Teacher Information

Students will likely predict low numbers of drops to begin with, but eyes widen as the water bulges above the top of the cup when more and more drops are added. Water molecules have an attraction for each other (called cohesion). This bond forms a skin-like surface and is called "surface tension." Water on the surface of the glass will bulge above the rim as the molecules cling together. Gravity soon overcomes this force, however, and the water spills over.

Water forms in drops because of surface tension.

Integrating

Math, language arts

Science Process Skills

Observing, inferring, predicting, communicating, comparing and contrasting, formulating hypotheses, identifying and controlling variables

Hands-On Earth Science Activities

Name _____   Date _____

 # Science Investigation

Journaling Notes for Activity 2.8

1. Question: How can you make water pile up on a cup?

2. What we already know: _____

_____

3. Hypothesis: _____

_____

4. Materials needed: _____

_____

5. Procedure: _____

_____

_____

_____

_____

_____

6. Observations/New information: _____

_____

_____

7. Conclusion: _____

_____

_____

_____

Water

How Many Nails Can You Put into a Full Glass of Water?

(Take home and do with family and friends.)

Materials Needed

- Eight-ounce glass
- Water
- Paper and pencils
- 200 nails 5 cm (2 in.) long (or smaller)

Procedure

1. Fill an eight-ounce glass with water. Make sure the water is level with the top of the glass. (If you lay a pencil across the top of the glass, the water should barely touch the pencil.)
2. Predict how many nails you can put into the glass before water spills over the top. Write your prediction.
3. Carefully put the nails in one at a time, head first to avoid splashing. What happened?
4. What can you say about this?

For Problem Solvers

Try the same activity with paper clips and with pennies. Be sure you write your predictions before you begin putting items in the water. Are you improving your prediction skills?

Do this project as a Science Investigation. Use a blank copy of the "Science Investigation Journaling Notes." Write your name, the date, and your question at the top. Plan your investigation through step 5 (Procedure) and have it approved by your teacher. Complete the Journaling Notes as you perform your investigation. Share your project with your group and submit your Journaling Notes to your teacher if requested.

Teacher Information

Students will probably be able to put many nails into the glass. Smaller nails, pennies, or paper clips will also work well. Water molecules have an attraction for each other, called cohesion. This attraction forms a bond at the surface, called surface tension. Water on the surface of the glass will bulge above the rim as the molecules cling together. Gravity soon overcomes this force, however, and the water spills over.

Water forms in drops because of surface tension.

Integrating

Math

Science Process Skills

Observing, predicting, identifying and controlling variables

How Does Pepper Swim?

Materials Needed

- Saucer
- Pepper
- Liquid detergent
- Water
- Toothpicks

Procedure

1. Cover the bottom of the saucer with water.
2. Sprinkle pepper lightly on the surface of the water.
3. Dip the tip of a toothpick into the center of the water. What happened?
4. Now dip the tip of another toothpick into the liquid detergent.
5. Dip the toothpick with detergent on it into the middle of the saucer. What happened?
6. Try to explain what you saw and why it happened.

For Problem Solvers

Place a staple very carefully on its side on the surface of the water. Add a drop of detergent and see what happens. Use hot water. Try cold water. Try soft water. Try distilled water. Predict what will happen each time you try a new idea; then try it and test your prediction. What do you think will happen if you fill a cup with water to the point that the water is bulging and then add a drop of detergent? Try it.

Teacher Information

Pepper will float on the surface of the untreated water. Because of adhesion (attraction of unlike molecules for each other), water molecules cling to the side of each pepper particle. The attraction of water molecules to each other at the surface (surface tension) results in a tugging effect on

the pepper particle all the way around. Adding detergent breaks the surface tension on the near side, and the pepper is pulled to the edge of the dish by the tugging of water molecules on the other side of the pepper particle.

Integrating

Language arts

Science Process Skills

Observing, inferring, predicting, communicating, formulating hypotheses

How Can You Make a Soap Motorboat?

(Take home and do with family and friends.)

Materials Needed

- Craft stick
- Eyedropper
- Liquid detergent
- Large bowl or pan of clean, fresh water

Procedure

1. Break one end from a craft stick. Use it for a boat, letting the rounded end be the front of the boat.
2. Float your boat near the center of the pan of water. (See Figure 2.11–1.)
3. Use the dropper to put a small amount of detergent on the back of the boat. What happened? Discuss your ideas with your group.

Figure 2.11–1. Stick Floating in Pan

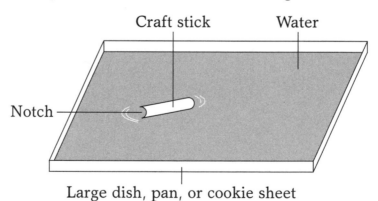

For Problem Solvers

Do more research about surface tension and then explain the actions of the boat in terms of surface tension. Did the soap push the boat?

Lay a paper clip very carefully on a pan of water. Put a drop of liquid soap or detergent in the water near the paper clip and observe. Can you make other objects float that normally do not float on water? With each item, predict whether it will float or not before you try it. Can you explain what's happening?

Teacher Information

The drop of detergent will dissolve, breaking the surface tension of the water behind the boat. Water molecules tug on the boat at the front, pulling it through the water.

Note: If liquid detergent is not available, scrape a bit of soap from a wet bar of hand soap onto the tail end of the boat. It will work just the same. Before attempting to repeat any activities involving soap or detergent, rinse everything thoroughly in clean water, being certain that no soap film is left from the previous activity.

If you prefer, you can carve the front of the boat into a point and make a notch in the broken end for the back of the boat, but you won't want to let students use sharp knives. The non-carved boat works fine.

Integrating

Language arts

Science Process Skills

Observing, inferring, classifying, predicting, communicating, identifying and controlling variables, experimenting, researching

How Can You Pour Light?

(Enrichment activity)

Materials Needed

- Tall, slim jar with a lid (olive jars work)
- Flashlight
- Hammer
- Nail
- Newspaper or light cardboard
- Masking tape or plastic tape
- Water

Procedure

1. With the hammer and nail, make two holes in the lid of the jar. The holes should be near the edge but opposite each other. One hole should be quite small. Work the nail around in the other to enlarge the hole a bit.

2. Fill the jar about two-thirds full of water and put the lid on.

3. Put tape over the holes in the lid until you are ready to pour.

4. Lay the jar and flashlight end to end, with the face of the flashlight at the bottom of the jar.

5. Roll the newspaper or cardboard around the jar and flashlight to enclose them in a light-tight tube. Tape the tube together so it will stay.

6. Slide the flashlight out of the tube, turn it on, and slide it back into the tube.

7. Hold the apparatus upright and remove the tape from the lid. Pour the water with the larger nail hole beneath the smaller one. Water will pour from the larger hole, with the smaller one serving as an air hole.

8. What happened to the beam of light as the water poured into the pan?

9. Do you have any idea what caused this? Discuss your ideas with your group.

For Problem Solvers

Use your creativity with this activity. Try different containers for the water and different light sources. Try putting some food coloring in the water. Does that provide the same effect as if you put a colored filter over the flashlight?

Do some research on fiberoptics. Is there any similarity between the way fiberoptics function and the function of the device you made with a flashlight and a jar?

Teacher Information

Although light travels in straight lines, it is reflected internally at the water's surface and follows the path of the stream of water. Because of the phenomenon of internal reflection, fiberoptics can be used to direct light anywhere a wire can go, even into the veins and arteries of the human body.

Refraction occurs as light changes speed in passing from one medium to another.

Reflection commonly refers to the bouncing of light within a single medium, in this case water and plastic or glass.

Integrating

Math, language arts

Science Process Skills

Observing, inferring, communicating, formulating hypotheses, experimenting

How Can a Water Drop Make Things Appear Larger?

(Take home and do with family and friends.)

Materials Needed

- Thin copper wire 15 to 20 cm (6 to 8 in.) long
- Nail 8 cm (3 in.) long
- Water
- Book

Procedure

1. Make a small loop in the end of the wire. You may want to wrap it around the nail to make it the correct size.
2. Capture a drop of water in the loop.
3. Use the drop of water in the loop to look at print in a book. What happened? What can you say about this?
4. Gently tap the wire. Try to get most of the water drop out of the loop (a little must remain across the loop).
5. Look at the print again. What happened? What can you say about this?

For Problem Solvers

Experiment with the idea of using a drop of water as a magnifier. Place a drop of water directly onto the print on a magazine page. Put a drop of water on a sheet of clear plastic and move it onto a page of print. Using a hand lens, carefully observe the shape of the drop. What is its shape?

Do some research and learn what you can about lenses. Find out what the shape of the water drop has to do with the way things appear when you look through it.

Teacher Information

This activity can be used to introduce the concept of light being bent as it passes from one medium to another. The water drop acts as a convex lens and makes objects appear larger. The thin film in the loop works as a concave lens and makes things appear smaller.

For younger children, you may want to put a drop of water on printed paper. The print will be magnified.

Figure 2.13-1. Convex and Concave Lenses

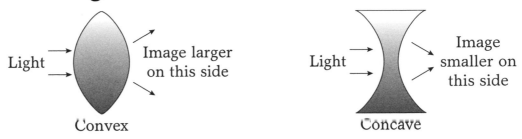

Integrating
Reading

Science Process Skills
Observing, inferring, comparing and contrasting

How Can Water Make a Coin Appear?

(Take home and do with family and friends.)

Materials Needed

- Opaque bowl
- Coin
- Water

Procedure

1. Put the coin in the bowl. Mark the spot so you're sure it doesn't move.

2. Put the bowl on the table and crouch down until you can no longer see the coin. (Don't go down too far—just until you can no longer see the coin.)

3. Have a friend slowly pour water into the bowl without disturbing the coin. What happened?

4. What can you say about this?

Teacher Information

Light travels in straight lines in air, but when it passes from air to water, it slows down and is bent. As water is poured into the bowl, the light will bend and more of the bottom of the bowl will be exposed. The coin will appear. (See Figure 2.14–1.)

Figure 2.14–1. Light Bends as It Passes from Water to Air

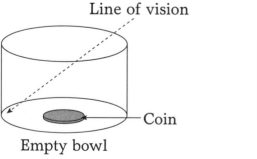

Line of vision

Coin

Empty bowl

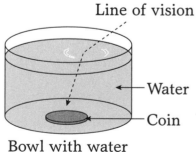

Line of vision

Water

Coin

Bowl with water

Science Process Skills

Observing, inferring

What Do Bears Know That Many People Don't?

Materials Needed

- Eight-ounce water glasses (clear)
- Pencils
- Water

Procedure

1. Use an eight-ounce glass about two-thirds full of water.
2. Put a pencil in the glass. Observe the pencil above and below the water level.
3. What can you say about this?
4. Why do you think this activity might be called "What do bears know that many people don't?" Think of a bear trying to catch a fish it sees in the water.

For Problem Solvers

Challenge your friends to a test of skills at spear fishing. Put some water in a dishpan or sink. Place a coin (that's the fish) at the bottom of the pan. Use a meter stick, a metal rod, or any other straight and narrow shaft as a spear. Place the tip of your spear on the edge of the pan, but not in the water. Aim at the fish, and quickly push the spear to the bottom of the pan, being sure to keep the spear at the same angle as when it was aimed.

Talk about eagles and bears and their ability to strike at the right place when catching a fish. How do you think they learned to do that?

Teacher Information

When the pencil is put in the glass of water, it appears to bend as it enters the water. This is because the light is bent as it enters the water. Actually, the part of the pencil that is in the water is not where it appears to be when viewing it from an angle. Bears seem to know this and use it when fishing. They seem to know where the fish is even though it isn't exactly where it appears to be.

Children may also notice that the pencil appears larger under the water when viewed from the side of the clear container. This is because the curved surface of the glass and the water in it act as a convex lens.

Integrating
Language arts

Science Process Skills
Observing, inferring, estimating, communicating

What Can You Learn from an Egg?

(Take home and do with family and friends.)

Materials Needed

- Egg
- Glass full of water
- Salt

Procedure

1. Put the egg in a glass of water.
2. Add salt a tablespoon at a time and stir until something happens to the egg. What happened?
3. Can you explain what happened? Discuss your ideas with your group.

For Problem Solvers

Put fresh water (from sink) and salt water in two separate glasses and add a few drops of food coloring (different colors) to each. See whether you can devise a plan to show the egg sinking in fresh water and floating on salt water in the same glass.

Teacher Information

When the egg is put in the untreated water, it will sink to the bottom of the glass. As salt is added to the water, the egg will rise in the water. This is because dissolving salt into the water increases the density of the water until the egg is able to float.

Floating an egg in brine solution is the method some people use to tell when the brine is just right for pickling.

Your problem solvers might try pouring the fresh water very carefully into the salt water. It will take a little while for the two to mix, so for a short time the fresh water should separate out and be on top of the salt water, with the egg floating on the salt water and the fresh water above the egg.

Integrating

Math, language arts

Science Process Skills

Observing, inferring, comparing and contrasting

How Can We Use a Soda Straw to Compare Density of Liquids?

(Teacher-directed activity)

Materials Needed

- Ten-ounce clear plastic cups (several)
- Water
- Isopropyl alcohol
- Salt
- Food coloring
- Soda straws
- Gummed label (or masking tape) with numbered marks every $\frac{1}{4}$ inch along its length
- BBs
- Clay

Procedure

1. Fill one clear plastic cup about two-thirds full of water.
2. Prepare a soda straw as a hydrometer, as follows:

   a. Press a small piece of clay into one end of the drinking straw.

   b. Use your pencil to push the clay about .5 cm ($\frac{1}{4}$ inch) into the straw.

   c. Put two BBs in the same end of the straw, followed by another small piece of clay to seal the BBs in place. (See Figure 2.17–1.)

   d. Prepare another hydrometer, using three BBs.

   e. Prepare a third hydrometer, using four BBs.

Figure 2.17-1. Soda Straw Prepared for Use as a Hydrometer

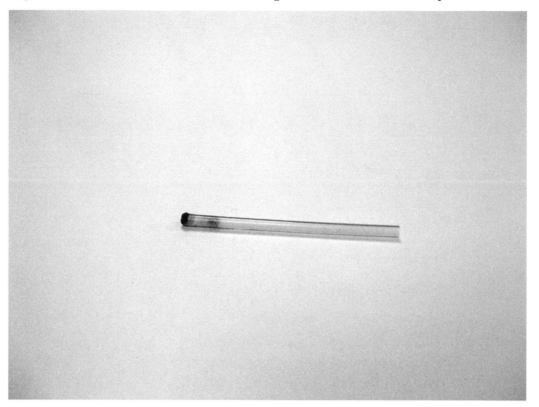

3. Test each of the hydrometers in the cup of water. The hydrometer needs to stand upright in the water without touching the bottom of the cup. If necessary, prepare other hydrometers with one and with four BBs, until you find one that works for you. (See Figure 2.17–2.)

4. Notice where the water level is on the hydrometer. Remove the hydrometer from the water, dry it, and apply the gummed label with the center of the label at the water level.

5. Fill two more plastic tumblers about two-thirds full, one with salt water and the other with rubbing alcohol. Put a few drops of food coloring in the salt water and in the rubbing alcohol, each a different color.

6. Place your hydrometer in the cup of water and record the hydrometer number that is nearest the water level.

7. Test the salt water and the rubbing alcohol and record the hydrometer numbers at the surface of each liquid.

8. Explain the density of the three liquids, comparing each liquid with the other two.

Figure 2.17-2. Hydrometer Standing in Cup of Water

For Problem Solvers

Do this project as a Science Investigation. Obtain a blank copy of the "Science Investigation Journaling Notes." Write your name, the date, and your question at the top. Plan your investigation through step 5 (Procedure) and have it approved by your teacher. Complete the Journaling Notes as you perform your investigation. Share your project with your group and submit your Journaling Notes to your teacher if requested.

Fill more ten-ounce cups with other liquids, each about two-thirds full. You could try cooking oil, pancake syrup, and others that are available to you.

Line up the liquids in order of least dense to most dense, according to your prediction. (Include the water, salt water, and rubbing alcohol that you have already tested.) Use your hydrometer to compare the liquids, and then arrange them in order, with the liquid of least density on the left and the liquid of greatest density on the right. Did you predict them accurately?

Make a list of the liquids you found to be more dense than water. Make a separate list of those you found to be less dense than water.

Gather a variety of small objects that are made of plastic, wood, metal, and so forth. Place these items in the liquids, one at a time. Try to find at least one item that will float on each liquid, but not on the next liquid to the left.

Hands-On Earth Science Activities

Pour a small amount of the most dense liquid into an empty jar. Using a bulb-type basting tool, carefully transfer about the same amount of a second liquid into the first and see whether one liquid will float on the other. Try a third liquid. After you have three or more liquids layered in the same container, select one object that you think will float at each level and carefully drop those objects into the jar. Explain to your teacher what happened, and share your newly found knowledge with the class.

Read about the Great Salt Lake. What unique experience can swimmers have there?

Share with a friend or family member what you have been doing with density. Be sure to explain to them what density is.

Teacher Information

Note: The BBs suggested for this activity can be replaced by any small weight that will fit into the soda straw.

Any object that floats in a liquid displaces an amount of liquid equal to its own weight (the Archimedes Principle). If the specific gravity (density) of the liquid is greater than that of the object, the object floats. If the density of the object is greater than that of the liquid, it will sink. The hydrometer will float at varying levels, sinking just far enough to displace its own weight.

Hydrometers are used with automobiles to test battery acid and antifreeze, using the Archimedes Principle. In these applications, the hydrometer is simply testing the density of the battery acid and of the antifreeze. In each case, the density increases as the concentration of the needed substance increases.

It is easier for swimmers to float in ocean water than in freshwater. Salt increases the density of water. Swimmers bob like a cork in the Great Salt Lake because of high salt content. Very simply, a high concentration of salt water has a higher density than that of the human body. If salt water gets in the eyes, it will burn. A shower following a swim in the Great Salt Lake is necessary, as a film of salt is left on the skin after the water evaporates. (The tiny brine shrimp [about one-fourth inch long] that cover your body as you exit the water and fill your swimsuit are a bonus!)

Integrating

Math, language arts

Science Process Skills

Observing, inferring, classifying, measuring, predicting, communicating, comparing and contrasting, using space-time relationships, formulating hypotheses, identifying and controlling variables

How Does Temperature Affect the Speed of Molecules?

Materials Needed

- Two clear tumblers per small group
- Food coloring
- Paper and pencils
- Two droppers
- Hot water
- Cold water

Procedure

1. Put very cold water in one tumbler and hot water in the other. Fill each about half full.
2. Draw four or five drops of food coloring into each of the two droppers. Put as near the same amount in each as possible.
3. Hold a dropper over each tumbler and squeeze to empty the contents of both at exactly the same time.
4. Compare the movement of the color in the two containers. In which tumbler did the color spread more rapidly?
5. If you have time, try different colors and different water temperatures. Record your observations.
6. Discuss your results with your group.

For Problem Solvers

Now measure the temperatures of your hot and cold water and measure the time required for the food coloring to completely disperse through the water. Put water in a third container, being sure that the temperature is different from either of the first two by several degrees. Predict the time required for the color to spread throughout the water in the third container. Test your prediction.

Do all of the colors spread through the water at the same speed? What is your hypothesis? Design a test to find out. Then try it. Was your hypothesis correct?

Teacher Information

As temperatures increase, molecules move faster. The food coloring will diffuse noticeably more rapidly in the hot water than in the cold water. In this activity, water temperature is the variable. You might have students try the same activity with color as the variable. For instance, use two tumblers of cold water and put red in one and green (or blue) in the other.

You might also consider having students use a stopwatch and a thermometer and record the actual time required for maximum diffusion (equal color throughout, as judged by the students).

Try it with different measured temperatures and graph the results. Have students use results already shown on the graph to predict diffusion time for each new temperature.

Integrating

Math, language arts

Science Process Skills

Observing, inferring, measuring, predicting, communicating, comparing and contrasting, using space-time relationships, formulating hypotheses, identifying and controlling variables, experimenting

What Happens When Water Changes to a Solid?

(Teacher-supervised activity)

Materials Needed

- Two pint-sized glass jars (alike if possible)
- One jar lid that seals
- Plastic ice trays
- Small medicine or spice bottle with pop-off (not safety) cap
- Water
- Freezer compartment
- Plastic bags (3 per group)
- Copies of the "Science Investigation Journaling Notes" for this activity for all students

Procedure

1. As you complete this activity, you will keep a record of what you do, just as scientists do. Use a copy of the "Science Investigation Journaling Notes" and write the information that is called for, including your name and the date.

2. For this activity you will find out what happens when water changes to a solid. For item 1, the question is provided for you.

3. Item 2 of the Journaling Notes asks for what you already know about the question. If you have some ideas about what happens when water changes to a solid, write your ideas.

4. For item 3, you need to think about what you wrote for item 2 and decide what you think happens when water changes to a solid. Write what you know about the question, and that will be your hypothesis.

5. Now continue with the following instructions. Complete your Journaling Notes as you go. Steps 6 through 11 will help you with the information you need to write on the form for items 4, 5, and 6.

6. Completely fill both jars, the ice tray, and the small bottle with water.

7. Screw the cap tightly on one jar and snap the cap onto the small bottle.

8. Place each jar and the small bottle in separate plastic bags.

9. Place all four containers upright in the freezer compartment. Leave for 24 hours.

10. Remove all four containers from the freezer.

11. Examine and compare the four containers.

12. What has happened to the water? What are your observations? Why do you think this happened? (This is item 6 on the form.)

13. For item 7 of the form, think about your hypothesis (item 3) and write what actually happened. Was your hypothesis correct? Did it turn out the way you expected?

For Problem Solvers

How much does water increase in volume as it freezes—2 percent, 3 percent, 5 percent, 10 percent, 20 percent? What do you think? Write your hypothesis, then find a way to measure it. Will you use a plastic bag as your container as you investigate this question, a glass jar, or what? Explain the reason for your choice. Will you completely fill the container with water? Why, or why not?

Teacher Information

Water, like other materials, expands as it gets warmer and contracts as it cools. Unlike other material, however, water expands as it approaches the freezing point. The water in the open jar will be frozen, but the jar will likely be intact since the top was left open to permit expansion. The surface of the ice cubes will be higher than the surface of the liquid water was before the container was placed in the freezer. The jar with the lid on will be cracked and broken or the lid will be bulged or forced off. The snap top will likely be pushed off the small bottle.

Because water expands as it freezes, water-cooled engines require a coolant with a lower freezing point (antifreeze) in cold climates. Most engines also have "freeze plugs," which are designed to pop out, just like the top of the small bottle, to prevent serious damage to the engine. In cold climates, outdoor water pipes are usually turned off and drained during winter months to prevent breakage.

Integrating

Math, language arts

Science Process Skills

Observing, measuring, predicting, communicating, comparing and contrasting, using space-time relationships, formulating hypotheses

Water

Science Investigation

Journaling Notes for Activity 2.19

1. Question: What happens when water changes to a solid?

2. What we already know: _____

_____

3. Hypothesis: _____

_____

4. Materials needed: _____

_____

5. Procedure: _____

_____

_____

_____

_____

6. Observations/New information: _____

_____

_____

7. Conclusion: _____

_____

_____

_____

How Can You Make a "Worm"?

(Take home and do with family and friends.)

Materials Needed

- Drinking straw with sealed paper wrapper intact
- Water
- Eyedropper
- Small dish

Procedure

1. Tear one end off the paper wrapper of the drinking straw so the end of the straw can be seen.

2. Put the closed end of the straw on a table and carefully slide the paper wrapper down the straw until it is wrinkled, but no more than 5 cm (2 in.) long. (See Figure 2.20–1.)

3. Place the wrinkled "worm" on a small dish and use your eyedropper to put three or four drops of water along its back.

4. What happened, and why do you think it happened this way? Discuss your ideas with your group.

Figure 2.20–1. Straw, Paper Wrapper, Dish, and Eyedropper

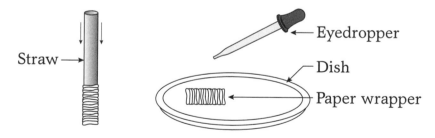

Teacher Information

When a few drops of water are put on the wrinkled paper, the "worm" will begin to grow and sometimes crawl. This is because the water spreads through the dry compressed paper and causes it to relax and expand.

Capillary action, of which this is one example, occurs because of the attraction of liquids to solids. It's the reason liquids climb up a wick against the force of gravity. If you lay a shoelace over the side of a cup of water, with one end in the water and the other end on the table top, the water will move up one end of the shoelace and down the other end, leaving a puddle of water on the table.

The study of surface tension in physics and chemistry also involves principles of capillary action.

Integrating

Language arts

Science Process Skills

Observing, inferring

Hands-On Earth Science Activities

How Do Raisins Dance?

(Take home and do with family and friends.)

Materials Needed

- Clear, carbonated soda
- Pint-sized or larger fruit jar
- Several raisins

Procedure

1. Add clear, carbonated soda to the jar until it is about two-thirds full.
2. Put several raisins into the jar with the soda. Observe for several minutes. What happened? What can you say about this?

Teacher Information

When the raisins are put into the soda, they will sink to the bottom of the jar. Gradually, small bubbles of carbon dioxide gas from the soda will collect on the skins of the raisins. Enough bubbles of gas will soon have collected on the surface of the raisins to make them buoyant, and they will float to the surface of the soda. As soon as the raisins reach the surface, the bubbles pop and the raisins sink to the bottom. This action will continue for some time.

Integrating

Math, language arts

Science Process Skills

Observing, inferring

How Does Lake Water Compare with Seawater?

Materials Needed

- Seawater (or salt water)
- Lake water (pond water if lake water is not available)
- Two pans per small group
- Measuring cups
- Hand lenses
- Blank copies of the "Science Investigation Journaling Notes" for all students

Procedure

1. Do the following as a Science Investigation. Obtain a blank copy of the "Science Investigation Journaling Notes." Write your name, the date, and your question at the top. Plan your investigation through step 5 of the form (Procedure) and have it approved by your teacher. Complete the Journaling Notes as you perform your investigation. When you are finished, share your project with your group and submit your Journaling Notes to your teacher if requested.

2. Pour one-half cup of seawater into one of the pans.

3. Pour one-half cup of lake water into the other pan.

4. Let all of the water evaporate.

5. Compare and describe what is left in the bottom of the two pans.

6. Examine the residue in both pans with a hand lens.

7. What do you think is in seawater that is not in lake water?

For Problem Solvers

Put one-half cup of tap water in a third pan. Let the water completely evaporate, and compare the residue with the residue of the seawater pan and the lake-water pan. Write notes on your observations, as you compare and contrast the residue in the three pans.

Now examine the residue in the three pans with a microscope. Look for crystals. If you found crystals with a hand lens, look for more detail about their shape, color, relative size, and any other characteristics you find.

Teacher Information

Seawater contains salt and small amounts of other minerals, which will be left as a light-colored residue in the bottom of the pan after the water has evaporated. For those who do not live near the ocean, a sprinkling of salt in tap water will make a good substitute.

The lake water will have other residues, but salt crystals will likely not be found in it. Encourage students to pay attention to detail as they observe and as they describe their observations, both verbally and in writing. This will be an excellent experience in comparing and contrasting as they find distinguishing characteristics of water from the different sources.

The tap-water pan might have a slight residue as well, depending on the minerals that are in the local water supply and whether the water has been treated by a water softener. You might choose to allow your students to taste the residue from prepared salt water. Water from the other sources should not be tasted, to be cautious of possible harmful substances.

Small amounts of minerals in our water supplies are common. These are leached out of the ground as water from snow and rain seeps through the ground and flows through streams and rivers to become our water supply. Most runoff water eventually flows to the oceans, so that's where the majority of salt and other minerals are deposited. Over great periods of time, the concentration of these minerals in the ocean increases. Lakes that collect runoff water but have no outlet to the ocean tend to build high concentrations of minerals. The Great Salt Lake is one of these. It is named for its salt content, but many other minerals are harvested from the water as well.

Integrating

Math, language arts

Science Process Skills

Observing, inferring, measuring, using space-time relationships

Water

Which Changes Temperature More Easily, Land or Water?

(Close teacher supervision required.)

Materials Needed

- Two plastic dishpans, identical in size and shape
- One thermometer
- Two heat lamps, same type and wattage
- Paper and pencils
- Water and soil

Procedure

1. Fill one dishpan about two-thirds full with water.
2. Fill the other dishpan to the same level with soil.
3. Let both dishpans stand overnight in the same indoor location, to stabilize temperature.
4. Position one heat lamp over each dishpan, about 25 cm (10 in.) above the surface. Be sure the heat lamps are at the same position and height above each dishpan. They must also be the same type and wattage.
5. Measure and record the temperature of both the water and the soil, about 5 cm (2 in.) below the surface.
6. Measure and record the temperature from the same position every 10 minutes for two hours. Each time you measure, be sure you measure one right after the other.
7. Make a graph of the temperatures.
8. Turn the heat lamps off for a few minutes while you discuss the following questions.
   a. From your findings, does land change temperature more easily than water, or does water change temperature more easily than land?
   b. How do you think temperatures of large areas of land and water might affect air temperature?
   c. How do you think air temperature might affect the temperatures of land and water surfaces?

9. Record your ideas and discuss them with your teacher.

10. Now measure the air temperature 2 to 3 cm (1 in.) above each of the two surfaces. Compare these and discuss any differences you find.

Teacher Information

Caution: Due to the use of electricity and hot lamp bulbs, very close supervision is needed.

Students will likely find that, given a similar environment, soil changes temperature more readily than does water, and that air temperature is affected by the temperature of the underlying surface. The underlying surface, in turn, is affected by air temperature, although this is not demonstrated in the above activity since the heat source used here is radiant heat, not just warm air.

Air is heated over warm surfaces and cooled over cooler surfaces. As air temperature increases, the air expands and rises. Cooler air sinks. When these actions occur over large bodies of land and water, huge pockets of air move, as warm, light air rises and cool, heavier air moves in to fill its place. We call it wind, and such heating and cooling actions have far-reaching effects on weather conditions. This is true both locally and globally, as air masses interact with land and water masses throughout the world. Air temperature affects surface temperature, and surface temperature affects air temperature. These are among the factors that together create continuous worldwide currents of air and water.

Integrating

Math, language arts

Science Process Skills

Observing, inferring, measuring, using space-time relationships

How Are Ocean Currents Affected by Wind?

Materials Needed

- Large glass baking dishes
- Water
- Soda straws
- Two or three rocks, about 5 to 10 cm (2 to 4 in.) high per small group
- Several tiny "boats" (these can be plastic or paper punch-outs from a paper punch, or other small items that float)
- Paper and pencils

Procedure

1. Fill the baking dish about half to two-thirds full of water and place the rocks in the water. The rocks will represent islands. The rocks need to be large enough, or the water shallow enough, that the rocks appear above the surface of the water.

2. Place the dish on a table where everyone in your group can see.

3. Give each of three or four people a soda straw and decide who will blow first.

4. The first person to blow should get in a position that the straw can be held in a horizontal position with the tip of the straw near the surface of the water and near the edge of the water.

5. Place the tiny boats in the water near blower number 1. Now blow lightly, just enough to make ripples in the water. Blow in only one direction, no matter what the boats do.

6. As the blowing occurs, everyone should observe the water movement, which will be indicated by the movement of the boats. These movements of the water are called *currents*.

7. Make a drawing of your "lake," including the islands, and draw arrows to show the movement of the water current (as seen by the movement of the boats).

8. After about 30 seconds of blowing, shift to blower number 2. Blower 2 should use his or her own straw, but blow across the water from the same position as Blower 1 and in the same direction. Do not blow on the boats; blow on the water.

9. After all blowers have had their turn, discuss your observations as a group. Consider the following questions, along with others you would like to discuss.

   a. Examine your drawings. Did the boats (and the water current) seem to move in any direction other than in the direction of the blowing of air?

   b. Did any of the boats move around an island?

   c. Compare the movement of the water currents of the different observers, as shown in their drawings. Are they all alike? Which one do you think is most accurate?

   d. Did water that was not directly receiving the wind seem to move, as well as the water that was directly in line with the wind?

Teacher Information

If many students are involved in this activity, the glass baking pan can be placed on an overhead projector; then the whole class can see.

Air masses and water masses continually interact, shifted about by movements that are energized by the sun, either directly or indirectly. Polar regions receive much less of the sun's energy than do the equatorial regions. Both water and air expand and rise as they are heated, then contract and sink as they are cooled. Both are continually rising, then falling, then rising, then falling, with change in temperature. Each affects the other in an endless cycle.

In this activity, students witness currents of surface water that result from winds blowing across the water. They should observe that there were water currents even in areas of the "lake" where the wind was not blowing directly. These areas were affected by the movement of the water that was directly blown by the wind. As the blown water entered the area of calm, the calm water was forced to move.

Integrating

Math, language arts

Science Process Skills

Observing, inferring, measuring, using space-time relationships

How Are Ocean Currents Affected by Temperature?

(Close teacher supervision required.)

Materials Needed

- Fish tank
- Water
- Soda straws
- Food coloring
- One-quart plastic bag full of ice per small group
- Masking tape
- Heat lamp
- Paper and pencils

Procedure

1. Fill the fish tank about two-thirds full of water.
2. Place the bag of ice in the water at one end of the tank, and anchor the top of the bag to the end of the tank with the masking tape.
3. Place the heat lamp at the opposite end of the tank, about 30 cm (1 foot) from the tank, pointing toward the end of the tank, and turn it on.
4. Put several drops of food coloring in the water on the end with the heat lamp.
5. Observe the food coloring, and record any movement that you see. Make a drawing of the way it is now. Record the time.
6. For one hour, examine the food coloring every five minutes and place arrows indicating any movements of the food coloring that you observe. Consider the water in the tank as the ocean, with the ice representing a polar region and the heat lamp representing a region near the equator. Record the time with each observation.
7. After one hour, discuss your observations as a group. Consider the following points, along with others you would like to discuss.

   a. Compare your observations.

   b. When the food coloring first began to move, which direction did it go? Describe the general directions and changes in direction in

122   **Hands–On Earth Science Activities**

the movement of the food coloring. Include the amount of time taken up with each of the movements noted.

    c. Trace the movement of the food coloring again. This time identify, the best you can, the reason for the movement in a particular direction. Each time you identify a change in direction, describe the reason you think it changed.

8. Discuss your observations with your teacher, and share with the class the things you learned in doing this activity.

Teacher Information

This activity models the movement of ocean water in response to changes in water temperature. The major impetus in these changes comes from the differences in the amount of energy received from the sun in the equatorial regions as compared with the polar regions. At and near the equator a tremendous amount of solar energy is absorbed into the ocean. As the water is heated, it expands, becomes less dense, and moves toward the surface. Near the poles, the water becomes very cold, contracts, becomes more dense, and sinks into lower layers of ocean water.

In the fish tank, the water circulated in a very short time, as seen by the movement of the food coloring. The ocean is so massive that some of the more dense water can actually remain in the lower, colder layers for many years before it returns to the layers nearer the surface.

Another major factor in the movement of ocean currents is salinity. One might suppose that with the system of ocean currents the level of salinity would be uniform throughout, but a difference of only one or two parts of salt per thousand parts of water makes a difference in the density of the water. This results in layering, with the water having a slightly greater salt content sinking beneath layers of lower salinity.

Such layering comes about by temperature differences as well as differences in salinity, and the mixing often occurs much more slowly than one might expect. Thus, at the bottom will be the colder layers of water of higher salinity, with the warmer, less salty layers riding on top. Layers separated by temperature can remain separated for many, many years, as is true also of layers separated by salinity differences. Still, there is a lot of mixing of the layers; surface layers that become very cold and dense sink, and they mix with other layers as they do.

Integrating

Math, language arts

Science Process Skills

Observing, inferring, measuring, using space-time relationships

Can You Solve This Water Word Search?

Try to find the following Water terms in the grid below. They could appear in horizontal (left to right), vertical (up or down), or diagonal (upward or downward) position.

moisture	water	vaporize
evaporation	humidity	condense
condensation	dissolve	liquid
cloud	droplet	boiling point
freeze	impurities	density

```
M  J  D  R  O  P  L  E  T  B  E  D
K  D  I  S  S  O  L  V  E  O  C  E
C  O  N  D  E  N  S  A  T  I  O  N
L  I  Q  U  I  D  F  P  L  L  N  S
O  V  W  A  T  E  R  O  O  I  D  I
U  A  E  W  I  R  E  R  P  N  E  T
D  P  D  Q  R  U  E  A  M  G  N  Y
K  O  S  R  U  T  Z  T  J  P  S  A
L  R  A  T  P  S  E  I  H  O  E  S
P  I  C  Y  M  I  J  O  Y  I  I  D
O  Z  X  U  I  O  K  N  G  N  N  F
I  E  Z  H  U  M  I  D  I  T  Y  G
```

Name _____   Date _____

Can You Create a New Water Word Search of Your Own?

Write your Water words in the grid below. Arrange them in the grid so they appear in horizontal (left to right), vertical (up or down), or diagonal (upward or downward) position. Fill in the blank boxes with other letters. Trade your Word Search with someone else who has created one of his or her own, and see whether you can solve the new puzzle.

_____   _____   _____

_____   _____   _____

_____   _____   _____

_____   _____   _____

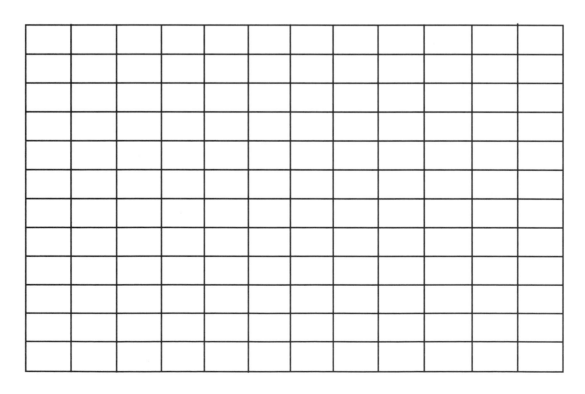

Water

Answer Key for Water Word Search

```
M  J  D  R  O  P  L  E  T  B  E  D
K  D  I  S  S  O  L  V  E  O  C  E
C  O  N  D  E  N  S  A  T  I  O  N
L  I  Q  U  I  D  F  P  L  N  D  S
O  V  W  A  T  E  R  O  O  I  D  I
U  A  E  W  I  R  E  R  P  N  E  T
D  P  D  Q  R  U  E  A  M  G  N  Y
K  O  S  R  U  T  Z  T  J  P  S  A
L  R  A  T  P  S  E  I  H  O  E  S
P  I  C  Y  M  I  J  O  Y  I  I  D
O  Z  X  U  I  O  K  N  G  N  N  F
I  E  Z  H  U  M  I  D  I  T  Y  G
```

Do You Recall?

Section Two: Water

1. What determines whether an object will float on water?

2. Where does water go when it evaporates?

3. What is condensation?

4. Why can a cup be overfilled with water without spilling over?

5. If you put a drop of water on a word on a magazine page, what happens?

6. Why does an egg sink in tap water but float in salt water?

7. What happens to water as it freezes to a solid?

8. What common substance is found in seawater but not lake water?

9. Why does air temperature cause currents in the atmosphere?

10. What are some factors that affect ocean currents?

Answer Key for Do You Recall?

Section Two: Water

Answer	Related Activities
1. The amount of water the object displaces	2.1
2. Into the air	2.2
3. Water comes out of the air, forming clouds or collecting on objects.	2.3, 2.4, 2.5
4. Water molecules cling to each other (cohesion).	2.8–2.11
5. The letters are magnified.	2.12–2.15
6. Salt water is more dense.	2.16, 2.17
7. It expands.	2.19
8. Salt	2.22
9. Changes in temperature cause changes in density, thus causing air pockets to rise and fall.	2.23
10. Temperature, wind, salt content	2.24, 2.25

Hands-On Earth Science Activities

Weather

To the Teacher

Weather is crucial in our lives. It influences where we live, what (and if) we eat, what we wear, what we do, and sometimes how we feel. Weather appears as a part of the first recorded history of man. Early civilizations grew and developed in favorable climates. The history of man is interwoven with myths, legends, stories, customs, religious beliefs, poetry, art, music, dance, and many other expressions that tell the story of man's continuing concern with the mysteries, beauties, and dangers of the often-unpredictable nature of weather.

Today, sophisticated weather instruments circle the earth to report weather conditions on a global scale. Countless weather stations, with both professional and amateur meteorologists, study and report on a daily basis, yet the news still carries reports of unpredicted weather events. This section should help students understand some of the many variables that must be taken into account in a study of weather and to appreciate its importance in our lives.

This study draws heavily on information from the "Air" and "Water" sections and should follow them as closely as possible. You may even see a need to repeat some of the activities from those sections.

Several activities require simple construction. Please take time to read all of the activities before you begin. Parents and other resource people can be a great help in gathering and assisting as you build a weather station and a convection box. You might want to construct several of each of them, depending on your situation.

Using the weather station and other sources to predict weather should take two to four weeks. However, it should not require too much time each day, so another section could be undertaken at the same time.

We hope you will use poetry, stories, music, and art liberally throughout the study.

Finally, please don't blame the weather on the weather forecaster!

The following activities are designed as discovery activities that students can usually perform quite independently. You are encouraged to provide students (usually in small groups) with the materials listed and a copy of the activity from the beginning through the "Procedure." The section titled "Teacher Information" is not intended for student use, but rather to assist you with discussion following the hands-on activity, as students share their observations. Discussion of conceptual information prior to completing the hands-on activity can interfere with the discovery process.

Regarding the Early Grades

With verbal instructions and slight modifications, many of these activities can be used with kindergarten, first-grade, and second-grade students. In some activities, steps that involve procedures that go beyond the level of the child can simply be omitted and yet offer the child an experience that plants the seed for a concept that will germinate and grow later on.

Teachers of the early grades will probably choose to bypass many of the "For Problem Solvers" sections. That's okay. These sections are provided for those who are especially motivated and want to go beyond the investigation provided by the activity outlined. Use the outlined activities, and enjoy worthwhile learning experiences together with your young students. Also consider, however, that many of the "For Problem Solvers" sections can be used appropriately with young children as group activities or as demonstrations, still giving students the advantage of an exposure to the experience and laying groundwork for connections that will be made at a later time.

Correlation with National Standards

The following elements of the National Standards are reflected in the activities of this section.

K-4   Content Standard A: Science as Inquiry

As a result of activities in grades K-4, all students should develop

1. Abilities necessary to do scientific inquiry
2. Understanding about scientific inquiry

K-4   Content Standard D: Earth and Space Science

As a result of activities in grades K-4, all students should develop understanding of

1. Properties of earth materials
2. Objects in the sky
3. Changes in earth and sky

5-8   Content Standard A: Science as Inquiry

As a result of activities in grades 5-8, all students should develop

1. Abilities necessary to do scientific inquiry
2. Understanding about scientific inquiry

5-8   Content Standard D: Earth and Space Science

As a result of activities in grades 5-8, all students should develop understanding of

1. Structure of the earth system
2. Earth's history
3. Earth in the solar system

How Can You Make Rain?

(Teacher-supervised activity)

Materials Needed

- Quart-sized glass jars
- Aluminum or iron pie tins
- Hot water
- Ice cubes

Procedure

1. Pour a cup of hot water into a quart-sized glass jar. *Caution:* Be careful with the hot water. (No lid is needed.)

2. Put some ice cubes in a pie tin and place it on top of the jar. (See Figure 3.1–1.)

3. Observe for several minutes. What happened? Discuss your ideas with your group.

Figure 3.1–1. Jar with Water in Bottom and Ice Cubes on Top

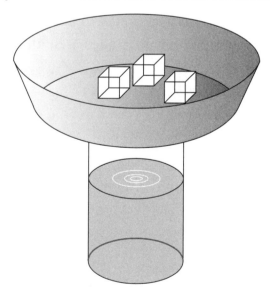

Hands-On Earth Science Activities

Teacher Information

The hot water will heat the air in the jar and add moisture to it. The moisture-laden hot air will rise. As it nears the cold pie tin, the air will cool and condense. In time it may actually begin to "rain" outside the jar, as water drops form on, and fall from, the part of the pan overhanging the jar.

Integrating

Math, language arts

Science Process Skills

Observing, inferring, measuring, estimating, communicating, comparing and contrasting, using space-time relationships, identifying and controlling variables

How Can You Make a Cloud?

(Teacher demonstration)

Materials Needed

- One two-liter plastic bottle with cap
- Wooden matches
- Water

Procedure

1. Put a small amount (about one-fourth cup) of water into the bottle.
2. Light a match. Hold it down in the bottle to make smoke. Most of the smoke will occur after the flame goes out.
3. Put the lid on the bottle. (See Figure 3.2–1.)
4. Shake the bottle to add moisture to the air inside the bottle.
5. Squeeze the bottle, then release it quickly and observe what is inside the bottle.
6. Squeeze and release several times. What's happening inside the bottle?
7. Share your observations and ideas with others who are interested in this activity.

Figure 3.2-1. Two-Liter Bottle with Small Amount of Water and Small Amount of Smoke

For Problem Solvers

Experiment with different temperatures of water and different amounts of smoke in the bottle for this activity. Also do some research and learn all you can about how clouds form in the atmosphere. What causes changes in pressure in the atmosphere, and how does this affect temperature? What do pressure and temperature have to do with cloud formation?

Teacher Information

Squeezing the bottle increases the air pressure inside the bottle. Rising air pressure increases the temperature of the air. As air temperature increases, the air is able to contain more moisture. Releasing the pressure on the bottle reduces the temperature of the air and decreases the ability of the air to hold moisture. The smoke particles that are suspended in the air act as condensation nuclei, and moisture condenses, or collects, around them. Each time you release the pressure, a cloud forms, and when you squeeze the bottle the cloud disappears.

Smoke and dust particles in the atmosphere act as condensation nuclei when moisture content is high and temperature decreases. Changes in atmospheric pressure create changes in atmospheric temperature, similar to the way these changes occur in the mini-atmosphere in the bottle.

Integrating

Reading, social studies

Science Process Skills

Observing, inferring, communicating, researching

How Can You Make a Thermometer?

Materials Needed

- Commercial thermometer
- Flasks or small-mouthed glass bottles (cough medicine, juice bottle)
- One-hole rubber stoppers to fit bottle
- Clear, thin, stiff plastic tubing at least 30 cm (12 in.) long (balloon sticks are just right)
- Warm water
- Red food coloring
- 8-inch by 10-inch index cards (or larger card)

Procedure

1. The first thing most people notice about weather is the temperature. Thermometers, which measure temperature, are easy to make. You might have learned from earlier science activities that liquids expand when they are heated and contract when they are cooled.

2. Fill the bottle with warm water. Add several drops of red food coloring.

3. Insert the plastic tube through the stopper and fit the stopper tightly in the bottle. Water should be forced into the tube as you press the stopper into place.

4. Using the stopper, adjust the water level so the water will rise nearly halfway up the tube.

5. Make a slit near the bottom of the index card and another near the top and slide it behind the tube. The card should either rest on the stopper or be taped in place, as shown in Figure 3.3–1.

6. Wait about an hour for the water to reach room temperature.

7. Consult the commercial thermometer and mark the present temperature with a line on the index card beside the water level in the tube.

Figure 3.3-1. Homemade Thermometer

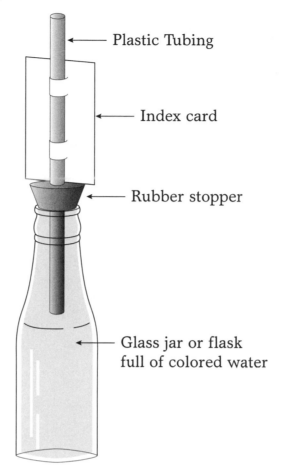

Plastic Tubing

Index card

Rubber stopper

Glass jar or flask
full of colored water

8. Each morning and afternoon, compare the commercial thermometer with the one you made. Mark the card each time, and record the temperature shown on the commercial thermometer.

9. You should soon be able to put the commercial thermometer away and use your homemade thermometer for temperature readings.

For Problem Solvers

Check the temperature on your thermometer each morning, noon, and night for at least one month. Try to do it at about the same time each day. For the first few days, compare the temperatures shown on your thermometer with those of a commercial thermometer to be sure you have calibrated your thermometer accurately. You will gain confidence in your thermometer as you use it.

Make a graph of day-by-day temperatures, using your homemade thermometer. Be sure to check the temperature at the same time each day. Estimate the temperature each time before you read the thermometer.

What are the temperature limits of your thermometer? At what temperature does the liquid rise to the top of the tube, if it does, and at what temperature does it drop out of sight at the bottom? Design a way to find out, and compare your results with those of others who are doing this activity.

Your thermometer works on the principle of expansion and contraction of liquids with temperature change. Do some research and find out what other ways are used to measure temperature. Learn what you can about instruments people have used for this purpose through the years.

Teacher Information

Ordinary methyl alcohol (or rubbing alcohol) may be substituted for water if the thermometer is to be left outside in below-freezing temperatures. *Caution:* Methyl alcohol is poisonous if taken internally.

The water expands because the molecules move more rapidly and push against one another as they are heated. As water cools, the molecules move more slowly and require less space, so the water contracts.

Balloon sticks are perfect as thermometer tubes. They are stiff, they fit the one-hole rubber stopper, and they are readily available at party-supply outlets.

Integrating

Math, reading, social studies

Science Process Skills

Observing, inferring, measuring, estimating, communicating, comparing and contrasting, using space-time relationships, identifying and controlling variables, experimenting, researching

How Can We Detect and Measure Changes in Atmospheric Pressure?

(Teacher-supervised activity)

Materials Needed

- Wide-mouthed jars (plastic is preferred, but it must be rigid)
- Round balloons
- Heavy-duty rubber bands
- Commercial barometer
- Soda straws
- Index cards
- Milk cartons cut into stands
- Toothpicks
- Glue (latex cement)
- Scissors
- Pencils

Procedure

1. Cut the narrow neck off a balloon and stretch the balloon very tightly over the mouth of the plastic jar.
2. Hold the balloon in place by placing the rubber band below the threads of the jar.
3. Glue one end of the soda straw to the center of the balloon in a horizontal position. Glue a toothpick in the end of the straw as a pointer. (See Figure 3.4–1.)
4. Attach the index card to the horizontal stand and bring it near the pointer.
5. Make a mark on the index card in the place indicated by the pointer.

Figure 3.4-1. Homemade Barometer

Straw — Toothpick — Index Card

Balloon —

Rubber band —

— Milk carton stand

— Glass jar

6. Consult your commercial barometer or call the local weather station to determine today's barometric pressure. Write the number beside the mark on your index card.

7. Repeat steps 5 and 6 every day for a week. What is happening? Discuss this with your teacher and class.

For Problem Solvers

In this activity, you made a barometer. Each time you read this barometer, the temperature of the air in the room must be the same. Think about that statement and see whether you can explain why it is true. Discuss your hypothesis with your friends, then with your teacher. Then keep a thermometer near your barometer so you can be sure of the temperature before you read the barometer.

Do some research and find out what other types of instruments are used to measure atmospheric pressure. Find out how they work.

Keep track of the barometer movement each day. Is it moving up or moving down? Whenever there is a change in atmospheric pressure, write a description of current weather conditions, then write your prediction of weather conditions for the next day. See whether you can identify a pattern of weather change following pressure changes. As the atmospheric pressure goes up, is the weather getting milder or stormier? As the atmospheric pressure comes down, is the weather getting milder or stormier?

Teacher Information

Before discussing the barometer, you may want to remind students of the air pressure activities in the section on "Air." Atmospheric pressure varies and is one indicator of approaching weather changes. Generally, decreasing barometric pressures accompany storm fronts, while rising pressures indicate fair weather.

When the balloon is stretched tightly over the bottle, the pressure inside the bottle will be the same as that of the atmosphere in the room. As the atmospheric pressure increases or decreases, it will change the amount of pressure on the balloon and cause the straw to move up or down. Because some air will pass through the balloon diaphragm, the air should be balanced by reattaching the balloon every few days.

Changes in air temperature will cause the air inside the barometer to expand and contract, making the diaphragm move up and down and invalidating the accuracy of this device as a barometer. Keeping a thermometer nearby and always reading the barometer at the same room temperature can control this effect. Following this procedure, you know that any change in the reading is due to change in atmospheric pressure, not change in temperature.

Integrating

Reading, language arts

Science Process Skills

Observing, inferring, communicating, comparing and contrasting, formulating hypotheses, identifying and controlling variables, researching

How Can We Measure Moisture in the Air?

Materials Needed

- Empty half-gallon milk cartons with the tops cut off
- Soda straws
- Small metal washers
- 5-inch by 7-inch index cards
- Freshly washed human hair at least 20 cm (8 in.) long
- Four paper fasteners
- Glass beads with hole
- Glue (latex cement works well)
- Rulers
- Toothpicks
- Pencils

Procedure

1. Use two paper fasteners to attach the index card to the carton so it extends beyond the edge of the carton. (See Figure 3.5–1.)
2. Push a paper fastener through the end of the drinking straw and then through the bead. Near one edge of the carton, measure up from the bottom 10 cm (4 in.) and push the paper fastener into the carton.
3. Slide the small metal washer over the straw just beyond the opposite edge of the carton.
4. Use a paper fastener and glue to attach the hair to the top of the carton near the same edge as the washer. Tie and glue the hair to the straw at a point directly below.
5. Glue a toothpick in the end of the straw as a pointer.
6. When you finish, your model should look like Figure 3.5–1.

Figure 3.5-1. Homemade Hair Hygrometer

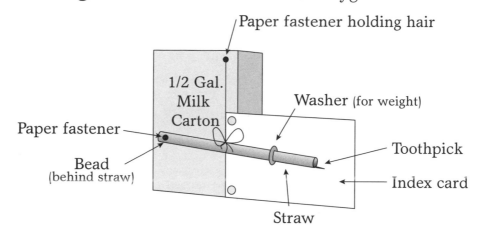

7. This is a hair hygrometer. A hygrometer is an instrument that measures moisture in the air, or "humidity."

8. Make a pencil mark on the index card at the end of the pointer (toothpick). Check it occasionally and record any changes you observe.

9. Discuss the changes with your group. What information is your hair hygrometer giving you?

For Problem Solvers

Do this project as a Science Investigation. Obtain a blank copy of the "Science Investigation Journaling Notes." Write your name, the date, and your question at the top. Plan your investigation through step 5 (Procedure) and have it approved by your teacher. Complete the Journaling Notes as you perform your investigation. Share your project with your group and submit your Journaling Notes to your teacher if requested.

Is there a difference in how well different types of human hair work in this activity? Does light-colored hair stretch when it gets wet more than darker hair does? Does coarse hair respond differently from finer hair? Design an experiment to find the answers to these questions. Discuss your design with other interested students, then discuss it with your teacher and carry out your experiment.

Calibrate your hair hygrometer by comparing it each day to a commercial instrument. Then record the humidity reading for one month and graph the data.

Do meteorologists use human hair to measure moisture in the air? Do some research and find out.

Teacher Information

Some people with long hair notice that their hair is longer when it is wet than when it is dry. Hair actually absorbs moisture and becomes longer in humid air. As air dries, the hair contracts. The soda straw moves up and down with the changes in length of the hair attached to it and the top of the milk carton. The washer attached to the straw provides extra weight to help it move down freely as the hair stretches in moist conditions. The pointer and index card will make small movements easier to detect.

You might want to make several hygrometers, using different colors and textures of clean hair. If there are differences in the hair, your encyclopedia can tell you why. Consult the Internet for this information as well.

Integrating

Reading, language arts

Science Process Skills

Observing, inferring, measuring, communicating, comparing and contrasting, using space-time relationships, researching

ACTIVITY 3.6

What Is Another Way to Measure Humidity?

Materials Needed

- Two identical commercial thermometers (preferably Celsius)
- Shoelace (with tips cut off) 20 cm (8 in.) long
- Two rubber bands
- Clear plastic bottle

Procedure

1. Cut a small hole in the side of the bottle (see Figure 3.6–1).
2. Use the rubber bands to fasten the two thermometers to the outside of the bottle.
3. Put some water inside the bottle.
4. Moisten the shoelace. Wrap one end around the bulb of one thermometer, and put the other end of the shoelace in the water.
5. After several minutes, compare the temperature of the thermometers.
6. What happened? Can you think of a way to explain this? Discuss this with your teacher and the class.

Figure 3.6–1. Wet/Dry Bulb Hygrometer

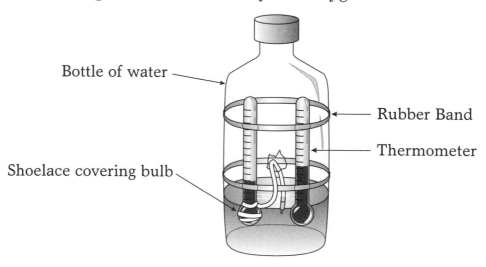

Bottle of water

Rubber Band

Thermometer

Shoelace covering bulb

Weather

For Problem Solvers

Do this project as a Science Investigation. Obtain a blank copy of the "Science Investigation Journaling Notes." Write your name, the date, and your question at the top. Plan your investigation through step 5 (Procedure) and have it approved by your teacher. Complete the Journaling Notes as you perform your investigation. Share your project with your group, and submit your Journaling Notes to your teacher if requested.

Why is there a difference in the temperature readings of these two thermometers? Moisten the back of your hand, then blow on it. Explain why this instrument can be used to indicate moisture in the air. Discuss your hypothesis with someone else who is doing this activity.

Meteorologists use an instrument that is a lot like this one. They call it a wet/dry bulb hygrometer. In this activity you made a wet/dry bulb hygrometer.

Table 3.6–1 is a relative humidity table that you can use with your homemade wet/dry bulb hygrometer. Find the dry bulb temperature along the bottom of the table and the wet bulb temperature at the left end of the table. The number on the table that is at the intersection of these two temperatures is the relative humidity.

Record both morning and afternoon relative humidity readings for one month (same times of day each day) and graph your data. If a commercial relative humidity instrument is available, graph the readings from it also. Compare the data from the two instruments.

Note: Be sure the wet bulb thermometer has been wet for at least a few minutes before you take your readings.

Table 3.6-1. Relative Humidity Table

Dry Bulb Temperature °C

Wet Bulb Temperature °C

WB \ DB	10	11	12	13	14	15	16	17	18	19	20	21	22	23	24	25	26	27	28	29	30	31	32	33	34	35	36	37	38	39	40	41	42	43	44	45
1	6	1																																		
2	15	9	4																																	
3	25	18	12	7	3																															
4	34	27	21	15	10	6	2																													
5	45	37	30	23	18	13	9	5	1																											
6	55	46	39	32	26	21	16	11	7	4	1																									
7	66	56	48	41	34	28	23	18	14	10	7	4	1																							
8	77	67	58	50	43	36	30	25	20	16	13	9	6	3	1																					
9	88	78	68	59	51	44	38	32	27	23	19	15	11	8	6	3	1																			
10	100	89	78	69	60	53	46	40	34	29	25	21	17	14	11	8	5	3	1																	
11		100	89	80	70	62	54	48	42	36	31	26	22	19	16	13	10	8	5	3	2															
12			100	90	80	71	63	56	49	43	37	32	28	24	21	18	14	12	9	5	4	4	2	1												
13				100	90	80	72	64	57	50	44	39	34	30	26	23	19	16	14	11	9	7	5	4	2	1										
14					100	90	81	72	65	58	52	46	41	36	32	28	24	21	18	15	13	11	9	7	5	4	3	2								
15						100	91	81	73	66	59	53	47	42	37	33	29	26	23	20	17	15	12	10	9	7	6	4	3	2	1					
16							100	90	82	74	67	60	54	48	43	39	35	31	27	24	21	19	16	14	12	10	9	7	6	4	3	2				
17								100	91	82	74	67	61	55	50	45	40	36	32	29	26	23	20	18	15	13	12	10	8	7	6	5	4	3	2	1
18									100	91	83	75	68	62	56	51	46	41	37	34	30	27	24	22	19	17	15	13	11	10	8	7	6	5	4	3
19										100	91	83	76	69	63	57	52	47	42	38	35	31	28	25	23	20	18	16	14	13	11	10	8	7	6	5
20											100	91	83	76	70	63	58	53	48	44	40	36	33	30	27	24	22	19	17	16	14	12	11	10	8	7
21												100	92	84	77	70	64	59	54	49	45	41	37	34	31	28	25	23	21	19	17	15	14	12	11	9
22													100	92	84	77	71	65	59	55	50	46	42	38	35	32	29	26	24	22	20	18	16	15	13	12
23														100	92	85	78	71	66	60	55	51	47	43	39	36	33	30	28	25	23	21	19	17	16	14
24															100	92	85	78	72	66	61	56	52	48	44	40	37	34	31	29	26	24	22	20	18	17
25																100	92	85	79	72	67	62	57	52	48	45	41	38	35	32	30	27	25	23	21	19
26																	100	92	85	79	73	67	62	58	53	49	45	42	39	36	33	31	28	26	24	22
27																		100	93	86	79	73	68	63	58	54	50	46	43	40	37	34	31	29	27	25
28																			100	93	86	79	74	69	64	59	55	51	47	44	41	38	35	32	30	28
29																				100	93	86	80	74	69	64	60	55	51	48	44	41	38	36	33	31
30																					100	93	86	80	75	70	65	60	56	52	49	45	42	39	36	34
31																						100	93	87	81	75	70	65	61	57	53	49	46	43	40	37
32																							100	93	87	81	76	70	66	61	57	53	50	47	44	41
33																								100	93	87	81	76	71	66	62	57	54	51	47	44
34																									100	93	87	82	76	71	67	62	58	55	51	48
35																										100	94	87	82	77	72	67	63	59	55	52
36																											100	94	88	82	77	72	68	63	59	56
37																												100	94	88	82	78	73	68	64	60
38																													100	94	88	83	78	73	68	64
39																														100	94	88	83	78	73	69
40																															100	94	88	83	78	74
41																																100	94	89	83	78
42																																	100	94	89	83
43																																		100	94	89
44																																			100	94
45																																				100

Teacher Information

After a few minutes, the wet bulb will have a lower temperature, because evaporation is a cooling process. This instrument is called a wet/dry bulb hygrometer. Meteorologists often whirl wet and dry thermometers together in the air. The handle and instrument containing the thermometers are together called a sling psychrometer. Your hygrometer works the same way, but not as rapidly. Students will often assume that the water is colder than the air and is making the wet bulb cooler. Actually, it is being cooled by the evaporation of moisture into the air.

Relative humidity is usually reported in percent. One hundred percent is the total amount of moisture air can contain at a given temperature. Twenty percent relative humidity would indicate that the air contains only 20 percent of the moisture that it could contain at the current temperature. If the relative humidity is very high (90 percent, for instance), a slight drop in temperature, which decreases the amount of water the air is able to hold, might increase the relative humidity to 100 percent and trigger a rainstorm.

The drier the air, the faster the evaporation from the wet bulb thermometer, cooling the thermometer and resulting in a lower temperature reading. The dry bulb thermometer remains unaffected by moisture content in the air. Therefore, the drier the air is, the greater will be the difference in temperature readings between the wet bulb and the dry bulb, which will indicate lower humidity (amount of moisture in the air).

Evaporative coolers (swamp coolers) operate on this same principle. As water evaporates, the water molecules that are moving most rapidly are the ones that escape into the air. You might say they have reached escape velocity. More rapid movement means higher energy, which also translates into heat. Thus, the molecules having the most heat are the ones that escape, leaving behind those of less-rapid movement, less heat, less energy. With the water molecules of greater energy being removed from the water through evaporation, those left behind have less energy and the water is cooler. Air is forced through this cooler water by a fan. This cools the air, and the cooled air circulates through your living space. Evaporation occurs rapidly in very warm, dry air, but very slowly in conditions of high humidity. Therefore, evaporative coolers are quite effective in dry climates, but you will seldom see them in areas where humidity is high.

Integrating

Reading

Science Process Skills

Observing, inferring, communicating, comparing and contrasting, formulating hypotheses, researching

Hands-On Earth Science Activities

How Can We Compare the Wet/Dry Bulb and Hair Hygrometers?

Materials Needed

- Hygrometers from Activities 3.5 and 3.6
- Empty aquarium or large cardboard box lined with plastic garbage bags
- Pan of hot water (use with caution)
- Warm, moist bath towel
- Paper
- Pencils

Procedure

1. Mark the position of the pointer on the index card of the hair hygrometer.
2. Compare and record the temperatures and difference in the wet/dry bulb hygrometer.
3. Put an open pan of hot water in the aquarium or box.
4. Carefully lower the hair hygrometer into the box and cover the box top with the warm, moist towel. What do you think is happening inside the container? Can you predict what will happen to the hygrometers?
5. After waiting five minutes, gently remove the hygrometer from the box and on the index card mark the position of the pointer.
6. Repeat steps 3, 4, and 5 exactly, using the wet/dry bulb hygrometer, except at the end record the temperatures and the difference between them.
7. What kind of environment (conditions) did you create inside the container?
8. What can you say about the reactions of your hygrometers? Discuss your ideas with your group.

Figure 3.7-1. Aquarium with Pan of Water and Warm, Moist Towel

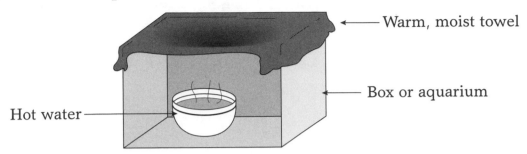

Warm, moist towel

Box or aquarium

Hot water

For Problem Solvers

Do this project as a Science Investigation. Obtain a blank copy of the "Science Investigation Journaling Notes." Write your name, the date, and your question at the top. Plan your investigation through step 5 (Procedure) and have it approved by your teacher. Complete the Journaling Notes as you perform your investigation. Share your project with your group, and submit your Journaling Notes to your teacher if requested.

This activity will help you to decide which of the hygrometers you prefer. Do the activity several more times, but vary the amount of moisture in the box by varying the amount of moisture you put in the towel. Also, include a commercial hygrometer with the two homemade devices. Estimate the humidity each time before you read the instruments and record your estimate. Record the readings from all three and graph your data. Include your estimates in your graph. Which of the two homemade instruments is more consistent with the commercial instrument? Are your estimates becoming more accurate?

Teacher Information

If possible, do this on a day that is "normal" for your climate. The pan of hot water and moist towel will create a very humid environment. The hair should lengthen and show a measurable difference on the card. The temperature of the wet bulb hygrometer should increase more than that of the dry bulb, but with little difference (both will go up some). The normal readings at the beginning of the activity, plus the moist reading at the end, should give students the beginning of a scale upon which they can record daily "readings" of the humidity.

Using the wet/dry bulb hygrometer with the relative humidity table should give a fairly accurate reading of relative humidity, rather consistent with a commercial hygrometer or sling psychrometer. The hair hygrometer could be calibrated to provide actual relative humidity values, but for our purposes it is probably more valuable simply as an indicator of change in relative humidity, as students observe the rise and fall of the pointer.

Integrating

Math, language arts

Science Process Skills

Observing, inferring, measuring, estimating, communicating, comparing and contrasting, using space-time relationships, formulating hypotheses, identifying and controlling variables, experimenting, researching

What Does a Wind Vane Do, and How Can You Make One?

(Teacher-supervised activity)

Materials Needed

- Pencils with erasers
- Soda straws
- Hatpins (or simple straight pins)
- Construction paper
- Scissors
- Fans
- Tape

Procedure

1. Draw a pointer for your wind vane on the construction paper.

2. Draw a tail fin. Make the tail fin larger than the pointer.

3. Cut out both the pointer and the tail fin.

4. Cut a slit in each end of the drinking straw, about 2 to 3 cm (1 in.) from the ends.

5. Slide the pointer in one end of the straw and the tail fin in the other end. Secure them with tape. This is the arrow for your wind vane. (See Figure 3.8–1.)

6. Lay your arrow on your finger and find out where it balances. Mark that point on the straw and push the pin through the straw at the point. Be sure the pin, the pointer, and the tail fin are all lined up vertically together.

7. Push the pin into the eraser of your pencil. You now have a wind vane.

8. Turn on the fan. Using the pencil as the handle, test your wind vane by holding it in the breeze in front of the fan. The arrow should point into the wind (toward the fan), showing which direction the wind is coming from.

9. When the wind blows, take your wind vane outdoors and let it show which way the wind is coming from.

Hands–On Earth Science Activities

Figure 3.8-1. Wind Vane

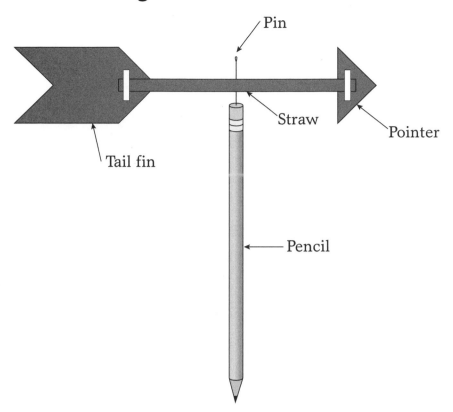

Teacher Information

This is a simple wind vane that even small children can make and use. Be sure the tail fin is larger than the pointer, because that's what turns the arrow around to face the breeze. If the arrow doesn't turn freely, work the straw around on the pin just a little bit to make the hole in the straw slightly larger.

The idea of the wind vane is that you can tell which direction the wind is blowing without being out in the wind. The pencil supporting the arrow can be pushed into the ground, tied to a post, or otherwise anchored outdoors. Students can "read" the wind direction as they observe from indoors through the window.

Caution: With the use of scissors and straight pins, close supervision will be needed.

Integrating

Art

Science Process Skills

Observing, communicating

What Is Another Design for a Wind Vane?

(Teacher-supervised activity)

Materials Needed

- Two strips of heavy cardboard 45 cm (18 in.) long by 15 cm (6 in.) wide
- One piece of half-inch plywood about 15 cm (6 in.) square
- One piece of 2-inch by 2-inch lumber about 20 cm (8 in.) long
- Pencil
- Scissors
- Glass portion of eyedropper or very thin glass bottle of about the same size
- Two eight-penny nails
- Heavy-duty wire cutters (side-cut pliers)
- Drill
- Drill bit, same diameter as the nails (or slightly smaller, not larger)
- Wood glue

Procedure

1. You can construct an instrument to help you chart wind direction.
2. On one strip of cardboard, draw an arrow with a small point and large tail.
3. With scissors, cut out the arrow and use it as a pattern to make a second arrow.
4. Glue the two arrows together, leaving an unglued portion in the middle to accept the dropper between the layers.
5. Find the balance point by balancing the arrow on your finger. Put a mark at that point on the arrow.
6. At the balance point, insert the eyedropper between the two layers of the arrow. The eyedropper is the bearing upon which the arrow will turn. Glue the two layers of the arrow tightly together around the bearing (eyedropper).

154

7. Stand the 20-cm (8-in.) long piece of wood on end in the center of the square base and glue it in place. Then turn it upside down and use the hammer to drive a nail through the base into the upright. The glue and nail will together make a strong joint.

8. Drill a hole down into the top center of the upright. Cut the head off the nail with the wire cutters, and pound the nail into the hole, with the point of the nail up. The nail should fit firmly into the drilled hole, and it must extend above the upright far enough that the bearing of the arrow will rest on the point of the nail. Get a longer nail if necessary. Having drilled the hole in the upright, you should be able to tap the nail into place with very little or no damage to the point of the nail; it only needs to be a snug fit.

9. Place the arrow on its stand, with the dropper over the nail, and your wind vane should be ready to use. The arrow should turn freely in all directions. It should now look something like Figure 3.9–1.

Figure 3.9-1. Homemade Wind Vane

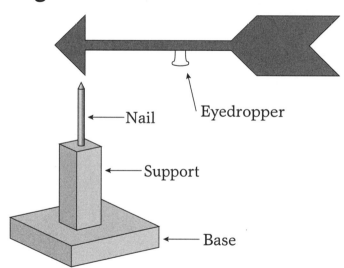

For Problem Solvers

Watch for wind vanes of all kinds. Look on the tops of homes and all other buildings, in yards, and on fences. Keep a record of how many of each type you see. Which design seems to be the most popular? If there is a small airport near you, try to go there and find out what kind of wind vane they use for pilots to see.

Learn about windsocks. Try making a windsock with a coat hanger frame and a nylon stocking with the foot cut out.

Teacher Information

Caution: Close supervision is recommended for safety reasons because of the use of glass (eyedropper) and of sharp objects (nails), which could cause injury if broken or used carelessly.

Wind vanes have been popular for centuries. Often they are beautiful, intricately designed works of art used to decorate barns, houses, churches, and public buildings. A rooster perched on top is a common identifying characteristic. A collection of pictures of wind vanes, both common and elaborate, would make an attractive bulletin board display.

Tubular pieces of cloth called windsocks are often used at small airports. They are designed to fill with air as wind speed increases, and to turn into the wind.

Integrating

Social studies

Science Process Skills

Observing

How Can You Make a More Sensitive Wind Vane?

(Take home and do with family and friends.)

Materials Needed

- Stirring straws (a section about 5 cm [2 in.] long)
- Round toothpicks
- Cube of clay, about 2 to 3 cm (1 in.) on each side
- Paper fins, about 4 cm by 15 cm (1.5 in. by 6 in.)
- Squares of plastic or paper with slick surface, a little smaller than the surface of the cube of clay
- Tape (transparent or masking)
- Cardboard bases for the clay, about 5 cm (2 in.) square

Procedure

1. Using the toothpick, make a hole in the center of the small plastic square; then place the plastic square on the cube of clay. Place the clay on the cardboard base.

2. Push the toothpick through the hole in the plastic and into the clay. This is a stand for the fin. (See Figure 3.10–1.)

3. Tape the fin onto the section of stirring straw, then fold it into a V-shape and place the stirring straw over the toothpick. (See Figure 3.10–2.) Let's call it a "Micro Wind Vane." Micro means small; this one is smaller and more sensitive to light breezes than those you might have made before.

4. Blow your breath toward your micro wind vane, to be sure it turns freely to face the breeze.

5. Place the micro wind vane in a place where you think there are breezes at least some of the time. Observe, record your observations, and share them with your group.

Figure 3.10–1. Toothpick in Clay Stand

Figure 3.10–2. Micro Wind Vane

Hands-On Earth Science Activities

For Problem Solvers

Do this project as a Science Investigation. Obtain a blank copy of the "Science Investigation Journaling Notes." Write your name, the date, and your question at the top. Plan your investigation through step 5 (Procedure) and have it approved by your teacher. Complete the Journaling Notes as you perform your investigation. Share your project with your group, and submit your Journaling Notes to your teacher if requested.

Make several micro wind vanes and place them around your classroom. Observe carefully and write notes to keep a record of the various locations: areas of the room where there are detectable air currents a lot of the time; areas where air currents change direction frequently, such as when ventilation fans turn on; and areas that do not seem to have any detectable air currents at all. When a change in air current is indicated by movement of a micro wind vane, try to determine what happened to make the change: perhaps a person walked past the micro wind vane, someone opened a door or window, or a ventilating fan turned on.

If there are areas that seem to have no detectable air currents at all, move those micro wind vanes to other areas, perhaps even outdoors.

Teacher Information

The small piece of plastic or paper called for in the materials list is to provide a slick surface for the wind vane to rest on, minimizing resistance and allowing the wind vane to turn more freely. Aluminum foil could be used instead of paper for the fin; being lighter in weight can give it a slight advantage, with a little more sensitivity to air movement.

The completed micro wind vanes should be quite sensitive to low breezes in the classroom, as when the windows are open or circulating fans are on. A strong wind will simply blow it away.

Integrating

Math, language arts

Science Process Skills

Observing, inferring, classifying, measuring, predicting, communicating, comparing and contrasting, using space-time relationships, formulating hypotheses, identifying and controlling variables, experimenting

How Can You Use a Wind Vane?

(Teacher-supervised activity)

Materials Needed

- Copies of Figure 3.11–1, at least 8 inches by 8 inches in size
- Wind vane
- Directional compass
- Ruler
- Pencil

Procedure

1. Get a copy of the Wind Direction Chart from your teacher.

2. Go outdoors on a windy day and find an open area. Use the compass to determine north. Align your Wind Direction Chart so the north side of the chart faces north, and put your wind vane in the center of it.

3. Place a mark on the outer line of the Wind Direction Chart to indicate the direction the arrow of your wind vane is pointing. Remember, the wind vane points in the direction the wind is coming from. A north wind *blows from the north,* and an east wind *blows from the east.* Beside the mark you made to indicate wind direction, write the time of day.

4. Write the date at the top (north side) of your Wind Direction Chart.

5. Return to the same place and repeat steps 2 and 3 three more times in the same day. Each time, mark the wind direction on your Wind Direction Chart, and write the time of day.

6. Do this each day for one month, using a new paper each day. Each day, try to use the same times of day.

7. Make a bar graph that includes a bar for each of the directions that are on your Wind Direction Chart and how many days the wind blew in that direction.

8. Make a second bar graph that shows the four times of day you used to check the wind. Show how many times the wind was blowing during the month at each time of day.

9. Discuss your findings with your teacher and with your group.

Teacher Information

Depending on your climate and the time of year, wind direction may not change frequently. Twice a day may be sufficient to obtain the necessary information. Wind direction will be combined with data from the other instruments to develop a student-made weather station.

Integrating

Math, language arts, social studies

Science Process Skills

Observing

Figure 3.11–1. Wind Direction Chart

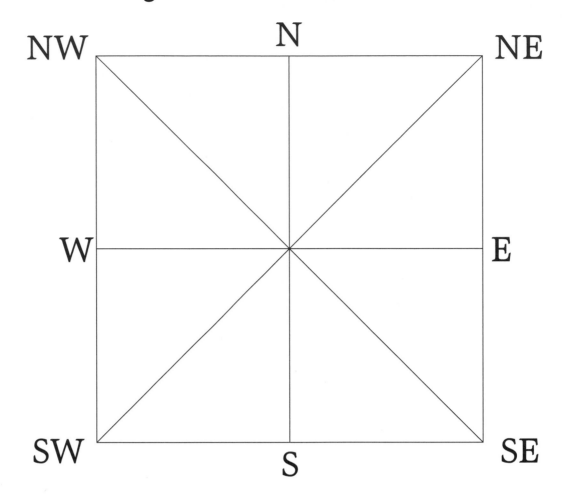

Hands-On Earth Science Activities

How Can Wind Speed Be Measured?

(Teacher-supervised activity)

Materials Needed

- Support base from Activity 3.9
- Two strips of lath 40 cm (16 in.) long
- Four four-ounce paper cups (three of one color and one of a different color)
- Thumbtacks
- Glass eyedropper or very thin glass bottle
- Wood glue
- Small 2 cm ($\frac{3}{4}$ in.) nails
- Hammer
- Drill

Procedure

1. Find the middle of each piece of lath. Cross one on top of the other, and glue them together. Use two small nails to hold them securely.

2. Have your teacher drill a hole in the exact center of the cross, large enough to accommodate the eyedropper or bottle.

3. Use the support base from Activity 3.9, or build another support base similar to it.

4. Glue a four-ounce paper cup to each of the four ends of the cross. Use thumbtacks, too, for extra strength. Be sure the open ends of all the cups face in the same direction.

5. Place the cross on the support base, resting the eyedropper over the nail. When completed, the cross with cups should spin freely.

6. This instrument is called an anemometer (see Figure 3.12–1), and it is used to measure wind speed.

Weather

163

Figure 3.12–1. Homemade Anemometer

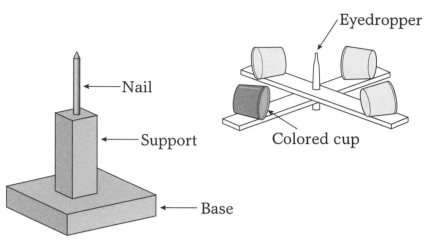

For Problem Solvers

Wind speed can be measured with instruments of different types. Can you think of another way to make an instrument that could indicate wind speed? It doesn't need to be like the one above. See what you can learn about other types of anemometers. Build one or more of them. Design your own anemometer.

Do some research and find out how meteorologists measure wind speed. Is there any resemblance between their instrument and yours?

Teacher Information

It is very important that the anemometer be balanced and spin freely. A parent or aide could be enlisted to use a hand drill to bore the holes in the crosspieces if you are making several of them.

Integrating

Reading, social studies, art

Science Process Skills

Observing, comparing and contrasting, measuring, identifying and controlling variables, experimenting, researching

How Does an Anemometer Work?

(Do this activity in moderate wind.)

Materials Needed

- Anemometer
- Stopwatch or watch with second hand
- Paper
- Pencil
- Masking tape

Procedure

1. Take the materials to an open area where a mild wind is blowing.
2. Put the anemometer on a flat surface where it will spin freely. Put a strip of masking tape on the flat surface under the cups so they will pass over it each time they spin around.
3. Use the colored cup as a counter and count the times it passes over the strip during a 60-second period.
4. Divide the number of times the colored cup passes over the strip by 10 and you will have the approximate speed of the wind in miles per hour.
5. Repeat steps 1 through 4 each day. Record the date, time, and wind speed for thirty days.
6. Discuss your findings with your teacher and with your group.
7. What implications does this information have in our lives?

For Problem Solvers

Here's another way you can calibrate your anemometer. On a calm, windless day, get someone to drive you to a back road that has very little traffic. Hold your anemometer out the window while the driver holds the speed at exactly 5 miles per hour. Count and record the revolutions of the anemometer in one minute. Do the same at 10 mph, 15 mph, 20 mph, and your anemometer is calibrated. Don't go too fast, or your anemometer will blow away!

Teacher Information

Friction will be an important factor in the accuracy of the anemometer. You can calibrate the accuracy to some degree if on a very calm day you hold the anemometer out the window of a car at various speeds while counting the number of spins. If the car is driven for one minute at 5, 10, and 15 miles per hour, you should have enough data to compare with the stationary recordings. The anemometer must be held far enough away from the car so air currents caused by the car do not disturb it.

This calibration should obviously be done on a road with very little traffic.

Integrating

Math, language arts, social studies

Science Process Skills

Observing, measuring, using space-time relationships

How Can Rainfall Be Measured?

Materials Needed

- A can that is at least 15 cm (6 in.) tall
- Ruler or meter stick
- Paper
- Pencil

Procedure

1. When rain is expected, take the can outdoors and leave it in a place where there are no buildings, walls, trees, or other obstructions nearby.
2. As soon as possible after the rain stops, use the ruler to measure the amount of water in the container.
3. Rainfall is usually reported in inches or centimeters.
4. Keep a chart for 30 days, listing the date and the amount of rainfall.
5. If you are studying weather at a time when most of the precipitation is in the form of snow, you can measure snow depth with the meter stick if you are in an open area.
6. If you are measuring precipitation in the form of snow, sleet, or hail, you can collect it in a wastebasket or pail, bring it into a warm place to melt and measure the water content. Different types of snow contain varying amounts of water for a given volume.

For Problem Solvers

How many centimeters or inches of precipitation does your area get in a year, on the average? What times of the year does most of the precipitation come? Does most of it come in the form of rain, or is it mostly from snowfall? Find a rainfall map and compare your area with other parts of the nation and of the world.

Teacher Information

Some rain gauges use a funnel at the top of the collector. This is helpful in collecting rainwater, but you should take into account the diameter of the funnel versus the diameter of the container and correct your measurement accordingly. Divide the area of the funnel opening by the area of the opening of the container, and then divide the depth of the water in the container by the result of that computation. For example, if the area of the funnel is 100 square centimeters, the area of the container opening is 50 square centimeters, and the depth of the rainwater is 3 cm, the computation becomes $100 \div 50 = 2$; then $3 \div 2 = 1.5$. The amount of rainfall is 1.5 cm. If you are measuring in inches, the computation is the same except use the numbers representing all measurements in inches.

Moisture content is very important in measuring snow. Five cm (2 in.) of wet snow may contain more moisture than 20 cm (8 in.) of powdery snow. If a slight amount of rain falls, but is not measurable, it should be recorded as a "trace."

Integrating

Math, reading, social studies

Science Process Skills

Communicating, using space-time relationships, researching

Hands–On Earth Science Activities

How Can You Operate a Weather Station?

(Class-planning activity)

Materials Needed

- Large bulletin board for sample "Weather Chart" (See Table 3.15–1.)
- Meter stick
- Crayons
- Markers

Procedure

1. Now that you have instruments to measure the weather, plan a 30-day chart to record it. Use the sample "Weather Chart" in Table 3.15–1 as a starting point. You will need to decide the data you want to record each day and assign committees to record it.

2. The Weather Bureau uses standard symbols to indicate weather conditions. Your teacher can help you find a book to help you learn to use these symbols if you care to.

3. Leave four extra columns at the end to record weather reports from other sources and to record the actual weather.

4. In addition to the large bulletin board chart, you may want to make smaller copies for your own use.

5. Discuss your findings with your teacher and with your group.

6. In what ways does this kind of information affect our lives?

For Problem Solvers

With this activity, try your hand at predicting the weather. Make another column at the right end of the chart and label it "Tomorrow's Forecast." In this column write your forecast for each day, one day in advance. Pay particular attention to the barometric pressure each day. Notice the kind of changes in the weather that follow a rise in pressure, and the kinds of changes that follow a drop in pressure. This information will help you make your daily forecasts.

Teacher Information

The official Weather Bureau symbols are much more complicated and usually unnecessary to use for a short period of time. The chart in the example provides for fifteen days. This is a minimum recommended time for the study. Thirty days would provide a more accurate comparison. Daily readings should take only a few minutes, so other science projects could be planned for the remaining time.

Integrating

Math, language arts, social studies, art

Science Process Skills

Observing, inferring, classifying, measuring, predicting, communicating, using space-time relationships, formulating hypotheses, identifying variables

Table 3.15-1. Sample Weather Chart

Key *										Tomorrow's Forecast				Today's Actual Date
Symbol	Condition	Date	Time	Temp	Wind Speed	Wind Direction	Humidity	Air Pressure	Class	Commercial	Weather Bureau TV, Radio, News	Farmers Almanac		
○	Clear Sky													
◑	Partly Cloudy													
●	Rain													
✳	Snow													
	Thunder Storm													
	Drizzle													
	Fog													
	Warm Front													
	Cold Front													
	Dust Storm													
▷	Showers													
	Hail													
	Sleet													
◇	Smoke													
∞	Haze													

* (not an official key)

● more symbols = stronger conditions

*▷ symbol above symbol = mixed condition

What Is the Best Source of Information for Predicting Weather?

(Group activity)

Materials Needed

- Weather instruments constructed in previous activities
- Commercial weather instruments manufactured for home use
- *The Old Farmers Almanac*
- Pencils
- A single professional source for weather reporting, such as a newspaper, television, radio, the U.S. Weather Bureau, or Internet sites that report and forecast weather conditions
- Weather chart from Activity 3.15

Procedure

1. Your teacher will tell you about four different methods you can use to predict weather. Choose one of the four and form a "weather team."

2. For the next several weeks, meet with your group, study the information you have collected from your source for the day, and record on the chart your group's prediction of what tomorrow's weather will be.

3. At the end of the week, compare each of the predictions with actual weather as it occurred. If your predictions were not accurate, try to think of ways to improve them.

Teacher Information

The main objective of this activity is to help students become aware of some of the major factors that are considered in weather forecasting.

Commercial weather instruments for home use are sold in many stores. They usually consist of a thermometer, aneroid barometer, and hygrometer. If they are not available in your classroom, you can probably borrow a set from someone in your school or community.

In selecting a professional source, try to locate an individual with whom you can work. This person can become an excellent resource and may be able to assist by providing materials and arranging field trips. If you make daily contact with an agency by telephone, be certain only one student is selected to make the call.

Long-term predictions are not included in this activity. However, this would be an appropriate time to introduce the use of current technology such as weather satellites, weather sites on the Internet, and the rapidly advancing weather radar systems.

Integrating

Reading, language arts, social studies

Science Process Skills

Observing, communicating, using space-time relationships, formulating hypotheses, identifying variables, researching

What Are Some Unusual Ways to Predict and Explain Weather?

(A just-for-fun activity)

Materials Needed

- Books and stories
- Traditions and myths
- Older adults

Procedure

1. Groundhog Day is known and observed almost everywhere in the United States. Find out all you can about this special day and share with your class.

2. Below are listed a number of other kinds of information people use to predict weather. How many do you know? Can you complete the sentences below?

   Woolly caterpillars tell us _____.

   Amount of fur or fat on animals tells us _____.

   The Native Americans say _____.

   My grandmother's arthritis _____.

   My grandfather's corns _____.

   The animals (squirrels, birds, and other wild animals) are _____.

   A ring around the moon means _____.

   Red sky at night, sailors' delight; red sky at morning, sailors take _____.

   A "rain dance" is _____.

   When north winds blow, _____.

3. Form a committee and find out as much as you can about folk methods for predicting and changing weather.

4. With your teacher's help, make an illustrated book on folk weather.

Teacher Information

Although it is not scientific, this activity may help children become aware of the many ways people have used to understand, predict, and influence the weather. Weather conditions in some manner influence many factors in our lives, including where we live, what we do from day to day, and our safety. Technology has enabled us to walk on the moon, circle the earth in an hour, see an event as it happens anywhere on earth—and even to be more confident of the accuracy of weather forecasts.

In your book of folk weather, be sure to include songs, poems, stories, and pictures to portray the feelings of mystery, power, beauty, wonder, and awe of that remarkable phenomenon we call weather.

Finally, remember the old saying, "It always rains on the weatherman's picnic."

Integrating

Reading, language arts, social studies

Science Process Skills

Communicating, researching

How Do Heating and Cooling Affect Air Currents?

(Teacher-supervised activity)

Materials Needed

- Ten-gallon aquarium and sheet of cardboard to cover the top (or a cardboard box approximately the same size)
- Two glass lamp chimneys
- Large cup or small pan
- Incense or hemp rope to produce smoke
- Roll of 5-cm (2-in.) wide plastic tape
- Transparent plastic wrap if a cardboard box is used instead of an aquarium
- Matches
- Small bowls
- Hot water
- Warm water
- Very cold water
- Knife or scissors

Procedure

1. If an aquarium is used, fit the cardboard covering snugly on top.
2. Use a lamp chimney to draw a circle near each end of the cardboard top.
3. Cut out the circles and fit a lamp chimney in each. (See Figure 3.18–1.)
4. If you use a cardboard box, cut off the top flaps and use the plastic wrap to make a window in that side of the box. Seal the wrap and all other openings in the box with plastic tape. Lay the box on its side and make holes in the top for lamp chimneys, as explained in steps 2 and 3. In one end of the box, cut a door that can be opened and closed. (See Figure 3.18–2.)

Hands-On Earth Science Activities

Figure 3.18-1. Aquarium with Lamp Chimneys in Cardboard Top

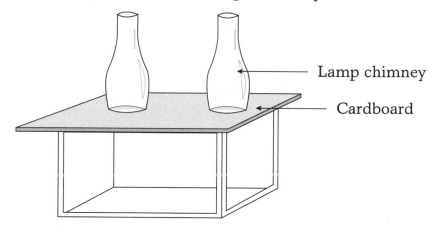

Lamp chimney

Cardboard

Figure 3.18-2. Box with Lamp Chimneys and Transparent Side

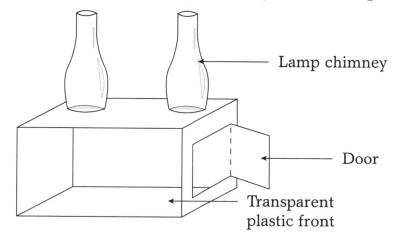

Lamp chimney

Door

Transparent
plastic front

5. Whether you use an aquarium or a cardboard box, seal any space around the lamp chimneys with tape. You now have a convection box.

6. Light the incense or rope and put it in a large cup or small pan in the center of the box. Observe what happens.

7. Place a cup of warm water in the box under one lamp chimney. What happened?

8. Repeat steps 6 and 7 using very hot water and observe carefully.

9. Repeat steps 6 and 7 again, this time using very cold water, and observe carefully.

10. Using information you have learned about air, explain what happened.

For Problem Solvers

Draw a circle to represent the earth. Label the north and south poles. Draw and label the equator. Think about regions of the earth that are warm and regions that are cold. Consider the effect these temperature differences might have on air movement. Draw arrows showing the movements of air masses that you would expect to occur in the atmosphere, based on the warm and cold regions that you have identified.

Do some research on winds and learn about major wind patterns around the globe. Do air masses move the way you showed them? What other factors seem to influence wind patterns? Add arrows to your drawing, showing major global wind patterns.

Teacher Information

Before you begin this activity, you may want to review concepts from the section on "Air."

If lamp chimneys are not available, use tall juice cans or other similar substitutes. When warm water is placed under one of the lamp chimneys in the box, the air around it will be heated and rise. Cooler air will be drawn into the box through the other chimney. Smoke will clearly show the currents.

If you think of the bottom of the convection box as a large area of the earth's surface that heats and cools irregularly due to the shape and material (land, water) of its surface, perhaps you can visualize how large warm and cold air masses develop and cause constant movement of the air.

Each time the water is changed, the smoke should be exhausted from the box. When fresh smoke and a different temperature of water are used, allow several minutes for the atmosphere to change in the box.

Integrating

Reading, social studies

Science Process Skills

Inferring, predicting, communicating, using space-time relationships, formulating hypotheses, identifying, researching

What Can We Learn from a Convection Box?

(Upper-grade activity)

Materials Needed

- Lamp chimney convection box
- Two sheets of 9-inch by 12-inch newsprint
- Pencils
- Large cups
- Smoke source
- Hot water
- Cold water

Procedure

1. Study the convection box and draw a picture of it.

2. Use hot water and smoke to start air movement in the convection box, as seen in Figure 3.19–1.

3. Since we know that faster-moving air has lower pressure, where might a difference in air pressure be inside your box? Write "high" and "low" in the places where you think the pressures might be different. (See Figure 3.19–2.)

4. Since we know warm air can hold more moisture than cold air, where might the differences in humidity be inside your box? Write "moist" and "dry" where you think the air contains more and less moisture.

5. Draw another picture of the convection box.

6. Replace the hot water with ice water in the actual box.

7. Observe the behavior of the smoke. Repeat steps 3 and 4, marking the places in the box where you think air pressure and humidity might differ.

8. Under what conditions does the air move faster?

Weather

179

For Problem Solvers

Consider the effect of rising and falling air on atmospheric pressure. Label each of the areas that you think will have high pressure as a "high" and each low-pressure area as a "low."

Look at a globe. Also get some sticky notepaper or small papers and tape. In what areas of the globe will air masses most likely pick up large amounts of moisture from the earth's surface? Label these as "moist." Label as "dry" those areas where air masses will be least likely to pick up moisture. Consult a map, if you need help in locating water and land surfaces.

Teacher Information

The students should not see Figures 3.19–1 and 3.19–2 until they have completed the activity. Although it would require very sensitive instruments to measure the differences, they do occur.

Some students may have difficulty with the abstract thinking this activity requires. A class discussion and review at the end of the activity should help.

This activity may also help you determine how well children understand the basic principles of weather and air that have been developed up to this point.

Figure 3.19–1. Convection Box with Hot Water

Figure 3.19-2. Convection Box with Cold Water

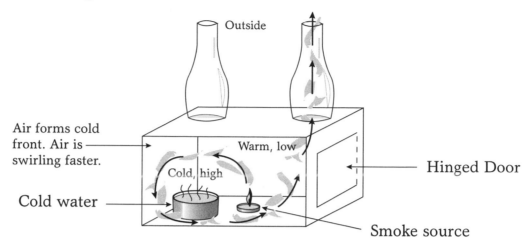

Integrating

Reading, social studies

Science Process Skills

Inferring, predicting, communicating, comparing and contrasting, using space-time relationships, formulating hypotheses, identifying variables, researching

What Makes Rain?

Materials Needed

- One copy of Figure 3.20–1 for each student
- Paper
- Pencils

Procedure

1. Study Figure 3.20–1. Can you see the relationships?
2. Write a story that describes what is happening from left to right in the picture. Can you explain why?

For Problem Solvers

Design and build a model that demonstrates the water cycle. You will need a closed box with a clear lid. This could be a plastic-lined cardboard box with clear plastic stretched over the top or a plastic box with a clear lid. Make a land form in your box. Include a mountain at one end of the box, sloped into a lake or sea at the other end. Plaster of Paris or papier mâché works well for making your land form, and all of this needs to be waterproofed. You can waterproof it by painting it with a sealer.

Now put some water in the lake and find a way to put a few ice cubes at the other end, up high. A plastic baggy could be mounted at the top of the box, over the mountain, for the ice cubes. This is your cloud; it represents the cold air in the upper atmosphere.

You need to include a warm sun. The sun could be a lamp, with the bulb positioned near the lake end, either protruding through the box or near the plastic cover.

Be patient for a while and watch the rain come down on the mountain and flow down into the lake. Share your model with others, and describe for them what's happening, step-by-step, through the water cycle. This is a model of the world's largest recycling operation.

Teacher Information

Figure 3.20–1 is a simplified diagram of one way weather can change. Reading from left to right: Sun shines on water, causing it to warm and evaporate. The air above is warm and moist and rises until it reaches the upper atmosphere and begins to cool. As it cools, moisture condenses and clouds begin to form. Prevailing winds that move from water to land carry the clouds inland, where they continue to pick up moisture.

When the clouds reach the mountain, they are forced upward into cooler air. As the air in the clouds cools rapidly, it must reduce its moisture content, which it does at lower elevations in the form of rain and at higher elevations in the form of snow (depending on temperature).

As clouds are forced up by a high mountain range, they may give up much of the moisture they contain, so less precipitation falls on the far side of the mountain. This area is called a rain shadow.

Warm air pockets have low pressure and tend to rise, while cold air pockets are heavier (high pressure) and tend to sink. Figure 3.20–1 shows air becoming colder and yet continuing to rise up the mountainside, increasing in relative humidity and releasing moisture along the way. For clarification, one must consider that the entire system shown here is a small part of a much larger system, in which cold air is forced upward by large-scale winds that often dominate the movements of smaller parcels within.

Your problem solvers will create water cycle models that will show the process of evaporation, condensation, and precipitation, somewhat as it occurs in nature.

Integrating

Language arts, social studies

Science Process Skills

Observing, inferring, communicating, using space-time relationships, identifying and controlling variables

Figure 3.20–1. Profile of Water, Land, and Mountains

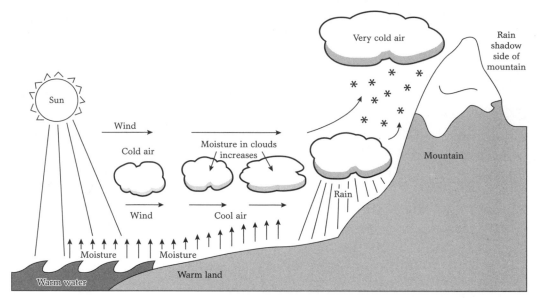

Hands-On Earth Science Activities

What Is a Cold Front?

Materials Needed

- One copy of Figure 3.21–1 for each student
- Crayons

Student Information

If all weather patterns were simple, the weather forecaster's job would be easy. Actually, different air masses form over water, ice, and dry land. Many different kinds of air masses are moving over the earth at different altitudes at the same time. When they collide, they often do not mix. At the point of impact, weather disturbances, sometimes of unpredictable extent, occur.

Procedure

1. Study the picture of colliding air masses. In this case, the cold air mass is somewhat like a moving mountain. Use your red crayon to write "warm" where you think warm temperatures would be found.

2. Use a blue crayon to write "cold" and "very cold" where you think cold temperatures might occur.

3. Use a green crayon to write "moist" where the most humidity will be found.

4. Use a yellow crayon to write "dry" where you think there is less moisture.

5. Use a black crayon to write "high" or "low" where you think air pressure differences might occur.

6. Compare and discuss your picture with your teacher and with other members of the class.

7. Why is it important to recognize some of the basic indicators of weather conditions? Discuss this question with your group.

For Problem Solvers

You can see by now that the earth's atmosphere is a very complex system. This activity considers movements of very large masses of air. On a smaller scale, can you see how winds are generated at a lake? Does water cool and heat faster or slower than the land surface? What effect would this have on air temperature after sunset? What about after sunrise?

With this in mind, examine the water cycle model you made for Activity 3.20. Which direction would you expect winds to blow in the morning? What about in the evening? Think about temperature changes that occur over land regions and over sea regions during the night and during the day. Share your ideas with others who are interested in this activity.

Teacher Information

The temperature will be warmer near the ground in the area before the approaching front. Temperatures behind and above the front will be colder.

As the cold front pushes the warm air upward, precipitation may occur. The type of precipitation will depend on the temperature of the air. The common weather prediction of "rain turning to snow" tells the progress of the cold front.

Because cold fronts move faster, the air pressure will be lower behind the front.

The humidity will be greater in areas before and following the front line.

If the cold front should stop over the town, it would be called stationary. Stationary lows and highs often determine weather for long periods of time over large regions of the country.

Occasionally, especially in mountainous areas, a cold front may become stationary with a warm air mass above it. The warm air forms a blanket and retards circulation of the cold air. This is called a "temperature inversion." If a temperature inversion occurs over a city, air does not circulate and smog will develop.

If you live in an area near a large body of water, such as an ocean or gulf, your weather is controlled to a great extent by the water mass. Since the air temperature over water does not change as much as it does over land, your temperatures could vary less. Latitude and ocean currents will be of greater importance. Severe storms will most often develop over the body of water and move onto land, especially in the southern latitudes. Weather is also greatly influenced by large lakes, rivers, mountains, and valleys.

A final evaluation for this study could be to have the students draw, label, and explain a picture of the last storm that occurred in their area.

Integrating

Math, language arts, social studies, art

Science Process Skills

Observing, inferring, predicting, communicating, using space-time relationships, formulating hypotheses, identifying, experimenting, researching

Figure 3.21-1. Colliding Air Masses

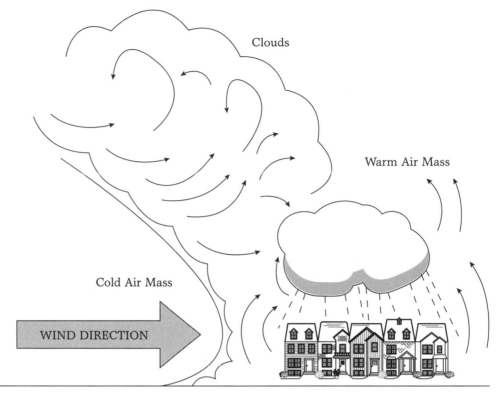

Clouds

Warm Air Mass

Cold Air Mass

WIND DIRECTION

Air circulates around cold front

Can You Solve This Weather Word Search?

Try to find the following Weather terms in the grid below. They could appear in horizontal (left to right), vertical (up or down), or diagonal (upward or downward) position.

weather	rain	snow
sleet	hail	freeze
cold	hot	humidity
cloudy	windy	frost
thermometer	hygrometer	barometer
anemometer	storm	

```
T  A  H  O  T  S  C  L  O  U  D  Y
C  H  B  E  F  D  F  R  E  W  T  T
V  I  E  E  F  R  E  E  Z  E  R  I
A  L  S  R  D  D  O  Q  W  E  E  D
S  N  O  W  M  L  Y  S  T  T  R  I
Z  H  Y  G  R  O  M  E  T  E  R  M
H  R  A  S  W  C  M  R  T  O  U  U
C  A  N  E  M  O  M  E  T  E  R  H
T  I  E  A  R  S  L  R  T  T  H  M
B  N  I  A  U  Y  I  T  D  E  O  P
T  U  B  O  W  E  A  T  H  E  R  M
B  W  I  N  D  Y  H  E  D  F  A  N
```

Can You Create a New Weather Word Search of Your Own?

Write your Weather words in the grid below. Arrange them in the grid so they appear in horizontal (left to right), vertical (up or down), or diagonal (upward or downward) position. Fill in the blank boxes with other letters. Trade your Word Search with someone else who has created one of his or her own, and see whether you can solve the new puzzle.

_____   _____   _____

_____   _____   _____

_____   _____   _____

_____   _____   _____

Weather

Answer Key for
Weather Word Search

```
T  A  H  O  T  S  C  L  O  U  D  Y
C  H  B  E  F  D  F  R  E  W  T  T
V  I  E  E  F  R  E  E  Z  E  R  I
A  L  S  R  D  D  O  Q  W  E  E  D
S  N  O  W  M  L  Y  S  T  T  R  I
Z  H  Y  G  R  O  M  E  T  E  R  M
H  R  A  S  W  C  M  R  T  O  U  U
C  A  N  E  M  O  M  E  T  E  R  H
T  I  E  A  R  S  L  R  T  T  H  M
B  N  I  A  U  Y  I  T  D  E  O  P
T  U  B  O  W  E  A  T  H  E  R  M
B  W  I  N  D  Y  H  E  D  F  A  N
```

Do You Recall?

Section Three: Weather

1. When clouds cool down, is it more likely to rain, or less likely? Why?

2. What causes the liquid in a thermometer to go up and down?

3. Why does atmospheric pressure increase as the air cools?

4. Why does a wet thermometer register colder than a dry thermometer?

5. What does a wind vane detect?

6. What weather instrument is used to measure wind speed?

7. What effect does temperature change have on wind?

Answer Key for Do You Recall?

Section Three: Weather

Answer	Related Activities
1. More likely to rain. Cold air cannot hold as much moisture as warm air.	3.1, 3.2, 3.20
2. The liquid expands as it gets warmer and contracts as it cools.	3.3
3. As air cools, it becomes more dense and is heavier.	3.4
4. Evaporation is a cooling process.	3.5, 3.6, 3.7
5. Direction the wind is coming from	3.8–3.11
6. Anemometer	3.12, 3.13
7. Air expands as it warms and contracts as it cools, causing large masses of air to move. We call it wind.	3.18, 3.19, 3.21

The Earth

To the Teacher

We live on a combination of rock, soil, and water known as the earth's crust. We depend on this relatively thin layer (along with air and sunlight) to provide our food, medicine, and clothing—and the materials to build our homes, cars, and other things. Geologists continually search the earth's surface for clues to the location of mineral resources and answers to questions about the origin, early history, and current changes of the surface of this planet. A study of its structure and evolutionary history helps to increase our appreciation for the earth and its resources.

Scientists are interested in the composition of the earth, the forces that shape and change it, and how it came to be as it is. From a career point of view, exposure to some of these ideas can help students begin to develop a perception of geology-related occupations and even stimulate possible early interests. From the standpoint of general interest, horizons are broadened within the mind as students acquire a glimpse of the significance and majesty of this great planet.

The first several activities of this unit are map oriented. The objective of these activities is not to present a thorough treatment of map reading, but to develop the concept of representing the earth, or small portions of it, on paper or another surface that can be used for observation and study. The map-related questions in this section deal with the problems arising from efforts to represent size and shape in miniature form. Even in the very early grades, students can begin forming concepts about the earth's magnitude and structure.

Children are natural collectors. This interest can be stimulated and broadened by encouraging them to watch for new kinds of rocks; then provide simple ideas for recognizing similarities and differences in rocks they find and categorizing them according to those recognized attributes.

Along with involvement in the activities of this section, emphasis should be placed on appropriate geologic concepts. The earth's crust, for instance, consists largely of rock layers that have been formed and layered by such factors as heat, pressure, and the effects of water and cementing material. Under the earth's crust is molten rock, called *magma*. Great pressures sometimes force magma to the surface, forming volcanoes. Other forces shift the outer layers of the earth's surface, causing earthquakes and forming mountains and valleys, sometimes causing much destruction in life and property.

Many locations are rich with nearby sites where geologic changes are evident—exposed rock layers on a mountainside or at an excavation site, a glacier-formed canyon, or a terrace that was once the beach of an ancient lake. These examples and many more stand as evidence of the ever-changing nature of the earth's surface. A geologist, forest ranger, or rock collector could provide fascinating information about local geologic interests.

Those living in the city are limited in availability of rocks for collection from natural settings, but a little creative effort can compensate rather well. Samples can be obtained from science supply catalogs or from local rock collectors. Possibly one or more students have collected rocks while on vacation that they would be pleased to bring to class and share with the group. Some teachers successfully add to their rock collections by asking family and friends to "bring me a rock" when they go on vacation. As a group, the class might acquire an impressive rock collection by simply writing to friends and relatives who live far away. Trips to a local museum can provide meaningful geologic field trips.

The following activities are designed as discovery activities that students can usually perform quite independently. You are encouraged to provide students (usually in small groups) with the materials listed and a

copy of the activity from the beginning through the "Procedure." The section titled "Teacher Information" is not intended for student use, but rather to assist you with discussion following the hands-on activity, as students share their observations. Discussion of conceptual information prior to completing the hands-on activity can interfere with the discovery process.

Regarding the Early Grades

With verbal instructions and slight modifications, many of these activities can be used with kindergarten, first-grade, and second-grade students. In some activities, steps that involve procedures that go beyond the level of the child can simply be omitted and yet offer the child an experience that plants the seed for a concept that will germinate and grow later on.

Teachers of the early grades will probably choose to bypass many of the "For Problem Solvers" sections. That's okay. These sections are provided for those who are especially motivated and want to go beyond the investigation provided by the activity outlined. Use the outlined activities, and enjoy worthwhile learning experiences together with your young students. Also consider, however, that many of the "For Problem Solvers" sections can be used appropriately with young children as group activities or as demonstrations, still giving students the advantage of an exposure to the experience, and laying groundwork for connections that will be made at a later time.

Correlation with National Standards

The following elements of the National Standards are reflected in the activities of this section.

K–4   Content Standard A: Science as Inquiry

As a result of activities in grades K–4, all students should develop

1. Abilities necessary to do scientific inquiry
2. Understanding about scientific inquiry

K–4   Content Standard D: Earth and Space Science

As a result of activities in grades K–4, all students should develop understanding of

1. Properties of earth materials
2. Objects in the sky
3. Changes in earth and sky

5-8   Content Standard A: Science as Inquiry

As a result of activities in grades 5–8, all students should develop

1. Abilities necessary to do scientific inquiry
2. Understanding about scientific inquiry

5-8   Content Standard D: Earth and Space Science

As a result of activities in grades 5–8, all students should develop understanding of

1. Structure of the earth system
2. Earth's history
3. Earth in the solar system

How Are Size and Distance Shown on a Map?

Materials Needed

- $8\frac{1}{2}$- by 11-inch paper
- Rulers
- Pencils

Procedure

1. Draw a map of your classroom. Be sure to include the furnishings, such as tables, chairs, bookcases, and desks.

2. Look carefully at your map. Compare it with the classroom. Do they look the same? Are they the same size?

3. If you mailed your map to a friend, what could you do to help your friend understand how large the room and the pieces of furniture really are? If others are doing this same activity, talk to them about ideas for including this information on your map.

4. When you think of an answer to step 3, fix your map so it will show how large things on it really are.

Teacher Information

A map is a representation of a room, a home, a building, a town, a portion of the earth, or sometimes all of it. This activity introduces a series of activities designed to help children understand how the earth, or portions of it, is represented in miniature form for observation and study. Depending on maturity level and prior experience with maps, students may need assistance in deriving a suitable answer for the question in step 3. One solution is to use a scale, letting each centimeter or inch on the map represent a certain distance in the classroom. Any workable solution should be accepted. If those given are impractical, students can be led to "discover" the use of a scale through discussion and use.

Integrating

Math, language arts, social studies, art

Science Process Skills

Observing, inferring, measuring, communicating, comparing and contrasting, using space-time relationships

The Earth

How Can You Show Your School Grounds on a Sheet of Paper?

Materials Needed

- $8\frac{1}{2}$- by 11-inch paper
- Rulers
- Pencils

Procedure

1. Draw a map of your school grounds, including the schoolhouse, ball field, playground, swings, and all other equipment. Use ideas you have already learned as you show the real size of things on your school grounds.

2. On your map of the school grounds, draw your classroom in the school building, showing its actual location in the building.

3. What changes does a mapmaker have to make in order to show larger areas on a map?

Teacher Information

Students should begin to get the idea that any area can be represented on a small sheet of paper. As the area increases in size, the scale must change, putting more actual distance into a given amount of space on the map. In discussion of step 3, be sure students realize that the mapmaker must decrease detail as greater areas are represented.

Integrating

Math, language arts, social studies, art

Science Process Skills

Observing, inferring, measuring, communicating, comparing and contrasting, using space-time relationships

How Can a Flat Map Show Three Dimensions?

(Individual or small-group activity)

Materials Needed

- Clay
- Pencils
- Paper or cardboard

Procedure

1. Form your clay into the shape of a mountain.

2. Now draw your mountain on paper. Think of a way to show the high and low places on your "map." If others are doing the same activity, talk about ways this could be done.

3. Put your clay mountain out of sight and trade papers with another person who is doing the same activity.

4. Looking at the map of your classmate's mountain, make a mountain out of clay the way you think his or her mountain looked, based on his or her drawing. Do not ask to look at the clay mountain that person made. As you make this mountain, the other person should be making one from your map.

5. When you are finished, each of you compare the mountain you made with the clay mountain the other person made the map from.

Teacher Information

The purpose of this activity is to help students discover ways to show a third dimension on a flat surface. This is commonly achieved with relief maps. Depending on maturity of students and prior experience with maps, they may or may not think to use shading or color coding. These methods could be suggested, but students should first be encouraged to devise their own ways to show the highs and lows of their mountains on paper. Original ideas that communicate the information, as well as the tried-and-true techniques, should be accepted and praised.

As a test of accuracy in their use of techniques for showing three dimensions, students might enjoy trading maps with a classmate. Each should leave his or her original mountain intact, get additional clay, and construct a second mountain from the borrowed map. Then each child should compare the second mountain with the classmate's original, to see how well the intended communication was given and interpreted.

Integrating

Math, language arts, social studies, art

Science Process Skills

Observing, inferring, measuring, communicating, using space-time relationships

What Are Contour Lines?

Materials Needed

- Clay
- Pencils
- Paper
- Thick books
- Thin books
- Rulers or meter sticks

Procedure

1. Form your clay into the shape of a mountain. Include hills and valleys, steep slopes, and gradual slopes.

2. Lay a thick book on the table beside your "mountain."

3. Using a ruler or meter stick as a guide, sight across the book to your mountain and put marks all the way around your mountain at the same level as the top of the book.

4. Draw a line around the mountain, connecting the marks you made for step 3.

5. Now stand above your mountain and look down at the line you drew. Does the line form a circle? What shape does it form? This is called a contour line.

6. Use a thinner book and draw a contour line further down the mountainside. Then stack two books and draw a contour line further up the mountainside. Draw still more contour lines if you wish, but keep them apart from each other.

7. Stand over your mountain and look down at the contour lines. Are they the same distance apart all the way around the mountain?

8. Draw your mountain on paper, including all contour lines as they appear from above. When you finish, you will have a contour map.

9. Trade contour maps with a classmate. Look at your classmate's map and try to visualize what the mountain looks like. Then look at the actual mountain and see whether or not you were right.

Teacher Information

The contour map is a very popular and practical way of illustrating elevation on a flat surface. This activity should add meaning to future experiences with maps, as students try to interpret actual contour maps to determine the highs and lows and the gradual and steep slopes. Students might enjoy creating each other's mountains from clay, using the contour maps as a guide.

Integrating

Math, language arts, social studies, art

Science Process Skills

Observing, inferring, measuring, communicating, comparing and contrasting, using space-time relationships

What Is a Contour Map?

Materials Needed

- Commercial contour maps, one per student
- Clay

Procedure

1. Examine the contour map you were given. How much elevation (height) is represented from one contour line to the next?
2. Select one section of the map. Study it carefully and try to visualize the area it represents.
3. Make a clay model of this section of the map.
4. Trade maps with a classmate. Examine and evaluate each other's work.

Teacher Information

This activity can be done individually or in small groups. Any contour maps can be used, but if maps can be obtained that represent a local area familiar to students, the experience will be more meaningful. Students might need help in determining the contour interval (amount of elevation change represented from one contour line to the next).

Some sample contour maps are provided (see Figures 4.5–1, 4.5–2, and 4.5–3) for your convenience, but a map within your locale would be more meaningful. If the maps used represent a local area, consider taking a field trip to that area. Students could then compare the maps with the actual terrain and evaluate their own interpretation of the map. If a class field trip is not possible, perhaps some students could take a field trip of their own, with the family or a group of friends.

If the class or group of students visits a local area with contour maps in hand, consider having them try to walk the contour lines for a distance. After determining the contour interval, each of several students could stand at the point best determined to be a contour line on the map. Then all in the group walk in unison around the terrain, being careful not to walk up or down the slope, each remaining as nearly as possible at the

same elevation as the starting point. The vertical distance between participants should remain constant, but the horizontal distance will vary as they walk along the terrain, as it varies on the contour map.

Your state Geological Survey Office is an excellent source for local maps.

Integrating

Math, language arts, social studies, art

Science Process Skills

Observing, inferring, measuring, communicating, using space-time relationships

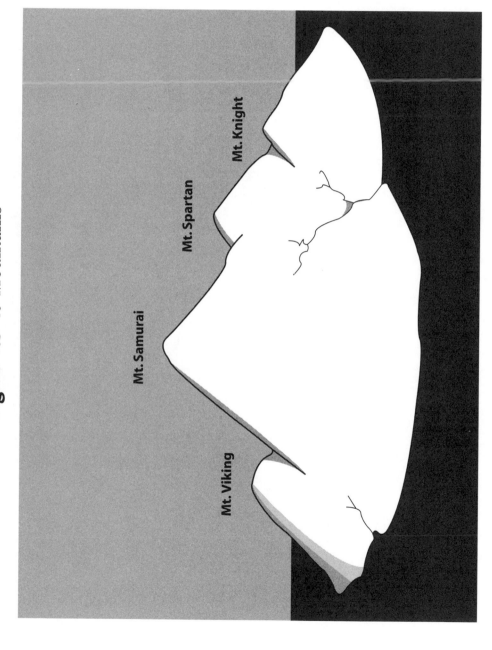

Figure 4.5-1. Mountains

Figure 4.5–2. Mountains with Contour Lines and Elevations

Contour Interval
C.I. = 500 feet

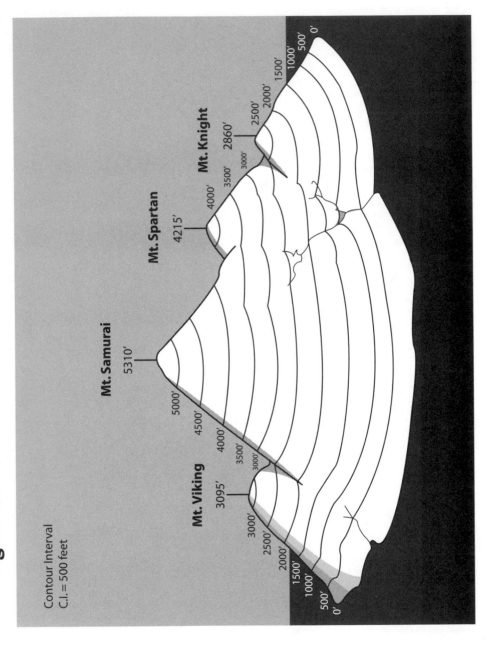

Mt. Samurai
5310'

Mt. Spartan
4215'

Mt. Viking
3095'

Mt. Knight
2860'

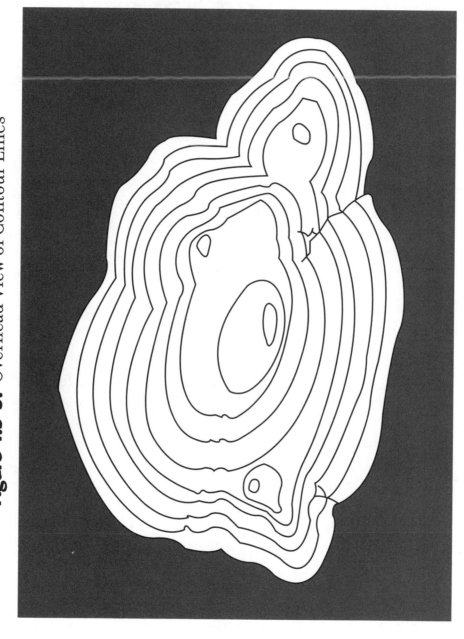

Figure 4.5-3. Overhead View of Contour Lines

How High and Low Are the Earth's Mountains and Valleys?

Materials Needed

- World relief map or globe
- Pencils
- Paper

Procedure

1. Study the relief map until you know how to determine the elevations of the different areas.
2. Write down several of the highest elevations you can find. Include the name of the mountain each one represents and the country it is in.
3. Write down several of the lowest elevations you can find and the name of the area each represents.
4. How much higher are the highest points than the lowest points?
5. The distance through the earth is approximately 8,000 miles. Draw a circle to represent the earth and make a mark to show how high above the line the highest mountain would be. Show the lowest point on the ocean floor also.
6. If others are doing this activity, compare notes and discuss your findings.

For Problem Solvers

Look at a ream of paper. Each sheet of paper is very thin, but the ream of 500 sheets is about two inches thick. If you think of the thickness of one sheet of paper as representing one mile, how many stacked-up sheets would be needed to represent the diameter of the earth? How many reams? If you let the top of the ream of paper represent the earth's surface at sea level, how many sheets of paper do you need to add to show how high the highest mountain is? How many sheets would you remove to show the deepest part of the ocean?

Hands-On Earth Science Activities

Using reams of paper or your own creative ideas, make a model of the earth that shows the highest and lowest parts of the earth's surface.

Teacher Information

Locating some of the highs and lows on the earth will help students visualize it better. Some might be surprised to find that, although the elevation differences between mountain peaks and ocean floors seem great, they actually represent very slight distortions of the earth's skin.

Integrating

Math, language arts, social studies, art

Science Process Skills

Observing, inferring, measuring, communicating, using space-time relationships

How Can a Flat Map Represent the Globe-Shaped Earth?

(Teacher-supervised activity)

Materials Needed

- World relief globe
- World relief map
- Fresh oranges
- Dull knives
- Pencils
- Paper

Procedure

1. Carefully remove the peel from your orange, keeping it all in one piece or in as large a piece as possible.

2. Try to lay the orange peel out flat on the paper. What happened?

3. Cut off a piece of orange peel about 2 to 3 cm (1 in.) square and lay it out flat on your paper. Did that work any better?

4. On the globe, compare the size of the United States with the size of Greenland.

5. Now compare the same two countries on the flat map. What do you find?

6. Think about what you did with the orange peel in step 2. What problems do there seem to be with representing a ball-shaped object on a flat surface?

7. If you were a mapmaker, what could you do to show the earth on a flat map?

For Problem Solvers

Put yourself in the place of the mapmaker. Brainstorm with others who are interested in this activity and try several different ways to represent the earth accurately on a flat surface. Share your ideas with your teacher and with the rest of the class.

Teacher Information

In doing this activity, students should begin to understand the problems involved with representing the spherically shaped Earth on a flat map. After students have considered the problem of representing a ball-shaped object on a flat map, discuss the ideas that were suggested. This would be an excellent time to discuss different types of projections used in map making. Bring samples to class if possible. Consider having students try to make one or more of these with their orange peeling (or a new one), by cutting along the "meridians," then flattening it out on paper. Discuss the advantages and disadvantages of the different types of projections.

Integrating

Math, language arts, social studies, art

Science Process Skills

Observing, inferring, measuring, communicating, using space-time relationships

How Does the Nature of the Earth's Surface Affect Atmospheric Temperature?

Materials Needed

- Relief maps
- Temperature maps
- Paper
- Pencils

Procedure

1. Study your temperature maps and identify at least ten areas that have high average temperatures.

2. Find these same areas on the relief map. Do they seem to be areas of high altitude, low altitude, medium altitude, or a mixture of all three?

3. Are these areas commonly near mountain ranges, near oceans, or far away from both? Or does it seem to be a mixture?

4. Are these areas near the equator or nearer to the North Pole or South Pole?

5. Next, identify at least ten areas that have low average temperatures. Do steps 2, 3, and 4 with them.

6. What can you say about the effect altitude seems to have on temperature?

7. What effect do mountain ranges and oceans seem to have on temperature?

8. What effect does latitude (distance from the equator) have on temperature?

For Problem Solvers

Do some research and find out how atmospheric temperature is affected by land masses and by oceans and other large bodies of water. What other surface features affect air temperature?

Hands-On Earth Science Activities

Teacher Information

Temperatures are affected by altitude. In general, the higher the altitude, the cooler the climate will be. Even near the equator, areas of higher altitude have cooler temperatures than do those near sea level. Oceans tend to have a moderating effect on nearby land masses, as water heats up and cools down more slowly than does land. Air masses coming from the oceans can have a great cooling or warming effect on temperature over land areas, depending on whether they are coming from the cold Arctic waters or from warmer ocean currents.

Latitude affects temperature more than any other single factor. Regions near the equator are said to have low latitude. High latitudes are near the poles. The higher the latitude of a region, the colder the climate will be. Low latitudes get the direct rays of the sun. Higher latitudes get slanted, less concentrated rays.

Integrating

Math, language arts, social studies

Science Process Skills

Inferring, communicating, comparing and contrasting, using space-time relationships, formulating hypotheses, identifying and controlling variables, experimenting, researching

How Do Mountains Affect Yearly Rainfall?

Materials Needed

- Relief maps
- Rainfall maps
- Paper
- Pencils

Procedure

1. Study your rainfall maps and identify at least ten areas that have high average rainfall.

2. Find these same areas on the relief map. Do they seem to be areas of high altitude, low altitude, medium altitude, or a mixture of all three?

3. Are these areas usually near mountain ranges, near oceans, or far away from both? Or does it seem to be a mixture?

4. Are these areas near the equator or nearer to the North Pole or South Pole?

5. Next, identify at least ten areas that have low average rainfall. Do steps 2, 3, and 4 with them.

6. What can you say about the effect altitude has on rainfall?

7. What effect do mountain ranges and oceans seem to have on rainfall?

8. What effect does latitude (distance from the equator) have on rainfall?

For Problem Solvers

Do this project as a Science Investigation. Obtain a blank copy of the "Science Investigation Journaling Notes." Write your name, the date, and your question at the top. Plan your investigation through step 5 (Procedure) and have it approved by your teacher. Complete the Journaling Notes as you perform your investigation. Share your project with your group, and submit your Journaling Notes to your teacher if requested.

Hands-On Earth Science Activities

Do some research and find out how annual precipitation is affected by altitude. Does latitude affect annual precipitation? What about longitude? What else do you think causes one region of the earth to have more or less precipitation than another? How does precipitation amount seem to coincide with population centers? Continue your research and see what you can learn. Share your information with others. If there are hills and valleys nearby, try to gather this information on your own area.

Teacher Information

Latitude determines which wind belt a region is located in and, to a large degree, whether the region will have warm, moist air creating rainy weather, or cool, dry air bringing dry weather. Rainfall is also affected by mountains, usually favoring the windward side of the mountain. As the air moves up the mountainside, it is cooled and condensed, and rainfall results. The leeward side of the mountain gets the air mass after much of the moisture has been condensed from the air. As winds blow inland from the ocean, the regions nearest the ocean get the most rainfall.

Integrating

Math, reading, language arts, social studies, art

Science Process Skills

Observing, inferring, communicating, comparing and contrasting, using space-time relationships, formulating hypotheses, researching

What Can You Learn from a Square Meter of Soil?

(Take home and do with family and friends.)

Materials Needed

- Meter sticks or measuring tape
- Small shovels
- Magnifying glasses
- Balls of string
- Tongue depressors
- Paper and pencils
- Encyclopedias and other resources

Procedure

1. Measure off one square meter (or one square yard) of soil.
2. Mark your plot of ground by outlining it with string, anchoring your string at the corners with tongue depressors.
3. Select a place to begin, perhaps at one corner.
4. Write down all the things you can find within your square meter (yard), including each type of grass, weed, insect, rock, and so forth. Describe or draw the different types of plant and animal life.
5. Dig into the soil. Add to your list anything else you find, such as worms, insects, roots, or rocks.
6. Pick up a handful of soil. Feel it and describe it on your paper. Is it hard, soft, spongy, moist, or dry? Does it pack into a ball when you squeeze it, or does it remain loose? Is it sandy?
7. Now examine your plants, insects, rocks, and soil with the magnifying glass and see how much additional information you can write down—things you did not notice without the magnifying glass.
8. Try to find out the names of some of the plants, animals, and rocks on your list. Use encyclopedias, field manuals, or resource people you think might know.

Teacher Information

We so often look without seeing. Students will be amazed at how much they learn from a tiny plot of ground, perhaps an area they have walked across, or near to, many times. Encourage students, especially those who show high interest in this activity, to select another plot and repeat the steps above. Suggest that the second plot be some distance from the first— at home, for instance. Compare information from the two. If interest continues, this activity could be repeated several times, with new information and new insights gained each time.

This could also provide an excellent opportunity to develop a study of how soil is formed from rocks and other materials.

Integrating

Reading, language arts, social studies

Science Process Skills

Observing, inferring, classifying, measuring, communicating, using space-time relationships, identifying and controlling variables, researching

ACTIVITY 4.11

How Is Soil Made?

(Take home and do with family and friends.)

Materials Needed

- Rocks
- Sand
- Magnifying glasses
- Leaves
- Soil
- Dishpan or bucket

Procedure

1. Examine the rocks and sand with the magnifying glass.

2. How are the rocks and sand alike? How are they different?

3. Each grain of sand was once a part of a rock and was broken off by natural forces. As the sand is ground finer and finer and mixed with organic material, such as decaying plant material, soil is formed. This process happens over a very long period of time.

4. Put a thick layer of sand in the pan or bucket.

5. Break up some leaves or other plant material into tiny pieces. You could even grind this material up between two rocks.

6. Mix the fine plant material into the sand. Use about the same amount of this material as the amount of sand you are using.

7. Compare your mixture with the soil. What similarities do you observe? What differences?

8. If you can, set your mixture and soil aside for several weeks. Then compare them again.

For Problem Solvers

Do some research and find out what soil ingredients are essential for most plants. Get some seeds for a fast-growing plant.

Prepare three or four different soil mixes—with different amounts of humus, different amounts of sand, and so on. Make a record of the quantities of each ingredient in each of your soil samples. Predict which of these types of soil your plant will grow best in. In this case, your prediction is your hypothesis, or your best guess as to which will do best. Test your prediction by experimenting by growing some seeds in each type of soil. Be sure that each sample has the same amount of water and sunlight, so you can be quite sure that any difference in growth is due to the difference in the soil.

After the plants begin to grow, measure and record the growth of the plants at least twice each week. Make a graph of their growth and use your graph to explain to others what you learned about soil and plant growth.

Teacher Information

Soil begins to form when rocks and similar materials on or near the earth's surface are broken down by environmental forces. The substance that results from this action is called "parent material." Parent material is broken down into mineral particles through a process called "weathering." There are two kinds of weathering: physical disintegration (caused by such forces as ice and rain) and chemical decomposition (such as when water dissolves certain minerals in a rock). Through the centuries, organic material mixes with the parent material, and the resultant matter resembles the parent material less and less.

Various environmental factors affect soil formation, including climate, land surface features, plants and animals present, kinds of parent material, and time. The mineral content of parent material helps determine the kinds of plants that grow in the soil.

Just as soil is constantly being formed, it is also constantly being destroyed by erosive forces such as wind and water.

Although this activity will not produce real soil, it will result in a soil-like material and will provide a glimpse of nature's soil-making process. If circumstances will allow, let the mixture stand for a period of several weeks or months. Leaves break down quite rapidly, and the substance will appear more like soil than when first mixed.

Consider having students crush their own rocks by using other rocks or hammers. If this is done, however, be sure adequate protection from flying chips is provided, especially for the eyes. Also be cautious of possible injury to fingers in the pounding process. Sand can similarly be ground into powder, resulting in a more soil-like mixture.

Other organic matter can be substituted for the leaves, or added to them.

Integrating

Math, reading, language arts

Science Process Skills

Observing, inferring, classifying, measuring, predicting, communicating, using space-time relationships, formulating hypotheses, identifying and controlling variables, experimenting, researching

The Earth

What Factors Affect Water Erosion?

Materials Needed

- Two identical erosion trays
- Sprinkler
- Two basins, such as plastic dishpans
- Water
- Several books
- Soil
- Leaves, sticks, and small rocks
- Paper towels

Procedure

1. Put an equal amount of soil on the two erosion trays.
2. Spread several leaves, sticks, and small rocks over the top of the soil in one tray.
3. Tilt both trays at the same angle and place the basins below the trays as illustrated in Figure 4.12–1. Sprinkle one quart of water over each one. First predict which tray will lose more soil.

Figure 4.12–1. Erosion Trays

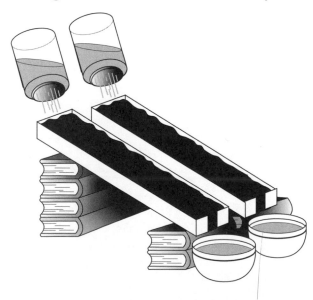

4. Use paper towels to filter out all the soil that was washed away in the quart of water. Was your prediction in step 3 correct?

5. Again place equal amounts of soil on the two trays. This time, leave the soil bare on each tray.

6. Lower one tray slightly and raise the other slightly. Which do you think will lose more soil during a "rainstorm"?

7. Sprinkle one quart of water over each of the two trays and filter out the soil that is washed away. Was your prediction correct?

8. Compare the amount of soil washed away in the four trays.

9. What can you say about soil erosion in the mountains and factors that affect it?

For Problem Solvers

Where in your area is water erosion a problem? In your own yard? In your schoolyard? On a nearby hillside? Think of a way to estimate the amount of soil that is lost each year. Do some research and find out some of the things people do to control erosion. Which of these methods do you think might work best in the area you identified? What could you and/or your class do to help? Organize a plan to make it happen, and carry out your plan. Check on the area each time there is a heavy rainstorm and see how well your project worked. Try to think of something you could have done to make it even better.

Teacher Information

In this activity students will learn that erosion occurs faster on steeper slopes and that erosion is retarded by plant growth and debris.

The "erosion trays" could be as simple as two or three layers of cardboard. They could also be made from a sheet of aluminum or sheet metal. Old plastic dishpans could be used by cutting the sides down partway and cutting one end out. Cookie sheets can also be used.

For the sprinkler, a watering can designed for flowers will work well, or simply use a quart jar and punch several holes in the lid.

Let students devise additional erosion activities using the same equipment. For instance, they could get a small slab of sod from the edge of the lawn and test it for erosion. Try some of the loose soil with leaves, sticks, and rocks mixed in as well as lying on top of the soil. Compare sandy soil with clay soil.

The Earth

Integrating

Math, reading, language arts, social studies, art, physical education

Science Process Skills

Observing, inferring, measuring, predicting, communicating, comparing and contrasting, using space-time relationships, formulating hypotheses, identifying and controlling variables, experimenting, researching

In What Order Do Materials Settle in Water?

Materials Needed

- One-quart or larger glass jar with lid
- Gravel (rocks of varied sizes)
- Water
- Soil
- Sand

Procedure

1. Add equal amounts of the soil, gravel, and sand until the jar is about one-third full.

2. Add enough water so that the jar is almost full.

3. Place the lid on the jar and shake it carefully to thoroughly stir the mixture.

4. Which of the materials inside the jar do you think will settle to the bottom? Which will be on top?

5. Stop shaking the jar and let it stand until all materials are settled and the water is somewhat clear.

6. Examine the materials in the jar and record the order in which they settle to the bottom.

7. How accurate were your predictions?

8. Shake the mixture again and find out whether the materials settle in the same order as the first time.

9. Try to explain why the materials settled out of the water in the order that they did. Do you think materials would settle in the same order at the bottom of the sea? What factors do you think would control the rate at which sediment settles to the ocean floor?

Teacher Information

If pieces of seashells or snail shells are available, add them to the materials in the bottle at step 1. Students will find that sediment will be rather consistent in order, with the largest rocks settling to the bottom and the fine sand and silt at the top. Some of the factors students should consider in step 9 are size of the particle, density of the particle, shape of the particle, and water currents.

Integrating

Math, language arts

Science Process Skills

Observing, inferring, classifying, predicting, communicating, comparing and contrasting, formulating hypotheses, identifying and controlling variables

How Are Rocks Classified?

Materials Needed

- A collection of rocks
- Encyclopedia
- Other reference books as available

Procedure

1. What colors are the rocks in this collection?
2. Classify (sort) the rocks by putting them into groups according to their color.
3. Do the rocks have different textures? Are some rough, some smooth, some shiny, and some dull? If so, classify them again according to their texture.
4. As you lift the rocks, do they all seem to have about the same density? In other words, do they seem to be about the same weight relative to their size? If not, classify them again according to density.
5. Look at the rocks carefully and see whether you can think of any other characteristics you could use to classify them. If you think of any, sort the rocks again by those characteristics.
6. Look up "rocks" in the encyclopedia or other reference books and find out what characteristics geologists use to classify rocks. See whether you can tell what some of the rocks in this group are called.

For Problem Solvers

Find out which rocks are often used as building material. Which ones are popular as jewelry? In what other ways are rocks useful to people? Share your ideas with others.

Teacher Information

If some students have rock collections, this would be an excellent time to bring them to share with the class. These students are likely to have some degree of experience and expertise in collecting and identifying rocks that they can share with the group. In addition, a parent or brother or sister might be a "rock hound" and available as a resource person. Consider also the possibility of inviting a local geologist, forester, or manager of a rock shop.

As students learn to classify a few rocks, either by standard techniques or from ideas devised by the class, a field trip to a nearby canyon could provide a meaningful and lasting learning experience.

Don't overlook the value of the creative classification experience in the above activity. Resource people and reference books should come on the scene after students have had the opportunity to examine several rocks, describe them, identify similarities and differences, and reason out in their minds some logical classifying characteristics.

The following activities will get students involved in testing for some of the characteristics used by experts in classifying rocks.

Integrating

Language arts, social studies, art

Science Process Skills

Observing, inferring, classifying, communicating, comparing and contrasting

Hands-On Earth Science Activities

How Do Rocks Compare in Hardness?

(Teacher-supervised activity)

Materials Needed

- Variety of rocks
- Dull knife, piece of glass, and other "scratchers"
- Copies of the "Science Investigation Journaling Notes" for this activity

Procedure

1. As you complete this activity, you will keep a record of what you do, just as scientists do. Use a copy of the form "Science Investigation Journaling Notes" for this activity, and write the information that is called for, including your name and the date.

2. For this activity, you will find out how to determine which rock is harder than another. For item 1, the question is provided for you.

3. Item 2 of the Journaling Notes asks for what you already know about the question. If you have some ideas about how to tell which rock is harder, write your ideas.

4. For item 3, you need to think about what you wrote for item 2 of the Journaling Notes and decide which rocks you think are the harder ones. Write what you know about the question, and that will be your hypothesis.

5. Now continue with the following instructions. Complete your Journaling Notes as you go. Steps 6 through 16 below will help you with the information you need to write on the form for items 4, 5, and 6.

6. Select two rocks from the collection.

7. Try to scratch one with the other.

8. Which would you say is harder, the one that will scratch or the one that can be scratched?

9. Keep the harder of the two rocks and set the other aside.

10. Select another rock and use the same scratch test to compare it with the first one you kept.

11. Again keep the harder of the two rocks and set the other one aside.

12. Repeat the procedure until you have identified the hardest rock in the collection.

13. Now compare the other rocks and find the second-hardest one. Put it next to the hardest.

14. Continue this process until you have all the rocks lined up in order of hardness.

15. Use the scratch test to compare other objects with rocks. Some things you might try are your fingernail, a penny, a knife blade, and a piece of glass. *Caution:* Ask for your teacher's permission before using a knife blade, piece of glass, or any other sharp object.

16. Try to find other rocks that are harder or softer than any you have in this collection.

17. What have you learned about determining which rock is harder than another? (This is item 6 on the form.)

18. For item 7 of the form, think about your hypothesis (item 3) and write what you learned as you compared rocks for hardness. Was your hypothesis correct? Did it turn out the way you expected?

For Problem Solvers

Learn about the Mohs hardness scale. What does it do? Why is it used? Make a hardness scale of your own that will provide the same kind of information. What materials will you use? How does each one compare with the items used by the Mohs scale?

Compare your list of materials with the lists of some of your classmates. If you used some of the same items for your hardness scale, do you agree as to the hardness of these items on the Mohs scale?

Teacher Information

The label "rock" is often used rather loosely to mean either rock or mineral. Actually, rocks are made of minerals. Minerals have physical properties and chemical composition that either are fixed or vary within a limited range. A rock is often an aggregate of minerals.

Minerals are scaled in hardness in a range of 1 to 10, with 1 being very soft and 10 very hard. A common method of determining hardness is the "scratch test." Fingernails have a hardness of about 2.5, so if a rock will scratch the fingernail, the rock has a hardness greater than 2.5. If it will not scratch the fingernail, or if it can be scratched by the fingernail, the rock has a hardness less than 2.5. A penny has a hardness of 3,

Hands-On Earth Science Activities

so if a rock scratches the penny, it has a hardness greater than 3. Other common materials that can be used in the scratch test are steel knife blades (hardness about 5.5), glass (hardness about 5.5 to 6.0), and other rocks.

The Mohs hardness scale is helpful in comparing hardness of rocks. It uses the following minerals, representing degree of hardness of 1 to 10:

1. talc
2. gypsum
3. calcite
4. fluorite
5. apatite

6. orthoclase feldspar
7. quartz
8. topaz
9. corundum
10. diamond

Caution: In step 15 above, you will need to judge whether students are to use knife blades and glass in their comparisons. Other objects can be tested to see where they lie in the range of hardness.

Integrating

Reading, language arts

Science Process Skills

Observing, inferring, classifying, predicting, communicating, comparing and contrasting, researching

Science Investigation

Journaling Notes for Activity 4.15

1. Question: *Which rocks are harder than others?*

2. What we already know: _____

_____

3. Hypothesis: _____

_____

4. Materials needed: _____

_____

5. Procedure: _____

_____

_____

_____

_____

6. Observations/New information: _____

_____

_____

7. Conclusion: _____

_____

_____

_____

What Color Streak Does a Rock Make?

Materials Needed

- Collection of rocks
- Porcelain (nonglazed)
- Sheets of paper in various colors
- Colored pencils

Procedure

1. Select one of the rocks from the collection.
2. Try to make a streak on the porcelain with the rock.
3. Does it make a streak? If so, what color streak does it make?
4. Try to make a streak with each of the other rocks in the collection.
5. Does the color of the streak usually match the color of the rock that made it?
6. Put the rocks in groups according to the color of the streak.
7. Will any of your rocks write on paper? Try it. If you have one that will, draw a picture with it. Try different colors of paper as well as different types of rocks.

Teacher Information

One of the common tests made in classifying rocks is the streak test. A porcelain plate, called a streak plate, is used. The rock is rubbed on the streak plate to see what color dust it makes. A piece of white porcelain tile will suffice as the streak plate. Use the back of the tile, not the glazed side.

Caution: If you use a broken piece of porcelain as the streak plate, close supervision is needed to assure safety.

The color of the streak is frequently different from the color of the rock that made it.

If the rock collection includes talc, anthracite (coal), or gypsum, students should be able to write on paper with them.

Integrating

Language arts

Science Process Skills

Observing, inferring, classifying, predicting, communicating, comparing and contrasting

The Earth

How Do Rocks React to Vinegar?

Materials Needed

- Collection of rocks
- One plastic cup for each rock
- Vinegar
- Chalk

Procedure

1. Put a small sample of each rock in a separate cup. Put a small piece of chalk in a cup as one of the rock samples.
2. Pour a small amount of vinegar on each sample.
3. What happened?
4. Group the rocks according to the way they responded to the vinegar.

Teacher Information

This test is called the acid test and it is normally performed with dilute hydrochloric acid (HCl). Vinegar is a weak acid and a household product, and it works satisfactorily.

The acid test is used to identify rocks that contain calcium carbonate. Any such rock will fizz when vinegar (or dilute HCl) is applied. Limestone, marble, calcite, and chalk are made of calcium carbonate and will fizz in the presence of vinegar. *Before applying the vinegar, scratch the surface of each rock to expose fresh material.*

Integrating

Language arts

Science Process Skills

Observing, inferring, classifying, predicting, communicating, comparing and contrasting

Which Rocks Are Attracted by a Magnet?

Materials Needed

- Collection of rocks
- Magnets

Procedure

1. Select one of the rocks and touch it with a magnet.
2. Is this rock attracted by the magnet?
3. Test each rock in the collection to see whether any seem to be attracted by the magnet.
4. Make two groups of rocks—those that are attracted by the magnet and those that are not.

Teacher Information

Try to include at least one rock that contains iron, such as galena, in the collection of rocks used for this activity. If no rocks that are attracted by a magnet are available, this activity should be omitted.

If you have, or can acquire, a piece of lodestone, it would make an excellent addition to the collection for this exercise. Lodestone is nature's magnet. After the activity is completed as written, have students suspend the lodestone from a string and see how it responds to the magnet. It will be attracted or repelled, depending on the position of its poles, the same as any magnet behaves in the presence of another magnet.

Integrating

Language arts

Science Process Skills

Observing, inferring, classifying, predicting, communicating, comparing and contrasting

Which Rocks Conduct Electricity?

(Teacher-supervised activity)

Materials Needed

- Collection of rocks
- Dry cell battery
- Small light socket with flashlight bulb
- Two pieces of insulated wire about 20 cm (8 in.) long
- One piece of insulated wire about 5 cm (2 in.) long
- Small bolt or nail

Procedure

1. Connect the bulb to the battery with the pieces of wire, as illustrated in Figure 4.19–1, to be sure the battery and bulb are working properly. Be sure you can light the bulb before going on to the next step.

2. Use the third wire and connect the system again, this time with the bolt held between two wires, as shown in Figure 4.19–2. Be sure you can light the bulb this way before you continue. The bolt is a good conductor of electricity.

Figure 4.19-1. Flashlight Cell, Bulb, and Wires

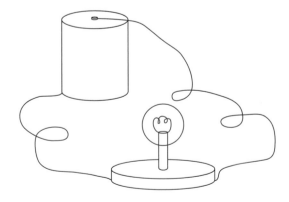

Figure 4.19-2. Bolt Added to the Circuit

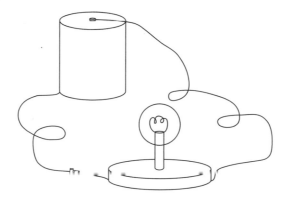

3. Remove the bolt and put one of the rocks in its place. Does the bulb light? If so, the rock is a conductor of electricity.

4. Sort the rocks into two groups, those that are conductors of electricity and those that are nonconductors. (If the bulb lights, the rock is a conductor.)

5. What similarities and differences do you see as you compare the conductors with the nonconductors? Discuss your ideas with your teacher and with your group.

Teacher Information

Some rocks conduct electricity (such as those containing significant amounts of copper, zinc, or iron). This is one of the characteristics scientists use in classifying and identifying rocks.

Integrating

Language arts

Science Process Skills

Observing, inferring, classifying, predicting, communicating, comparing and contrasting

How Can Rocks Be Dissolved in Water?

Materials Needed

- Small pieces of limestone
- Corrugated cardboard
- Plastic wrap or large plastic bags
- Pieces of clear glass
- Rainwater
- Vinegar
- Goggles

Procedure

1. Make a long trough of the corrugated cardboard and line it with plastic.
2. Prop one end of the trough so that it tilts slightly, as in Figure 4.20–1.
3. If the limestone is not in small pieces, break it up with a hammer or with another rock. If you do this, be sure to wear goggles.
4. Wash the pieces of limestone with clean rainwater and spread them along the trough.

Figure 4.20–1. Trough Lined with Plastic, Pieces of Limestone, and Glass

  **Hands-On Earth Science Activities**

5. Add clean rainwater very slowly, drop by drop, at the top of the trough.

6. Clean the clear glass well and place it under the lower end of the trough to catch several drops of water that have soaked through the limestone.

7. Let the water evaporate from the glass.

8. Examine the dry glass. What do you see? Is it still perfectly clean? If not, what is on it?

9. What if this same process occurs with mountains of limestone and millions of gallons of rainwater? What happens? What has this to do with the formation of limestone caverns?

10. Repeat the activity, using vinegar in the place of rainwater at step 5. If you notice any difference in the amount of material deposited on the glass, try to explain why.

For Problem Solvers

Have you ever visited a limestone cave? Find out about the one that is nearest to your area. Visit the cave if you can, but at least study about it. Ask a geologist or a rock hound how the formations are formed within the cave. Consider what you did for the above activity, and what you learned about limestone. Why is that important in understanding limestone caves?

Teacher Information

Caution: If students break rocks, be sure they wear protective eyewear to avoid small chips hitting their eyes.

Water containing weak acids will actually dissolve limestone, as is witnessed by the formation of many caves and caverns, both large and small. Once caverns have been formed, water keeps dripping into them and the rock material comes out of solution, forming stalagmites and stalactites.

The dissolving process is speeded up as the acid content increases. This is demonstrated by the use of vinegar. The acid involved is mostly carbonic acid, formed when water dissolves carbon dioxide. Other acids are contained in some air pollutants and washed out of the air by rain. This is called *acid rain,* and it can be harmful to plant and animal life and water supplies.

Similar action brings salt and other minerals from the mountains into lakes and oceans. Thus, ocean water is salty. The only plant and animal life found there are those that have a high tolerance for salt. The Great Salt Lake in Utah is salt-saturated for the same reason, and the only animal that can tolerate the high salt content is the tiny brine shrimp. Unlike

most regions, the Salt Lake Valley is in an internal drainage system. In most areas, runoff water is transported from stream to stream and from river to river, eventually making its way to the ocean. Runoff water that flows into the Salt Lake Valley stays in the Salt Lake Valley. As evaporation occurs, the minerals leached out of the mountains through runoff stays within the valley. Salt companies harvest enormous quantities of salt from the area each year. You have likely been using it to season your food. And incidentally, you might have been feeding your fish with brine-shrimp eggs, which are also harvested in large quantities from the Great Salt Lake.

Integrating

Language arts, social studies

Science Process Skills

Observing, inferring, communicating, comparing and contrasting, using space-time relationships, formulating hypotheses, identifying and controlling variables, researching

How Do Crystals Form?

(Teacher-supervised activity)

Materials Needed

- Heat source
- Metal saucepans
- Three ounces of powdered alum per person
- String
- Fruit jars
- Filter paper or cotton cloth
- Water
- Hand lenses
- Pencils
- Small rocks or other weights

Procedure

1. Measure one cup of water and pour it into the saucepan.
2. Heat to boiling point. *Use caution!*
3. Sprinkle the alum into the water and stir.
4. Pour the hot water into the fruit jar, straining it with the filter or cloth.
5. Tie a piece of string to a pencil. Tie a small rock (or other small weight) to the other end of the string. Lay the pencil across the top of the jar and let the string hang down into the water.
6. Let the solution stand for one full day, occasionally examining it to see what happens.
7. What formed in the jar? Look at it carefully.
8. Continue your observations for at least three or four days, discussing any changes that occur. Take notes, describing your observations.
9. Carefully remove the string from the jar and examine it with a magnifying glass. What do you see? Describe the shapes.

Figure 4.21-1. String Hanging into Water from Pencil

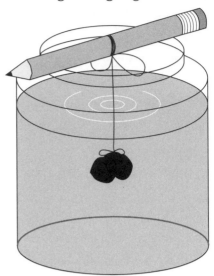

For Problem Solvers

Now repeat the activity, using table salt this time instead of alum. Do it as a Science Investigation. Obtain a blank copy of the "Science Investigation Journaling Notes." Write your name, the date, and your question at the top. Plan your investigation through step 5 (Procedure) and have it approved by your teacher. Complete the Journaling Notes as you perform your investigation. Share your project with your group, and submit your Journaling Notes to your teacher if requested.

Examine the crystals very carefully with a hand lens and compare them with the alum crystals. How are they the same? How are they different? Try the activity again, using sugar. Compare the results. Share your observations with others and see whether they agree with your comparisons.

Teacher Information

As the solution cools, alum crystals will form in the jar and on the string. Careful examination with a magnifying glass should reveal the crystals to be diamond-shaped.

Your problem solvers will repeat this activity, using table salt instead of alum. Salt crystals will form from a saturated salt solution, and the crystals will be cube-shaped. Students should discover this difference as they examine and compare. Then try the same activity with sugar. Students should begin to realize that each substance produces its own unique crystalline shape.

Hands-On Earth Science Activities

Be patient. Crystals form as the water evaporates to the point that the solution is super-saturated. If your solution is not saturated in the first place, more evaporation time will be required before crystals will form. Depending on the solution you started with and the weather (rate of evaporation), it might require several days for crystals to appear.

Integrating
Language arts, art

Science Process Skills
Observing, classifying, communicating, comparing and contrasting

What Type of Crystals Do Rocks Have?

(Take home and do with family and friends.)

Materials Needed
- Collection of rocks
- Hand lens

Procedure
1. Examine each rock with the hand lens.
2. Can you see any crystal structure?
3. Are the crystals lined up or are they arranged randomly?
4. Do the crystals seem to be somewhat interlocking (melted together), or do they appear to be glued together by a cementing material?
5. Put the rocks in groups according to your findings.

For Problem Solvers

Do some research in encyclopedias, field manuals, the Internet, and whatever sources you have. Find out about common types of rock crystals. How many of these do you have in your collection? Try to find more. Share your information with others who are interested in rock crystals.

Teacher Information

Igneous and metamorphic rocks have undergone intense heat in their formation, and the crystals are interlocking, or melted together by nature. Beautiful arrangements of quartz crystals are found in the centers of hollow rocks called geodes. Try to include at least one geode in the collection used.

Integrating
Language arts

Science Process Skills
Observing, classifying, communicating, comparing and contrasting, researching

Hands-On Earth Science Activities

What Is Conglomerate Rock?

Materials Needed

- Dry cement powder
- Dry sand
- Variety of rocks
- Plastic-lined shoeboxes
- Water
- Sticks
- Magnifying glasses

Procedure

1. Put one cup of powdered cement, one cup of dry sand, and one cup of cold water into the plastic-lined shoebox and stir with a stick. Be sure to mix it thoroughly.
2. Stir your rocks into the mixture.
3. Let the mixture stand for two or three days.
4. What happened to the mixture?
5. Take your mixture out of the shoebox and remove the plastic.
6. Use the magnifying glass to examine your mixture. Can you see some of the rocks you put in it? Can you see the sand? Discuss your observations.

Teacher Information

A conglomerate rock is made of various smaller rocks that have become cemented together by nature, quite like the block of concrete students make in this activity. For obvious reasons, the rocks used for this activity should not be from a rock collection that someone wants to keep.

A small conglomerate rock formed by nature would be an excellent visual aid to accompany this activity. A field trip to an area where students can find conglomerate rocks in nature makes an excellent learning activity. Students could also examine sidewalks, concrete walls, and bricks to compare and find evidence of the "conglomerate."

Integrating

Language arts

Science Process Skills

Observing, inferring, classifying, measuring, communicating, comparing and contrasting, identifying and controlling variables

How Can You Start a Rock Collection?

(Take home and do with family and friends.)

Materials Needed

- Hammer and chisel
- Canvas bag (or other strong bag)
- Goggles
- Egg cartons (at least three)
- Newspapers
- Marker

Procedure

1. Take your hammer, chisel, and bag and gather a few rocks to begin your rock collection. Around the schoolyard, at home, or on the way to school are good places to look. Try to find rocks of different colors and textures and with other differences that you can see or feel.

2. It will probably be necessary to break up some of the rocks in order to get the right size specimen, or just to allow a better view of what the rock really looks like. *Put the goggles on before you strike the rock with the hammer*, or put the rock in newspapers, a bag, or other covering to trap the flying pieces and avoid injury.

3. Sort your rocks into three main categories, as follows:

   a. *Sedimentary:* Have a layered appearance. Usually feel gritty and break easily.

   b. *Igneous:* Often crystalline appearance, never in layers.

   c. *Metamorphic:* Very hard, appear more crystalline than igneous rocks. Crystals of each mineral are lined up in bands or layers.

4. Label one egg carton "Sedimentary," one "Igneous," and one "Metamorphic," and put your rocks into the compartments of the appropriate egg carton.

5. Compare your rocks with each other and with the rocks in the collections of others, and discuss your observations.

Hands-On Earth Science Activities

Teacher Information

To add to an established rock collection, one might need to visit distant or hard-to-get-to locations, but the collection can be started anywhere. A stone quarry or area that has been excavated is an excellent location, but some very interesting rocks can often be collected around the yard at home, at school, or at the side of a road. Hillsides provide excellent prospects, as do stream beds. If rocks for student collection are not available in your area, try to find another source. For instance, students could write letters to friends and relatives in other parts of the country and ask for some small samples of rock common to their areas.

Students should be encouraged to collect rock specimens that are neither too large nor too small. The egg carton suggested for classification and storage helps in keeping size under control.

As students begin their rock collections, explain that it is very important to keep a record of information, such as collection location, date, collector, and rock type. An easy way to do this is to put a number on each rock, then write the information with that number in a notebook. You might consider adding white paint and a small brush to the supplies; a spot of white paint, allowed to dry thoroughly, facilitates writing on the rock with a pen.

Integrating

Math, language arts

Science Process Skills

Observing, inferring, classifying, measuring, communicating, comparing and contrasting, identifying and controlling variables

What Other Classifications of Rocks Are There?

Materials Needed

- Rock collections in egg cartons
- Vinegar
- Masking tape
- Markers
- Piece of white porcelain tile
- Rock identification charts and books
- Paper
- Pencils

Procedure

1. Use masking tape and a marker to put a number on each rock in the igneous collection.

2. List the numbers of the igneous rocks down the left side of your paper. Leave space at the right for recording information about the rocks.

3. Do the "scratch test" on each of the numbered rocks and record the rating on the paper.

4. Do the "streak test" on each of the numbered rocks and record the result on the paper.

5. Do the "acid test" on each of the numbered rocks and record the reaction on the paper.

6. Use rock and mineral identification charts in various references and decide what you think each rock is. Record your findings on your paper.

7. Now follow these same steps with your sedimentary collection and your metamorphic collection.

For Problem Solvers

Find ways to expand your rock collection. Find opportunities to go to new places and look for rocks. If there are hills and canyons in your area, explore them. Be sure you don't take any rocks illegally, as from private

Hands-On Earth Science Activities

property without permission or from a state park or national park. Write letters to people you know who are in other parts of the country. You could ask someone to help you find pen pals—people you don't even know. Trade small rock samples with them by mail. As you communicate with these people, tell them about your area. They will be interested to know what the land is like, what trees grow in your area, what kinds of birds and other wildlife are common, and so forth. Ask them to tell you about the area where they live. Report this information to your teacher and your class.

As your rock collection grows, try to identify your rocks. Talk to a geologist or to a rock hound. Check encyclopedias, field manuals, the Internet, and other references. See how many different types of rocks you can find and identify.

Teacher Information

Before beginning this activity, students should have already tried each of the tests (scratch, streak, and acid) in previous activities. They should also have collected a variety of rocks and sorted them into the three major categories, using egg cartons or other appropriate containers.

Having completed these preliminary activities, students should be prepared to make a serious effort to further classify the rocks in their collections. Encyclopedias and field manuals on rocks are excellent sources for identification charts. Don't overemphasize the importance of precise identification of the rocks. It's more important for students to consider the characteristics of each rock and identify the one that seems most likely, based on their observations. The label can change if warranted by newly acquired information. That, after all, is the way of science.

As an alternate way of labeling the rocks, consider adding white paint and a small brush to the supplies; a spot of white paint, allowed to dry thoroughly, facilitates writing on the rock with a pen. The masking tape method is easy, but the spot of white paint makes for a neater and more permanent label.

Integrating

Reading, language arts, social studies

Science Process Skills

Observing, inferring, classifying, communicating, comparing and contrasting, researching

How Can You Measure the Density of a Rock?

(Enrichment activity or for older students)

Materials Needed

- Variety of small rocks
- Gram balance
- Jar or soup cans
- Small trays or pans
- Water
- Paper
- Pencils

Procedure

1. Select a rock. It must fit inside your jar.
2. Weigh your rock on the gram balance and record the weight.
3. Determine the weight of a volume of water equal to the volume of your rock by following these steps:
   a. Place the tray on the balance. Weigh the tray and record its weight. Then place the jar on the tray.
   b. Pour as much water into the jar as you can get in it without over-flowing water into the tray. If any water spills into the tray, it must be cleaned up.
   c. Carefully put your rock into the jar of water. The water that is displaced by the rock will spill into the tray. It will have exactly the same volume as the rock.
   d. Carefully remove the jar without spilling any more water.
   e. Weigh the tray containing the water and subtract the weight of the empty tray to obtain the weight of the water that was displaced by the rock.
4. Divide the weight of the rock by the weight of the water it displaced.
5. What is the result? This number represents the specific gravity of the rock.
6. Follow the same procedure with rocks of other types and compare the specific gravity of the rocks.

For Problem Solvers

Specific gravity is a measure of density. The specific gravity of water is 1.0. Is the specific gravity of your rock greater or less than the specific gravity of water?

Find other small objects—some that seem to be heavy for their size and some that seem to be light for their size. For each one, predict whether it is lighter than water or heavier than water. Test your prediction by measuring the density of each object using the technique you learned by doing the above activity. Were your predictions right?

Teacher Information

Specific gravity is a number expressing the ratio between the weight of an object and the weight of an equal volume of water at 4 degrees Celsius (39 degrees Fahrenheit). If a rock weighs twice as much as an equal volume of water, its specific gravity is 2. If it weighs three times as much as an equal volume of water, its specific gravity is 3, and so on. Most common minerals have a specific gravity of from 2.5 to 3.0. Those outside these limits feel noticeably light or noticeably heavy.

If a gram balance is not available, try a postage scale or other sensitive scale.

Integrating

Math

Science Process Skills

Observing, inferring, comparing and contrasting, classifying, measuring, predicting

How Can You Make a Permanent Shell Imprint?

Materials Needed

- Seashells
- Pie tins
- Petroleum jelly
- Plaster of Paris
- Water
- Paper towels
- Newspapers

Procedure

1. Coat the bottom and sides of a pie tin with a thin layer of petroleum jelly so the plaster will release easily.

2. Coat your shell with a thin layer of petroleum jelly.

3. Lay your shell in the bottom of the pie tin. Place it with the rounded side up, as seen in Figure 4.27–1.

Figure 4.27–1. Shell, Rounded Side Up, in Pan

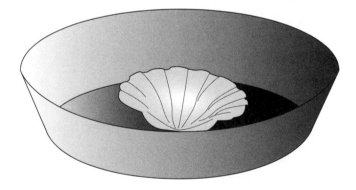

4. Mix plaster with water according to the instructions on the package. Prepare sufficient plaster to make a layer in the pan about 15 mm (at least $\frac{1}{2}$ in.) deep.

5. Pour the plaster carefully over the shell and let it harden (leave it at least one hour).

6. Turn the pie tin upside down on a table covered with newspaper and tap it lightly. The plaster cast with shell should fall out onto the table.

7. Remove the shell, but handle the plaster cast very carefully. The plaster will be quite soft until it has had at least a day to cure (harden).

8. After at least one day of curing time, carefully wipe the excess petroleum jelly off the plaster cast with a paper towel. Then wash the rest off lightly with warm water.

9. You now have an imprint of the shell in plaster, much like those often found in limestone and other sedimentary rock. (See Figure 4.27–2.) When found in rock, this imprint is called a fossil because it is evidence of an ancient animal.

Figure 4.27–2. Shell Imprint in Plaster

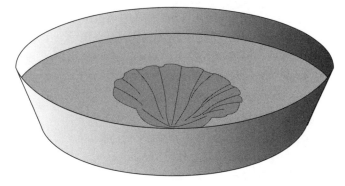

For Problem Solvers

Begin a collection of fossils, especially any that might be found in your area. Watch for opportunities to expand your collection. If you know a geologist or a rock hound, he or she will be able to help you start. Find out what kind of fossils you have and what period of time they represent. What conditions do you think the animal or plant lived in? Study about the fossils and find out whether scientists agree with you. Encyclopedias will be very helpful. Share what you learn with others who are interested in fossils.

Teacher Information

Plaster of Paris can be obtained at a local builders supply store or hobby shop. It is easy to work with and, if students follow the directions, the project should be successful. As the plaster cures, it will become quite warm, and then will cool. It should be allowed to cool completely before being removed from the mold (pie tin).

If you have an area nearby where fossils can be found, that would be an excellent field trip. Otherwise, perhaps a few fossil samples could be borrowed from a friend or purchased from a science-supply house. The experience of making a "fossil" will make a more lasting impression on the minds of students if they can see just how similar their "fossil" is to the real fossil formed by nature.

The imprint resulting from the above activity is a negative imprint. If a positive image is desired, spread a thin layer of petroleum jelly on the entire surface of the plaster, wrap and tie a piece of cardboard around it to provide sideboards to hold plaster, and pour another layer of plaster on top of the first. After it has cured, remove the cardboard, separate the two pieces of plaster with a knife blade, and you now have both a positive and a negative of the shell. Clean up the petroleum jelly after the plaster has cured thoroughly, as indicated above.

An imprint of a leaf can be made following the same steps.

Note: Depending on the shape of the shell, it sometimes works best to press the shell upside down into a layer of freshly poured plaster instead of pouring the plaster over the shell. You will have to make that judgment. Also, when using water to remove petroleum jelly, emphasize quickness over thoroughness, to avoid washing away some of the plaster.

Integrating

Reading, language arts, social studies

Science Process Skills

Observing, classifying, communicating, using space-time relationships, formulating hypotheses, researching

Hands–On Earth Science Activities

How Is Snow Compacted into Ice to Form Glaciers?

Materials Needed

- Tall, narrow jars with lids
- Rocks or other weights that can fit into the jars
- Scissors
- Cardboard
- Masking tape
- Fresh marshmallows (miniatures preferred)
- Pencils

Procedure

1. Fill the jar with fresh marshmallows, loosely packed.
2. Cut a cardboard circle to fit inside the jar without rubbing the sides.
3. Place the rocks, or other weights, on top of the cardboard circle.
4. Place a strip of masking tape on the side of the jar from top to bottom.
5. Make a pencil mark on the masking tape at the level of the cardboard.
6. Put the lid on the jar and set the jar in a safe place.
7. Twice each day for four days, check the jar and make a pencil mark on the jar at the level of the cardboard.
8. At the end of four days, discuss your observations with others. Tell how you think this is like the forming of a glacier.

For Problem Solvers

Do some research about glaciers. What makes a glacier a glacier? Where is the nearest one to where you live? What do glaciers do to alter the surface of the land?

Where do icebergs come from? Are they the same as glaciers? What is the difference between a glacier and an iceberg? Why do ship captains have to be careful when they are around icebergs? Draw a picture of an iceberg, showing how much of it is above the water and how much of it is below the surface of the water.

Teacher Information

As snow accumulates and remains for long periods of time, the weight of the snow compacts the lower layers into ice. If conditions are such that the accumulation continues season after season, a snowfield is formed. If it moves, it's a glacier. In this activity, the compacting action is demonstrated with marshmallows. The weights substitute for upper layers of heavy snow. The lid is used to keep the marshmallows from drying out so the compacting action can continue for a longer period of time.

Integrating

Reading, language arts, social studies, art

Science Process Skills

Inferring, communicating, researching

How Is the Earth Like Your Body?

(Total-group activity)

Materials Needed

- Pencils
- Lined paper
- Pictures of the earth
- Pictures of the moon

Procedure

1. Scientists often refer to our earth as a living planet. Unlike the moon, which is considered dead, the earth is constantly changing its surface, using energy from the sun to grow new life, repairing damage to itself, and adjusting its surface in response to many stresses from within. Compare the pictures of the earth and the moon. Can you see how one might be called living and the other dead?

2. Your body works in much the same way. Its surface changes, it has mountains and valleys, it is covered by a thin crust (skin), and it uses energy from the sun to grow. It also has the ability to repair itself when it is injured.

3. With your teacher and others, discuss what it means to be alive and why our earth is sometimes called a "living planet."

Teacher Information

Interesting discussions can accompany this activity. Encourage students to share their perceptions of the notion of the "living earth." In what ways do they think it is reasonable to think of the earth as a living planet, and in what ways do they think it is not reasonable? The concept of living things, once-living things, and nonliving things could enter into this discussion, tying in with material they have already studied or that they will yet study.

Integrating

Health, language arts, social studies

Science Process Skills

Observing, inferring, predicting, communicating, comparing and contrasting, using space-time relationships, formulating hypotheses

The Earth

How Is the Earth Like a Jigsaw Puzzle?

Materials Needed

- Globe of the earth
- Soccer ball
- Tennis ball cut in half

Procedure

1. Look at the three objects. They represent different models of the earth.

2. The thin outer cover of the tennis ball represents the earth's crust, the part on which we live. The model would be more accurate if we filled the rest of the ball with very hot metal, but we won't do that.

3. Examine the soccer ball. Notice it is not just a smooth, round ball, but appears to be made of many pieces. In some ways, the crust of our planet is like the soccer ball; scientists believe it is not a single, solid piece or cover, but many pieces, called *plates,* that fit together in different ways. This idea is called *plate tectonics.*

4. Now look at the globe of the earth. Pretend it is a big jigsaw puzzle. If you could move the continents around, could you find a way to make them somewhat fit together?

5. It is believed that millions of years ago the continents were joined together in some way and have gradually drifted apart. The movement of the continents is called *continental drift.*

Teacher Information

Caution: Carefully puncture the tennis ball before cutting it.

Some students may be unable to visualize the shapes of the continents in such a way that they can put them together.

Plate tectonics is the study of the formation and deformation of the earth's crust. Evidence of plate tectonics is considered to be one of the most significant scientific breakthroughs in the history of geology. Although some scientists have suggested related theories for over one hundred years, clarification of it into a unifying theory of the earth's dynamics is credited to research and writing of the 1960s. It explains the origin of mountains, the history of ocean basins, and the forces and changes within the earth's crust that bring about volcanoes and earthquakes.

Integrating

Reading, language arts, social studies, art

Science Process Skills

Observing, inferring, communicating, using space-time relationships

What Are the Earth's Plates?

Materials Needed

- Copies of Figures 4.31–1, 4.31–2, 4.31–3, and 4.31–4 for all students
- Scissors
- Drawing paper

Procedure

1. Study Figure 4.31–1. Notice the arrows suggesting slow movement of the mantle (molten rock) beneath the earth's crust.

2. Now study Figure 4.31–2. Many scientists believe that all of the land (the part of the earth's crust that is not covered by water) was together at one time. This very large continent is called *Pangea*.

3. Gradual movement of the magma broke the earth's crust into several segments, called *plates*. This process also divided Pangea into several segments. Can you see a resemblance between the segments shown for Pangea (Figure 4.31–2) and the shapes of the continents on a world map (see Figure 4.31–4)?

4. Examine Figure 4.31–3. With further movement of the magma, the segments of Pangea were repositioned and reformed.

5. Cut out the segments of Figure 4.31–3 and lay them on the world map (Figure 4.31–4). How closely do they match? What further changes seem to have happened in the positions and formation of the continents as they became the continents of today's world?

6. If similar changes continue to occur, what do you think the world will look like in the future? Draw a map of the world as you imagine it to be after another 50 million years. Since nobody knows for sure what the world will look like at that time, go for it! It's your world!

7. Compare your map with the maps created by others who are doing this activity. Discuss your maps and your thoughts with your group and with your teacher.

Teacher Information

Using Figure 4.31–1, help students understand that beneath the earth's crust is molten rock (magma). Slow-moving convection currents in the upper zone of the mantle are at work, as a continuous upwelling of energy comes to it from the earth's very hot core.

Some of the crust is exposed (*continental crust*) and some is covered by water (*oceanic crust*). The ocean floor is the surface of the oceanic crust.

Many scientists believe that hundreds of millions of years ago there was only one huge land mass on the earth. This supercontinent, as it was then, is called Pangea. Eventually the earth's crust began to break apart due to the convection currents within the magma. The resulting segments of the crust are called *plates*. The term *plate tectonics* is used in reference to the gradual shifting, reshaping, and repositioning of the plates with respect to each other.

We call the exposed areas of the plates *continents,* but it is important to remember that the plates also include areas of oceanic crust. The movement of the plates seems to be less than 10 cm (4 inches) per year. The changes in their position with respect to each other is not noticeable in the span of a lifetime, or even many lifetimes, except with careful scientific observation using precise instruments, but over a period of many millions of years it is significant.

Integrating

Math, reading, language arts, social studies, art

Science Process Skills

Observing, inferring, measuring, predicting, communicating, comparing and contrasting, using space-time relationships, formulating hypotheses, identifying variables

Figure 4.31-1. Inner Structure of the Earth

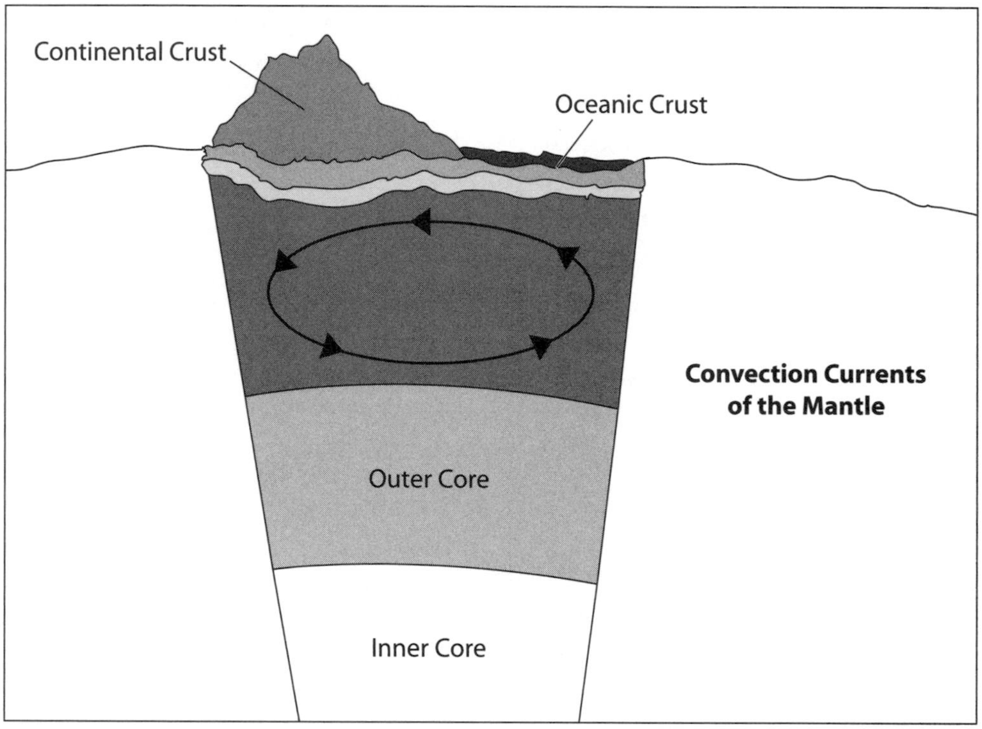

Continental Crust

Oceanic Crust

**Convection Currents
of the Mantle**

Outer Core

Inner Core

Hands-On Earth Science Activities

Figure 4.31–2. Pangea

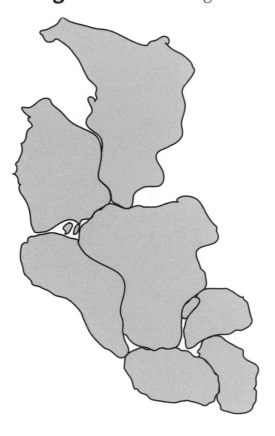

Figure 4.31-3. Plate Movement Over Millions of Years

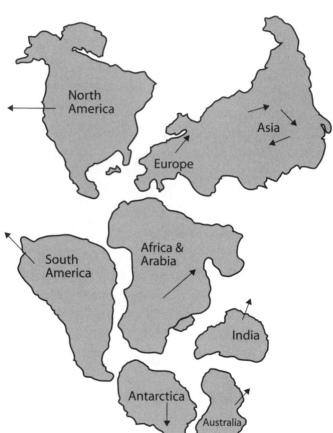

Hands-On Earth Science Activities

Figure 4.31-4. Continents Today with Likely Future Direction of Movement

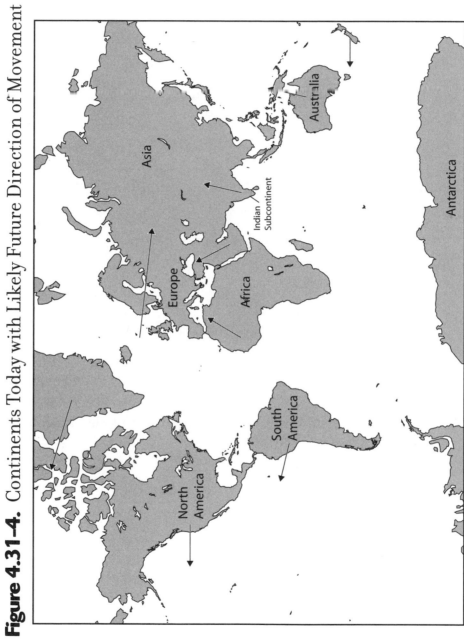

What Causes Earthquakes?

Materials Needed

- Several colors of clay (or fabric)

Procedure

1. Select one color of clay and make a flat sheet of it about 25 cm long by 10 cm wide and 5 mm thick (10 in. by 4 in. by $\frac{1}{4}$ in.).

2. Make similar sheets of other colors of clay, varying the thickness somewhat.

3. Stack several strips of clay on top of each other, as seen in Figure 4.32–1.

Figure 4.32–1. Stacked Clay Strips

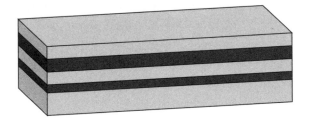

4. Put one hand on each end of the stack of clay and push toward the middle.

5. What happened?

6. If the layers of clay were layers of rock on the earth's surface, and they were forced together as you forced the clay in step 4, what would happen?

For Problem Solvers

In this activity, you demonstrated what happens as rock layers push together due to pressures in the earth's crust. Such action is called *convergent movement*. The earth's crust shifts in other ways, too, as the crustal plates move in response to convection currents within the mantle. Find out about divergent movement and lateral movement, and make a model

that you can use to demonstrate these movements. What else causes earthquakes? Can you think of any other ways to make models that show earthquake action?

What was the most recent earthquake that you have heard about? What damage was done? Could some of the damage have been avoided if buildings, roads, and bridges had been built the way earthquake experts recommend?

What should you do if you are where an earthquake strikes? Share your ideas and your research with your class.

Teacher Information

Any soft plastic clay will work for this activity. If sufficient clay is not available, carpet samples will do. You might think of other material that could be substituted, such as colored bath towels. Anything that can be layered and pushed together to show folding is adequate.

Movement of the earth's crustal plates is inevitable, as convection currents continue in the mantle beneath them. Although the layers of rock in the earth's surface are very hard and very heavy, heat and pressure under them are strong enough to cause them to shift, slide, and buckle. This results in earthquakes, and if one occurs in populated areas, much damage to life and property can occur.

You might want to let the layers of clay dry somewhat in order to better resemble the brittle rock layers as folding occurs, or wet the surface of each layer so that the layers are more likely to slide on each other as rock layers sometimes do.

If cracks are noted in the layers of clay, point out that these represent joints. Sometimes rock layers shift at joints. Cracks along which movement has occurred are called *faults*. If there is an earthquake fault reasonably nearby, a visit to it would make an excellent field trip. Students could construct a model of the earth layers from clay as they think the area of the fault might appear.

You might want to consider doing "cake quakes" with your students. (See Hardy and Tolman's "Cake Quakes! An Earth-Shaking Experience," *Science and Children,* September 1991.)

Integrating

Reading, language arts, social studies

Science Process Skills

Inferring, classifying, predicting, communicating, using space-time relationships, formulating hypotheses, researching

How Can You Make a Volcano Replica?

Materials Needed

- Large pans
- Rubber tubing 50 cm (20 in.) long
- Flour
- Salt
- Water
- Puffed rice
- Brown tempera paint
- Paintbrushes
- Pencils

Procedure

1. Make at least two quarts of salt-flour clay in the pan.
2. In the same pan, form the salt-flour clay into a volcano-like cone, leaving a cone-shaped hole in the center, as seen in Figure 4.33–1.
3. Use a pencil to form a small tunnel under one side of the volcano. Then insert the tube into the tunnel and bring it up in the center of the volcano so that the end of the tube comes up in the bottom of the cone. Seal the channel by pressing the clay around the tube.
4. When the model dries and hardens, paint it with brown tempera paint and with other colors if you have them and want to use them.
5. Pour some puffed rice into the cone.
6. Blow on the end of the tube, gently at first, then harder.
7. What happened? From the way your model works, tell what you can about real volcanoes.

Figure 4.33-1. Volcano Replica

Puffed rice

Rubber Tubing

For Problem Solvers

Volcanoes provide indisputable evidence of the energy that is under the crust we live on. The same energy that causes the crustal plates to move sometimes forces magma to the surface through cracks in the plates.

Make another design of a volcano model that will show how material from within the earth is thrust out by forces that are there. Use your creativity. Check your encyclopedia and other reference books that are available to you. Discuss your ideas with others who are working on the same activity. Together you will probably be able to think of several different ways to design a volcano model. Construct at least one of these and try it out. Check the Internet, but first try your own creativity.

Do you know where there is an active volcano, or one that has been active during your lifetime? If not, find out about one. Do some research, talk to people who know about it, and learn what you can about it. In what ways did it change the shape of the earth's surface? What damage did it do? What did people do to avoid being hurt by it? Is it expected to be active in the future? How soon? Share your information with others.

Draw a cross-section of this volcano, showing what you think is within the volcano and beneath it, deep in the earth's crust. Share your drawing with others who did the same activity.

Did you study about the "ring of fire"? If not, this would be an outstanding time to learn about it. The encyclopedia and the Internet would be excellent resources.

Teacher Information

In this model, air pressure forces the cereal out of the vent, simulating an eruption. In real volcanoes, the pressure is created by heat, steam, and movements beneath the earth's surface. This experience should be followed by a discussion of the similarities and differences between the model and a real volcano. Volcanic eruptions form mountains. Some islands, such as the Hawaiian Islands, are the tops of such mountains formed in the ocean.

A more realistic model can be made by using ammonium dichromate (crystal form) for the erupting material. (See Figure 4.33–2.) If you use this, certain changes should be made in the construction of the volcano. Instead of forming the inside cone, place a small tin can in the top and mold the clay around it. Omit the rubber tube and the puffed rice. You might want to make the volcano out of plaster of Paris instead of salt-flour clay. The ammonium dichromate is placed in the can and is to be lit with a match. You might need to add a bit of alcohol or lighter fluid to get it to light.

Caution: The operation of this volcano must be closely supervised, and the volcano must be used outdoors. Fumes from the ammonium dichromate are poisonous. Have students stand back before the volcano is lit. With proper supervision, this volcano is safe and provides a rather realistic impression of a volcanic eruption. Be sure to wash your hands thoroughly after this activity, as the ash produced during the eruption is poisonous, and the fumes from the ammonium dichromate is more so. The volcano should be placed on newspapers which are gathered up and thrown away when you are finished.

Hands-On Earth Science Activities

Figure 4.33–2. Volcano Made for Use with Ammonium Dichromate

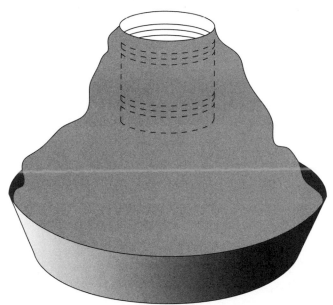

If you have access to a compressed air source, even a portable air tank, you should consider another style of volcano model that is safe, realistic, and easy to construct. Insert a rubber tube through the bottom of a cardboard box at the center and attach it with tape (the opening of the tube should be very near the bottom of the box). The box should be at least 30 cm (12 in.) square. Put a layer of sand in the box, at least 10 cm (4 in.) deep. Turn on the air slowly at first, and then increase the pressure. Too much air pressure will blow sand farther than you probably want it. A "volcanic" cone will form in a natural way, as the sand is blown up and falls back to the surface. (See Figure 4.33–3.)

Integrating

Math, reading, language arts, social studies, art

Science Process Skills

Observing, inferring, measuring, predicting, communicating, using space-time relationships, formulating hypotheses, researching

The Earth

Figure 4.33-3. Volcano Model Made for Use with Compressed Air

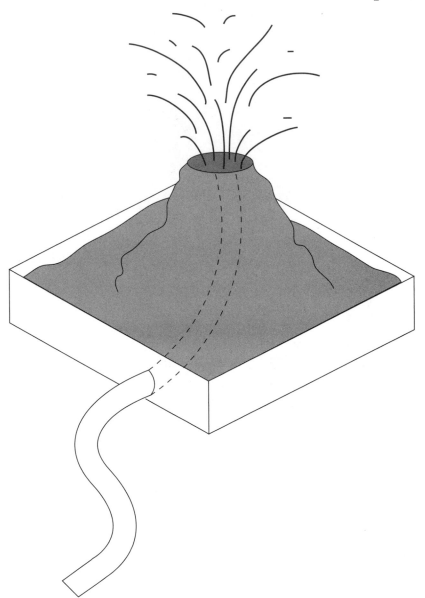

ACTIVITY 4.34

What Is the Rock Cycle?

(Teacher-supervised activity)

Materials Needed

- Two aluminum pie plates
- One piece of 2-inch by 4-inch board, about 4 inches long
- Measuring cup
- Hammer
- Crayons
- Crayon sharpener
- Hot plate
- Goggles
- Water (in case needed)
- Dull knife
- Copies of the "Science Investigation Journaling Notes" for this activity

Procedure

1. As you complete this activity, you will keep a record of what you do, just as scientists do. Use a copy of the form "Science Investigation Journaling Notes" at the end of this activity and write the information that is called for, including your name and the date.

2. For this activity you will learn about the "Rock Cycle." For item 1, the question is provided for you on the form.

3. Item 2 asks for what you already know about the question. If you have some ideas about what the rock cycle is, write your ideas.

4. For item 3, write a statement about the rock cycle, according to what you already know, and that will be your hypothesis.

5. Now continue with the following instructions. Complete your Journaling Notes as you go. Steps 6 through 17 below will help you with the information you need to write on the form for items 4 and 5.

6. Using the crayon sharpener, prepare about one and one-half cups of crayon shavings (different colors). The shavings will represent sediments that collect at the bottom of a lake.

7. Pour the "sediment" into one of the aluminum pie plates.

8. Place the second pie plate inside the first, on top of the sediment.

9. Place the board inside the top pie plate and strike it several times with the hammer, to press the sediment together.

10. Remove the board and the top pie plate and examine the sediment. What type of rock does this most closely represent? Record your observations on item 6 of the form.

11. Break off about one-third of the "rock" and set it aside for further observation later.

12. Place the second pie plate back on the first, with two-thirds of the sediment still inside. Using the board and the hammer again, pound it harder this time, putting a lot of pressure on the "rock" inside.

13. Remove the board and examine the rock. What type of rock does this most closely represent? Record your observations on item 6 of the form. Continue your writing on the back of the paper or on another paper as needed.

14. Break off about half of the "rock" that's left and set it aside with the first piece for further observation later.

15. With the hot plate on low heat, place the pie plate, with the remaining rock, on the hot plate and warm it enough to melt the sediment.

16. Let the sediment cool and solidify. When it has cooled, compare this "rock" with the first two. The first was pressed, and the second was pressed harder but not melted, and the third was melted. Identify similarities and differences between the three and record your observations. Continue your observations on item 6 of the form.

17. What type of rock does the second one most closely represent? Continue your observations on item 6 of the form.

18. Now break your three "rocks" into small pieces, into separate piles. What would happen if these small pieces of rock were swept away by a stream and deposited at the bottom of a lake, then subjected to pressure as before, and perhaps subjected to heat as well?

19. Discuss your ideas with others in your group and with your teacher. What do you think the "rock cycle" means?

20. For item 7 of the form, think about your hypothesis (item 3) and write about what you now know about the rock cycle.

Hands-On Earth Science Activities

Teacher Information

One of the laws of physics is that under ordinary circumstances matter can neither be created nor destroyed. There is only so much hydrogen and oxygen (of which water is formed), so much aluminum, and so much copper. For this reason we recycle aluminum cans to reuse the aluminum. This effort could result in more cans, or the same aluminum might become a tool for the kitchen, an airplane part, or any one of thousands of other items that include aluminum in their structure. We recycle newspapers and make cardboard or other paper products. We do this to conserve our natural resources.

Many materials are also recycled by natural processes. We hear a lot about the water cycle as a process of reusing the same water over and over again, in what is probably the largest recycling project of all time. But wait! As a recycling process, the water cycle has a competitor in the less-well-known rock cycle. Just as the water cycle reuses the same materials from nature to keep the earth supplied with water, the rock cycle reuses the same minerals over and over again in different forms. (See Figure 4.34–1.)

Figure 4.34–1. The Rock Cycle

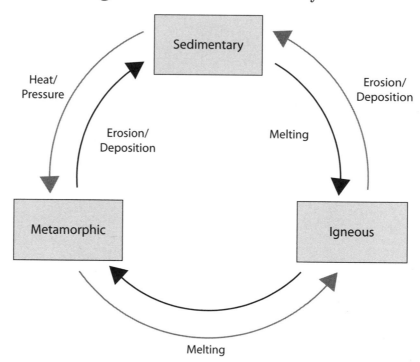

There are about two thousand known minerals, but most of the earth's crust is made of fewer than one hundred of these. In general, rocks are formed basically in one of three ways:

1. *Sedimentary rock* is formed through the processes of weathering and erosion. Tiny fragments of rock materials are moved by wind and water and deposited in lakes, trenches, and low-lying areas. Sediments collect gradually in layers where they are deposited. As these layers build up, great pressure is exerted on the low-lying materials, dissolved chemicals are added, and over time sand becomes sandstone, mud becomes shale, and small rocks mix with sand and mud to form conglomerates. All of these are classed as sedimentary rocks.

   Limestone is a type of sedimentary rock that forms in a different way. Instead of originating from deposition of fragmented rock materials, limestone is a hardened accumulation of coral and of shells and skeletons of sea animals. This typically forms in warm, shallow seas.

2. *Igneous rocks* result when magma is forced up to the surface, or near the surface, of the earth's crust, then cools and hardens. When lava is forced to the surface through cracks in the rock layers or is blown from a volcano, it is exposed to the air, cools quickly, and forms small crystals to produce the volcanic rocks pumice and obsidian. If instead of coming to the surface the lava squeezes between rock layers (usually forming a dome), it cools slowly and forms large crystals. When the surface material is eroded away, the underlying rock is exposed, usually a granite-type rock.

3. *Metamorphic rock* is changed in form. As rock layers shift, due to tremendous underground forces, sedimentary or igneous rock can be thrust deep under other rock layers or buried under lava flows. Being exposed to extreme heat and pressure, they can change form and become metamorphic rock. Some metamorphic rock is difficult to differentiate from igneous rock, but they will be harder than the original rock and they often have bands of different colors.

   Sometimes when we use models in an effort to clarify concepts, we inadvertently create misconceptions. Be sure to clarify that metamorphic rocks are not formed by a pounding action; the pounding in this activity is used in an effort to simulate the pressure that earth materials undergo with the shifting of rock structures.

Any of the three basic types of rock can become either of the other two, given the conditions to cause certain changes. If a geologic event occurs that forces sedimentary or metamorphic rock deep enough into

Hands-On Earth Science Activities

the crust that the material melts, it becomes magma. If and when it is again forced to the surface (or near the surface) it will cool and become igneous rock. Any rock that becomes weathered and eroded and collects in layers of sediment can become sedimentary rock by the process explained above.

And so goes the rock cycle, as the same mineral materials are reused over and over again, as sedimentary, igneous, and metamorphic rock. Both at the earth's surface and under the surface of the earth, the rock cycle constantly churns, not creating new rock material, but transforming one type of rock into another type of rock.

In reflecting back over the above activity, hopefully students will recognize the resemblance between crayon shavings and rock sediment and that when the shavings were pressed (by hammering) they became a representation of sedimentary rock. The sedimentary rock while undergoing greater pressure (more energetic hammering) might represent metamorphic rock and when melted became a representation of igneous rock. Any of the three basic types of rock can become any of the others, given the right conditions of weathering, erosion, compaction, and heat. Sedimentary rock can become a new sedimentary rock.

Integrating

Math, reading, language arts, art

Science Process Skills

Inferring, measuring, communicating, comparing and contrasting, using space-time relationships, researching

Science Investigation

Journaling Notes for Activity 4.34

1. Question: *What is the rock cycle?*

2. What we already know: _____

_____

3. Hypothesis: _____

_____

4. Materials needed: _____

_____

5. Procedure: _____

_____

_____

_____

_____

6. Observations/New information: _____

_____

_____

7. Conclusion: _____

_____

_____

How Old Is the Earth?*

(Teacher-directed activity)

Materials Needed

- 10 meters of butcher paper
- Markers or crayons
- Meter sticks

Procedure

1. Draw four lines the full length of the butcher paper. Make each line 10 meters long, spacing the lines evenly down the paper.

2. Draw one more line at the bottom. This one should be 5 meters long.

3. Mark off each line in centimeters, with heavier marks at 1-meter points.

4. Scientists think the earth is about 4.5 billion years old. On these lines, each centimeter represents one million years!

5. At the left end of the top line, make a mark. Near the line, write "The Earth Began About 4.5 Billion Years Ago. Each Centimeter Represents One Million Years."

6. At the right end of the bottom line, make a box 1 centimeter square. Color the box yellow or some other light color. Above this box write "The Last One Million Years."

7. In the box, toward the right side of the box, make a narrow, red vertical line, about the width of a pencil line.

8. Below the box, write "The width of the red line represents how long humans have been on the earth."

9. Talk about some of the things you know that people have done and how they have lived throughout history. They have lived in caves, hunted with spears and with stones, invented electricity, and so forth. All of these things, including today's space travel and vast technological advances, have occurred within the time represented by the red line. Draw pictures to illustrate some of these events.

---

*Adapted from Tolman, 2002, *Discovering Elementary Science: Method, Content, and Problem-Solving Activities,* 3rd ed., p. 486. Boston: Allyn & Bacon.

For Problem Solvers

Add to the time line. With each centimeter (one million years) it will be easy to find specific time periods. For example, the first life seems to have begun in the water long before the Cambrian period, which began about 570 million years ago (about 57 cm back from today). Dinosaurs lived during the Mesazoic era, which began about 245 million years ago (about 245 cm back from today) and ended about 66 million years ago (66 cm back from today).

Use the Internet and reference books, such as geology books or encyclopedias, that will help you to identify major events throughout history and about when they occurred. Add some of them to the time line. With major events from recent history you can just draw an arrow to the narrow red line in the box.

Teacher Information

Making a mark at each centimeter along 45 meters of line is a task, but won't take too long for students to do as a group. It will help them to get a feel for what a very long time the earth has been here and what a very small part of that time people have been present on it. Students should recognize that information about conditions long ago is not complete, and that scientists continue to study and learn. They will change what they teach as they receive new information.

As for the number of years that humans have inhabited the earth, scientists do not agree because evidence is not yet conclusive. Evidence does indicate that humans have been on the earth for many thousands of years, but that's only a small part of the million years represented by that final centimeter on the chart.

Integrating

Math, reading, language arts, social studies, art

Science Process Skills

Inferring, measuring, communicating, comparing and contrasting, using space-time relationships, researching

Hands-On Earth Science Activities

Name _____   Date _____

Can You Solve This Earth Word Search?

Try to find the following Earth terms in the grid below. They could appear in horizontal (left to right), vertical (up or down), or diagonal (upward or downward) position.

soil   rocks   erosion
color   hardness   crystal
conglomerate   sedimentary   density
fossil   metamorphic   glacier
earthquake   volcano   streak

```
C  F  E  R  O  C  K  S  R  E  T  M
C  O  N  G  L  O  M  E  R  A  T  E
H  S  L  A  S  E  R  D  E  R  M  T
A  S  V  O  C  V  B  I  L  T  R  A
R  I  O  U  R  P  N  M  A  H  E  M
D  L  L  I  Y  O  I  E  T  Q  I  O
N  W  C  V  L  K  S  N  S  U  C  R
E  E  A  R  E  L  A  T  Y  A  A  P
S  D  N  B  U  O  S  A  R  K  L  H
S  M  O  N  G  I  E  R  C  E  G  I
F  D  E  N  S  I  T  Y  C  Y  A  C
E  R  O  S  I  O  N  C  I  K  O  K
```

The Earth   **279**

Can You Create a New Earth Word Search of Your Own?

Write your Earth words in the grid below. Arrange them in the grid so they appear in horizontal (left to right), vertical (up or down), or diagonal (upward or downward) position. Fill in the blank boxes with other letters. Trade your Word Search with someone else who has created one of his or her own, and see whether you can solve the new puzzle.

_____   _____   _____

_____   _____   _____

_____   _____   _____

_____   _____   _____

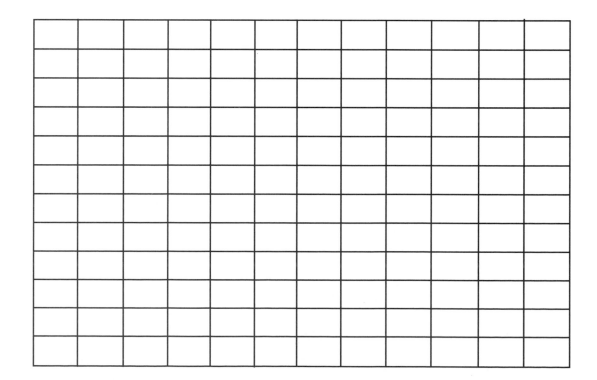

Copyright © 2006 by John Wiley & Sons, Inc.

Answer Key for Earth Word Search

C F E R O C K S R E T M
C O N G L O M E R A T E
H S L A S E R D E R M T
A S V O C V B I L T R A
R I O U R P N M A H E M
D L L I Y O I E T Q I O
N W C V L K S N S U C R
E E A R E L A T Y A A P
S D N B U O S A R K L H
S M O N G I E R C E G I
F D E N S I T Y C Y A C
E R O S I O N C I K O K

Do You Recall?

Section Four: The Earth

1. What is the purpose of a map?

2. What kind of map is used to show mountains and valleys?

3. What is the value of grass and other plant growth on a hillside during a rainstorm?

4. As a river washes gravel, silt, and sand into a lake, in what order will the three materials settle at the bottom of the lake?

5. What do we do when we classify rocks?

6. What are some of the characteristics usually considered in classifying rocks?

Do You Recall?

Section Four: The Earth (continued)

7. Are all crystal structures (such as salt crystals, alum, sugar, calcite, and others) alike?

8. What is a conglomerate?

9. When you measure the density of a rock, what information are you getting?

10. What causes earthquakes?

11. What is the rock cycle?

Answer Key for Do You Recall?

Section Four: The Earth

Answer	Related Activities
1. A miniature representation of a large area	4.1–4.7
2. Contour map or relief map	4.4, 4.6
3. Roots hold the soil in place, helping to prevent erosion.	4.12
4. Gravel on the bottom, then sand, and silt on top	4.13
5. Sort them into groups by specific characteristics	4.14
6. Hardness, color of streak, reaction to vinegar or dilute hydrochloric acid, magnetic properties, electrical conductivity	4.15–4.20
7. No, each crystal has a unique shape.	4.21, 4.22
8. A mix of different kinds of rocks cemented together	4.23
9. How much the rock weighs, compared to an equal volume of water	4.26
10. Movement of rock layers in the earth's crust	4.31, 4.32
11. The changing of rocks from one form or type to another	4.34

Ecology

To the Teacher

Ecology is both interdisciplinary and intradisciplinary. It is interdisciplinary because it involves content from the biological, physical, and earth sciences, plus many areas of the social sciences. It is intradisciplinary because the ecologist attempts to use information from many sources to produce a unique field.

Many of the ecological problems we read about, see on TV, or hear on the radio are global in nature. Some are highly sensitive and fall in the political realm. National and international relations often deteriorate over ecologically based issues. In this section we do not attempt to deal with moral, economic, or political issues. We deal with some basics of the science of ecology and attempt to help students realize their place, as individuals, in the ecological system.

The first portion of the section deals in very simple ways with nature's balance, food cycles, and food webs. The cycles of soil, water, and air are alluded to but not introduced formally. If you care to pursue these in greater depth, your library, along with the Internet, can provide ample resources.

People are introduced into an ecological system in this section. Liberties are taken with the term ecosystem to generalize it to apply to the student and his or her interaction with the immediate environment. Human interaction with the immediate environment becomes the focal point. Conservation, cooperation, and individual responsibility are emphasized. You may be tempted, as many are, to become preachy at this point; however, the effectiveness will be greatly increased if students are helped to discover these ideas on their own.

Many of these activities could be enhanced by the use of movies on nature and wildlife. Be aware that some movies show predators killing prey and portray life and death as they occur in a true ecosystem. Be sure to preview the movies and use only those you consider to be appropriate for your students.

Try to include as much art, music, poetry, and aesthetic experience as you can. Opportunities for enrichment are almost limitless.

The following activities are designed as discovery activities that students can usually perform quite independently. You are encouraged to provide students (usually in small groups) with the materials listed and a copy of the activity from the beginning through the "Procedure." The section titled "Teacher Information" is not intended for student use, but rather to assist with discussion following the hands-on activity, as students share their observations. Discussion of conceptual information prior to completing the hands-on activity can interfere with the discovery process.

Regarding the Early Grades

With verbal instructions and slight modifications, many of these activities can be used with kindergarten, first-grade, and second-grade students. In some activities, steps that involve procedures that go beyond the level of the child can simply be omitted and yet offer the child an experience that plants the seed for a concept that will germinate and grow later on.

Teachers of the early grades will probably choose to bypass many of the "For Problem Solvers" sections. That's okay. These sections are provided for those who are especially motivated and want to go beyond the investigation provided by the activity outlined. Use the outlined activities, and enjoy worthwhile learning experiences together with your young students. Also consider, however, that many of the "For Problem Solvers" sections can be used appropriately with young children as group activities or as demonstrations, still giving students the advantage of an exposure to the experience, and laying groundwork for connections that will be made at a later time.

Hands–On Earth Science Activities

Teachers of young children should particularly be aware that some movies show predators killing prey and portray life and death as they occur in a true ecosystem. To preview any movies being considered for classroom use is especially important at the early grades.

Correlation with National Standards

The following elements of the National Standards are reflected in the activities of this section.

K–4   Content Standard A: Science as Inquiry

As a result of activities in grades K–4, all students should develop

1. Abilities necessary to do scientific inquiry
2. Understanding about scientific inquiry

K–4   Content Standard D: Earth and Space Science

As a result of activities in grades K–4, all students should develop understanding of

1. Properties of earth materials
2. Objects in the sky
3. Changes in earth and sky

K–4   Content Standard F: Science in Personal and Social Perspectives

As a result of activities in grades K–4, all students should develop understanding of

1. Personal health
2. Characteristics and changes in populations
3. Types of resources
4. Changes in environments
5. Science and technology in local challenges

5–8   Content Standard A: Science as Inquiry

As a result of activities in grades 5–8, all students should develop

1. Abilities necessary to do scientific inquiry
2. Understanding about scientific inquiry

5–8   Content Standard D: Earth and Space Science

As a result of activities in grades 5–8, all students should develop understanding of

1. Structure of the earth system
2. Earth's history
3. Earth in the solar system

5–8   Content Standard F: Science in Personal and Social Perspectives

As a result of activities in grades 5–8, all students should develop understanding of

1. Personal health
2. Populations, resources, and environments
3. Natural hazards
4. Risks and benefits
5. Science and technology in society

What Is a Simple Plant-Animal Community?

Materials Needed

- 24-inch by 36-inch poster of Figure 5.1–1, labeled by the teacher and hung in the front of the room
- $8\frac{1}{2}$-inch by 11-inch unlabeled copy of Figure 5.1–1 for each student
- Crayons
- Pencils

Procedure

1. Compare your picture with the one on the poster. This is a basic grassland community. It has six important elements. As you read about each item below, color it on your paper.

2. Energy from the sun in the form of heat and light is the very first ingredient. Without it, nothing else could happen. Label and color the sun.

3. Air must be present in order for life to exist. Since air is colorless, write "air" on a blank spot somewhere below the sun.

4. Moisture in some form must also be present. How do you think this grassland is receiving moisture? Label and show it in some way on your picture.

5. Good soil is necessary for grassy or woody plants. Soil has dead leaves and sticks (humus) in it. There are also small animals called *scavengers,* such as worms, bugs, and beetles. Scavengers feed on dead plant and animal materials in the soil and break it down into smaller parts. Tiny bacteria and fungi called *decomposers* further break down materials into minerals that plants need in order to grow. Color and label the humus, scavengers, and decomposers.

6. Plants of many kinds grow above the ground. They all depend on energy from the sun, air, moisture, and rich soil. In turn they remove carbon dioxide from, and release oxygen into, the air. They give off moisture. Most plants use energy from the sun combined with moisture and rich soil to produce food. They are the primary producers of food on the earth. Without them, other forms of life could not exist. Color the plants and flowers in your picture.

7. Your grassland community is now working. Save it for use later on.

Teacher Information

In this part of the study of ecology, we will consider groups or types of living and nonliving things interacting with each other as communities. When we add animals as primary and secondary consumers, we will then have an ecosystem.

Ecosystems can be as simple as a balanced aquarium in a classroom or as complex as an entire region, country, or the world. Our studies will be confined to small communities and ecosystems to provide simple examples with which the students can relate.

As people are introduced into ecosystems, students will begin to understand how complex the problems can become.

Integrating

Language arts, social studies, art

Science Process Skills

Observing, communicating, comparing and contrasting, using space-time relationships

Figure 5.1-1. Profile of a Grassland Community

What Is a Pond Community?

Materials Needed

- Student copies of grassland picture from Activity 5.1
- Unlabeled copy of Figure 5.2–1 for each student
- Crayons
- Pencil

Procedure

1. Compare the picture you made of the grassland community and the new picture you have.

2. This is a picture of a pond community. It is sometimes called an ecosystem. Label and color all the nonliving elements, as you did in your last picture. If there are any new nonliving things, label and color them.

3. Use your picture from the last activity to label as many other similar things (grasses, scavengers, decomposers) as you can.

4. What new things are unlabeled and uncolored?

5. The animals in the picture do not produce food; they consume it. They are called *consumers.*

6. Animals that feed on primary producers (plants, grasses, and algae) are called primary consumers. Animals that usually feed on other animals are called secondary consumers.

7. In your picture, the small animals (shrimp, water flea, and snail) are primary consumers feeding on plants and algae. Label and color them.

8. The fish and frog are secondary consumers in this instance, since they feed on small primary consumers. Label and color them.

9. The snake is a higher-level secondary consumer that may eat either the frog or the fish. Label and color it.

10. The bird (in this case a blue heron) is an even higher level of secondary consumer because it may eat the fish, frog, or snake. Label and color it.

11. Whether an animal is a primary or a secondary consumer depends on what it eats, not on its size. The elephant is a primary consumer. A ladybug beetle is a secondary consumer.

12. Turn your paper over and draw a picture of the plants and animals in your classroom aquarium. Can you find both producers and consumers?

Teacher Information

If you do not have a freshwater aquarium or a good terrarium and have not developed one earlier in the year, this would be an excellent time to do so. As students learn more about ecosystems, they will be able to have first-hand experience with a simple model.

As we add primary and secondary consumers to the model, the system becomes far more complex. Up to this point, the terms *herbivore* (plant eater), *carnivore* (animal eater), and *omnivore* (eats both plants and animals) have not been introduced. They are not necessary to the understanding of ecosystems.

Integrating

Language arts, social studies, art

Science Process Skills

Observing, inferring, classifying, communicating, comparing and contrasting, using space-time relationships

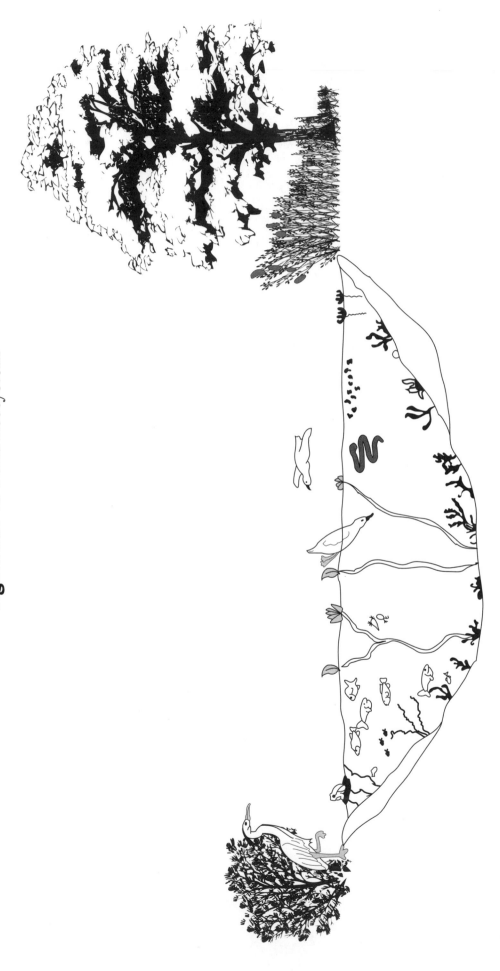

Figure 5.2-1. Pond Ecosystem

What Is a Simple Ecosystem?

Materials Needed

- Pictures of grassland community developed in Activity 5.1
- Pencil
- Crayons
- Copies of Figures 5.3–1, 5.3–2, and 5.3–3 for each student

Procedure

1. Figures 5.3–1 and 5.3–2 show animals that might live in a grassland community. Some are primary consumers and some are secondary consumers. Draw the ground animals on your picture of a grassland community. Color them.

2. Some birds are primary consumers. They eat berries and seeds. Others are secondary consumers who prey on primary consumers. Can you tell which is which? *Hint:* Look at their beaks and claws.

3. Now that we have added consumers, our grassland ecosystem is complete. However, we have two new kinds of animals. The smaller bird is a migratory animal who joins the ecosystem for a period of time when certain seeds or berries are ripe and then moves on to another location. On your picture of a grassland community, draw a migratory bird. Color it.

4. The second, larger bird is a predator. It preys on smaller animals. Notice its large, powerful claws and sharp beak. Some predators are migratory, but many are permanent residents, depending on the food supply. Draw the predator on your picture of a grassland community. Color it.

5. Figure 5.3–3 shows some larger animals that might be found in a grassland community. Two are primary consumers. One is a predator, or secondary consumer. If you know what they eat, then you know which is a primary consumer and which is a secondary consumer. On your grassland community, draw the new animals. Color them.

6. Now that you have developed both a pond and a grassland ecosystem, can you think of the reason why plants and animals live together and are dependent on each other?

Teacher Information

As consumers and migratory animals are added to an ecosystem, it becomes increasingly complex. Younger children may need to see colored pictures similar to the pictures of the animals they are asked to color. (Otherwise you may get purple ground squirrels!)

The existence of an ecosystem is directly related to energy and its transfer. The sun is the major source of energy. Lower forms of plants and animals spend most of their lives in producing and consuming energy. Reproducing the species, in many cases, is the only other function they perform. Some more advanced species do spend time in play.

Integrating

Language arts, social studies, art

Science Process Skills

Observing, inferring, classifying, communicating, comparing and contrasting, using space-time relationships

Figure 5.3-1. Animals

Figure 5.3–2. Animals

Figure 5.3-3. Animals

How Is Energy Transferred in an Ecosystem?

Materials Needed

- Complete grassland ecosystem from Activity 5.3
- Simple food chain chart (Figure 5.4–1)
- Simple food web (Figure 5.4–2)

Procedure

1. Study the picture of the grassland ecosystem you made before. Energy from the sun is the basis of life in the system. Why? Discuss this with your teacher and other members of the group.

2. Figure 5.4–1 is a diagram of a simple food chain showing how energy from the sun is used and stored in food molecules manufactured by the producers from nonliving materials. In turn, they are consumed by primary and secondary consumers. The waste products and remains of dead animals and plants are returned to the soil, where the scavengers and decomposers complete the cycle so that it can begin again.

3. There are many different ways food chains can work. Some consumers eat only certain producers. Other consumers eat both primary and secondary consumers. Ecologists call these many variables the food web. Just as a spider spins a web one strand at a time, food webs are made up of many food chains. Compare the food web (Figure 5.4–2) with the food chain (Figure 5.4–1).

4. Weather and chemicals produced from the nonliving portions of the ecosystem (air, water, soil) influence the conditions within the system. Can you think of other factors that might change the food web? What would happen if there were no mice?

5. Ecosystems are very complex. Can you see why ecology is an interesting and exciting science?

Teacher Information

Figures 5.4–1 and 5.4–2 are simple, but should still give students a feeling for the highly complex interrelationships that occur in nature. Also, chance is always part of the interplay.

Using charts may convey a feeling of a static process. Ecosystems are actually highly dynamic, with countless variables. Students may need additional experience in constructing ecosystems and applying them to life situations. Later in the section, parks, vacant lots, and even back-alley ecosystems will be discussed.

Integrating

Language arts, social studies, art

Science Process Skills

Observing, inferring, classifying, communicating, comparing and contrasting, using space-time relationships

Ecology

Figure 5.4-1. Food Chain

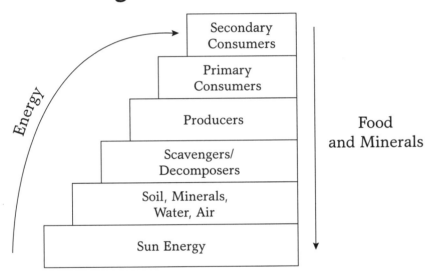

Figure 5.4–2. Simple Food Web

ACTIVITY 5.5

Where Do People Fit into an Ecosystem?

Materials Needed

- 3-foot by 6-foot poster of Figure 5.5–1 for each small group of students
- Cutouts of plants and animals, such as those in Figures 5.3–1, 5.3–2, and 5.3–3
- Colored pencils
- Pictures of people, houses, stores, domestic animals, and so on
- Thumbtacks
- Drawing paper

Procedure

1. Study the picture on the large bulletin board. This is the way your community may have looked before it was settled.
2. Identify the nonliving and living elements that make up the ecosystem.
3. Add a family to the system. What will they need to survive? Where will they get what they need?
4. Put a house and yard in the picture. Add a barn and barnyard. What animals will live in the barnyard? Where will the people get food? Where will they plant crops?
5. Add a second family with all the things the first family has.
6. What is happening to the ecosystem?
7. Add a third house, family, and barn.
8. Build a general store, house of worship, school, and post office near the homes.
9. Is this still an ecosystem?
10. What changes could you make in it? Discuss planning as a part of urban and suburban change.

For Problem Solvers

How has the ecosystem of your community changed with time? Do you know how and when your town or city actually began? What was the

Hands-On Earth Science Activities

area like before that? What animals and plants were common in the area? Which of these are no longer found there? Which ones were forced out of the ecosystem because of loss of natural habitat as people moved in? Was it covered by forest, grasslands, marshes, or what? Why did people settle this area? Do you know anyone who has been here for many, many years? If so, ask them to tell you what they know about the early days of this community. Think of some questions you want to ask before you begin and write them down. Perhaps you could record the interview and share the information with your class. Ask at the public library for information about the story of your town. Early photographs of the community might be available.

Before you begin your search for information about your town or city, write a brief description of what you think the area might have been like, who you think the first settlers might have been, and why you think they came. Draw a picture showing what you think it might have looked like at that time. Compare your picture with what you learn about the way it really was.

Teacher Information

Figure 5.5–1 was developed from a grassland-woodland area. In representing more arid or humid regions, you can vary the environment and the people according to existing conditions. Be sure to have cutouts ready as students add people and houses.

Some teachers who like to sketch have used light pastels and drawn figures and objects in darker colors as the housing develops. The wild animals, fish, trees, and bushes will need to be removable or be covered by cutouts. Involve students in the development of these materials if possible.

If you live in a large city or suburban area, the poster as shown in Figure 5.5–1 could finally be covered by a tall skyline or rambling homes.

The purpose of the activity is not to show how people destroy natural ecosystems. Rather, it should help students understand that with civilization natural ecosystems will change and that planning can help society preserve, conserve, and restore many ecosystems in the world. People are second-level consumers. As such, they have responsibilities to ecosystems if they are to continue to be supported by those systems.

Integrating

Reading, language arts, social studies, art

Science Process Skills

Observing, inferring, communicating, comparing and contrasting, using space-time relationships, formulating hypotheses, researching

Figure 5.5-1. Grassland/Woodland Ecosystem

How Do You Fit into a Personal Ecosystem?

(Class discussion)

Materials Needed

- Drawing paper
- Colored pencils
- Rulers

Procedure

1. We have learned how the ecosystem of your community has changed with time. Whether you live in a very small community or a very large metropolitan area, many things have changed, are changing, and will change. In the center of your paper make a small picture of yourself.

2. Next to you, make a picture of the people (family) with whom you live and any animals you own.

3. Place a rectangle around your picture. This represents the place where you live and is the first part of your personal "ecosystem."

4. Somewhere near your home, make a picture of your favorite out-door place to play (yard, park, playground, friend's yard, or alley). This is a second portion of your personal ecosystem.

5. Make a picture of your school with your classroom located in it. This is a third part of your personal ecosystem.

6. Next, draw small pictures of other places where you spend time regularly (house of worship, club, friends' places, grandparents' or other relatives' places).

7. Make boxes around all the pictures and draw lines connecting your "home" box with all the others. Estimate the amount of time you spend with each of the elements each week and write the time in hours and minutes if you can.

8. You are a second-level consumer, and this web of boxes and lines represents most of the "ecosystem" in which you live.

Teacher Information

You will probably need to use the chalkboard or overhead projector to show how to construct the web. Younger children will be unable to estimate time spent, and perhaps distance, but the size of the pictures they draw could substitute for length of time and importance to them. It is best not to "model" family size or structure by drawing in two parents, other children, and so forth.

The web, of course, is not intended to represent any type of true ecosystem. Its purpose is to provide focus for the following activities, which will be centered on individuals and their relationships to people and things around them.

Integrating

Language arts, social studies, art

Science Process Skills

Observing, communicating, comparing and contrasting, using space-time relationships

How Do You Live at Home?

Materials Needed

- Drawing paper
- Crayons
- Rulers
- Pencils

Procedure

1. Draw an outline of your home. Divide your home into rooms or living areas. Choose your favorite color and mark the space that belongs to you. If you share a bedroom, color your part of the room.

2. Use different colors to show places that belong to other individual members of the family.

3. Some spaces are shared with others in your family. Use different colors to show "community" areas. You might want to show some shared furniture, such as a computer and TV.

4. Some animals that live together in communities within an ecosystem have rules that govern their own space or territory and territory shared with others. With other animals, most rules for community living are controlled by instincts—unlearned behavior that is beyond their personal control. Insect communities, such as bees and ants, live in a complex social structure controlled by instinctive behavior. In human communities, most behavior is controlled by thinking or reasoning, that is, by rules.

5. On your paper, make a small colored line to identify the territories (areas or rooms) in your home and write several rules for living and sharing in each territory.

6. Look at the rules you have written. Are they different for your personal territory, for territory that is shared by other members of your family, or for guest territory, if you have any?

7. Save this picture for a later activity.

For Problem Solvers

Some animals identify a certain territory and claim that territory as their own. They defend it against other animals of their own species. We say these animals are *territorial*. Read about bears, and especially about their territorial habits. Find out what other animals you can identify as being territorial. Are people territorial? Are you territorial? If so, in what ways do you show it? Share your ideas with your teacher and your class.

Teacher Information

The following series of activities will help the student identify his or her place in various communities. The use of terms such as family, community, and ecosystem may help students realize that, just as with other animal relationships, they too have rights and responsibilities.

A positive approach to the use of rules instead of instincts should help children understand that rules are necessary and helpful for survival, protection, and comfort.

Discuss and compare rules and family lifestyles with your class. Accept and positively reinforce differences. Help students understand reasons for the rights, responsibilities, and rules in their family community.

Integrating

Reading, language arts, social studies, art

Science Process Skills

Observing, inferring, classifying, communicating, comparing and contrasting, using space-time relationships, formulating hypotheses, identifying and controlling variables, researching

Hands-On Earth Science Activities

How Do You Live in Your Classroom?

Materials Needed

- Drawing paper
- Pencils
- Crayons
- Rulers

Procedure

1. Use your ruler to draw an outline of your classroom.
2. Locate and color your personal space in the classroom.
3. Mark and color your teacher's personal territory in the room.
4. Use another color to show the personal space of other students in the room.
5. Look around the room and decide what is shared space in your classroom community. Draw pictures of and color the shared territory. If there is any space not being used, leave it blank.
6. Think about the nonliving parts of your classroom environment. How do you get light, moisture, and air? Is the temperature comfortable for community living? Under your picture, write a word or sentence to describe the nonliving parts of your classroom.
7. Since there are probably more members in your classroom community than in your home, what additional rules are necessary?
8. On your paper, list several important rules everyone needs to follow in order to live comfortably with others.
9. Discuss and compare your picture and rules with those of other members of the class.
10. Save your picture for use in a later activity.

Teacher Information

In any community, rules work only if they are understood, accepted, and supported by each individual. Even very young children need to understand reasons for community rules. In animal communities, the rules of instinct have probably developed from survival through natural selection. People have extended rules far beyond the instinctive survival level. Customs, traditions, mores, taboos, and religious beliefs are often translated into some kind of pattern of rules or laws with which a society is governed.

Integrating

Language arts, social studies, art

Science Process Skills

Observing, communicating, comparing and contrasting, using space-time relationships

How Does Our School Community Function?

(Class discussion and small groups)

Materials Needed

- Large pieces of chart paper
- Writing paper
- Pencils
- Portable tape recorders

Procedure

1. This activity may take several days to complete. With your teacher and other members of the class, make a drawing of your school on the chart paper. Show the classrooms and other spaces, such as the library, lunchroom, auditorium, multipurpose room, offices, teachers' room, custodial areas, and restrooms. If your school has special features that you like, be sure to put them in.

2. Form small groups (four or five people) and choose an area (territory) of your school community you would like to study. List people you'd like to talk to and special things to look for in your area. Share the list with your teacher. Prepare some questions to ask about your area. Be sure to ask how students can help support this part of the school community. Ask about problems that are of special importance in that territory.

3. Make an appointment with the person in charge of the area you have chosen (librarian, principal, custodian, lunchroom manager, school secretary) and arrange an on-site visit. Be sure to take paper and pencil and a tape recorder so you will be able to report back to your class.

4. After your visit, meet as a group and ask your teacher to help you prepare a brief report for the class. Include pictures and drawings.

5. Share your reports with the class. As other groups report, compare your findings with theirs.

6. Save all your material and notes for a later activity.

Teacher Information

Before you begin, be sure to discuss this activity with your principal and other members of the school staff who may be involved. Enlist their help in identifying special features and problems of their roles.

Students should realize that a well-functioning school community depends on the quality of each segment. A theme for this study might be "How do you help us? How can we help you?"

Be sure the students have specific questions to ask as they gather data for a report. As a part of the report, school staff members might be willing to visit.

Visualizing the whole school on a chart (step 1) may be difficult for younger children (some adults, too). Before you use a chart for class discussion, you may want to rule a light outline in pencil and use a black marker during the actual class discussion.

Integrating

Language arts, social studies, art

Science Process Skills

Observing, communicating, comparing and contrasting, using space-time relationships

Hands-On Earth Science Activities

How Is Your School Like an Ecosystem?

Materials Needed

- Pictures of grassland ecosystem developed in Activity 5.1 (one per student)
- Large poster paper for each student
- Pieces of 9-inch by 12-inch paper
- Pencils

Procedure

1. Look at your picture of a grassland ecosystem. Remember the important nonliving and living elements in it?
2. How is your school like an ecosystem? On your poster paper, make an outline of your school building.
3. Instead of a sun to provide energy, make a circle above the building and call it "Learning."
4. Inside the building, write the name of the major consumer of "learning."
5. Inside the building, write the names of the major producers of learning.
6. Near the outside of the building, write the names of organisms (people) who help the producers and consumers.
7. Farther away from the building, write the names of nonliving things that help the producers and consumers.
8. Still farther away, write the names of migratory producers who help but are not a permanent part of the system.
9. Can you think of other things that need to be added to the ecosystem? If so, put them in.
10. Compare your school "ecosystem" with a grassland ecosystem. Which do you think is more difficult to keep balanced?

Teacher Information

This activity is suggested with apologies to any purists in the field of ecology. There are many microecosystems within the school building and on the school grounds. However, the purpose of this analogy is to focus on the students' role in a system that functions to assist them. It is not unlike farmers and some large industries that use resources to provide consumer products. Most of these industries recognize their responsibilities to the ecological system on which they depend.

The following activity will help students identify specific problems in the school "ecosystem" and devise methods to solve some of them.

Figure 5.10–1 is a suggested model for your poster. Modify it to fit your own situation.

Integrating

Language arts, social studies, art

Science Process Skills

Observing, communicating, comparing and contrasting, using space-time relationships

Figure 5.10–1. A School as an Ecosystem

The following diagram shows concentric circles with labels. From outer to inner:

Sunlight, Other Taxpayers, School Board, Friends, Social Worker, Nurse, Psychologist, Supervisors, Air, Grandparents, Superintendent, Delivery Persons, Sanitation Workers, Water, Postal Workers, Firefighters, Food, Police, State and Local Officials, Heating and Cooling Plant Building, Furniture, Books, Cafeteria, Films, Film Strips, Television Equipment, Buses, Lavatories, Offices, Playground, Teachers' Room, Auditorium and/or Multipurpose Room, Water, Lights, Fuel, Clerk, Learning, Custodian, Secretary, Bus Drivers, Librarian, Lunch Room Workers, Teachers, Volunteers, Special Teachers, Students, Parents, Aides, Principal, Crossing Guards

Hands-On Earth Science Activities

Where Can We Begin?

(Introductory teacher demonstration)

Materials Needed

- Classroom wastebasket
- Tape recorder
- Blank recording tape
- Large photograph of the earth taken by astronauts as they stood on the moon

Teacher Information

This activity is suggested as a way to interest children in ecology as it directly affects their lives. It has proven successful in many classrooms. If you feel it is not appropriate for your group, just omit this activity.

1. Make a tape recording by someone with a deep, sonorous voice. This recording should have a few minutes of blank tape at the beginning. Place it in a battery-operated tape recorder, buried (but protected) under litter in your classroom wastebasket. Turn it on just before school begins or after lunch.

2. After the few minutes of blank tape, the wastebasket will say some of the following (adapt the taped message to fit your own situation):

   a. Call out several times (ask to be put on the table).

   b. Call attention to the kinds of things people are throwing away.

   c. Point out the condition of the classroom.

   d. Talk about hearing complaints from the garbage can where all school refuse is dumped; also the waste cans in the lunchroom.

   e. Call the attention of the class to the photo of the earth taken by astronauts as they stood on the moon. Point out that this is all we have—this fragile globe on which we live; when it's gone, what do we do?

f. Ask the students whether they have ever heard of a food chain or ecosystem. Remind them that they are supposed to be consumers, not wasters. Consumers make contributions. Offer to tell them some ways they can help.

g. Say, "Ms. or Mr. [teacher's name], tell everyone about the bulletin board you have on the wall."

Integrating

Language arts, social studies

Science Process Skills

Observing, communicating

What Is Litter?

Materials Needed

- Garbage bags
- Large poster paper (one per committee)
- Glue
- Tongs (one set per committee)
- Clean cotton gloves (one pair per committee)
- Plastic-covered table

Procedure

1. Divide into groups of four or five.
2. Choose an area near the school building such as the school grounds, curbs (not street), vacant lots, or sidewalk.
3. Take a garbage bag and spend 30 minutes collecting all materials that are not part of the natural environment in the area. Use the tongs or gloves to pick up things that are sharp or dirty. (Don't collect or touch dead animals.)
4. After 30 minutes, return to the classroom with the things you have collected.
5. Put everything on a plastic-covered table. Can you find ways to classify or organize them?
6. Use the poster paper and glue to make three-dimensional collages of the material.
7. Think of titles or slogans for the pictures.
8. Display them in your room and other parts of the school.
9. Wash your hands frequently during this activity.
10. The area you picked up is clean now. How could you keep it that way?

Ecology

Teacher Information

This activity is regularly used in schools. It seems most effective when the goal is to sensitize students to litter and how easily it accumulates. The most important message should be that each bit of litter represents a careless, lazy, or thoughtless person. Many careless, lazy, thoughtless people produce an ugly, littered, and often unhealthy environment. Students should realize that they, as individuals, are responsible for the control of litter.

Integrating

Language arts, social studies, art

Science Process Skills

Observing, inferring, classifying, measuring, communicating, using space-time relationships

What Is in the Air Besides Air?*

(Take home and do with family and friends.)

Materials Needed

- Paper plate
- Petroleum jelly
- Hand lonooo
- Microscopes

Procedure

1. Spread a thin layer of petroleum jelly on the top surface of the paper plate.
2. Set the plate outdoors for one day, in an area where it is exposed to the air and where it will not be disturbed. Predict what you might find on it the next day.
3. One day later, look at the plate very carefully. Do you see anything stuck to the petroleum jelly?
4. If something is there, describe what it looks like and where you think it came from.
5. Examine the plate with the hand lens. Do you see any more than you saw without the lens?
6. Discuss your observations with others.

For Problem Solvers

Do the same activity in different places, but do it as a Science Investigation. Get a blank copy of the "Science Investigation Journaling Notes." Write your name, the date, and your question at the top. Plan your investigation through step 5 (Procedure) and have it approved by your teacher. Complete the Journaling Notes as you perform your investigation. Share your project with your group, and submit your Journaling Notes to your teacher if requested.

---

*Adapted from Tolman, 2002, *Discovering Elementary Science: Method, Content, and Problem-Solving Activities,* 3rd ed., p. 168. Boston: Allyn & Bacon.

Put a plate in the classroom, another in the furnace room, and others in other classrooms and at home, both indoors and outdoors. There might be still other places you will want to check for pollutants in the air. Be sure to label each plate with its location. See whether you get the same results in the different locations.

As you examine your collections with magnifiers, do you see any differences in the particles from one collection area to another, or even possibly on the same plate?

Teacher Information

You will need to caution children to be careful to keep the petroleum jelly off their clothes, to avoid stains. Students should also wash their hands after the activity.

It will be interesting to compare the dust and pollutants that come out of the air in different locations. If someone lives near a factory, be sure he or she brings a sample from home. With appropriate supervision, perhaps someone could collect a sample at a busy intersection, if a place can be found to hide the plate, yet leave it exposed to the atmosphere. After the activity begins, have students predict what they will find each time they try a new location. Be sure to have them record their observations and their predictions as they continue.

Have your students think of ways to use numbers in comparing the amount of pollution collected on the various plates. Then graph the results, identifying the locations where the data were gathered. You might want to compare pollutants collected during the day with those gathered through the night, and perhaps areas near roadways during rush hours and non–rush hours.

Is there a local newspaper that might be interested in reporting the class project? If there are great differences in pollutants found from one area to another, discuss possible causes and perhaps even actions that might be taken for improvement. Such a class project can sometimes provide a meaningful service to the community.

Integrating

Math, language arts, social studies

Science Process Skills

Observing, inferring, classifying, measuring, predicting, communicating, comparing and contrasting, using space-time relationships, formulating hypotheses, identifying and controlling variables, experimenting, researching

How Does Our Water Become Polluted?

(Teacher-demonstration; advance preparation needed)

Materials Needed

- One clear two-liter plastic bottle with cap
- Scissors
- Drill, with $\frac{1}{8}$-inch bit or smaller
- Sandy soil
- Small package of punch powder
- 0.5 liter (1 pint) tap water

Preparation for Teachers

1. Using the scissors, cut the two-liter bottle into two sections, with the bottom section being slightly taller than the top.
2. Drill three or four drain holes in the cap, as shown in Figure 5.14–1.

Figure 5.14-1. Two-Liter Bottle Cut into Two Pieces

Ecology

3. With the cap on the bottle, insert the top of the bottle upside down into the bottom section. You now have a funnel with a catch basin. With the holes in the lid we'll call it a soil filter, because that's what we're going to use it for.

4. Fill the top part of your filter about half full of sandy soil. (See Figure 5.14–2.)

5. Place about half of the small package of punch powder on top of the soil, being very careful to avoid the edges and keep the powder toward the middle of the soil surface.

6. Add another 2 cm ($\frac{3}{4}$ in.) of soil, being sure the punch powder is well covered and not visible. The soil sample is now "contaminated" with punch powder.

7. Now you are ready to display and demonstrate the soil filter to your students.

   a. Ask students to predict what water would look like if it were allowed to flow through the soil. Record their predictions.

   b. Have someone slowly pour about 500 ml (2 cups) of tap water through the filter, as seen in Figure 5.14–3.

   c. Discuss observations and implications.

Figure 5.14–2. Sandy Soil in Top Portion of Bottle

Hands-On Earth Science Activities

Figure 5.14-3. Water Pollution

For Problem Solvers

Try to arrange for an interview with someone from your state's Division of Water Quality or from a local person responsible for water quality, such as your city mayor or the city engineer. Before you go for the interview, discuss with your class the questions you might ask. Write your questions and be well prepared. Find out what we, as citizens, can do to help take better care of our water supply.

Take good notes and/or record the interview, and report to the class. You might even be able to arrange for the person you interview to visit your class or your school.

Teacher Information

Sometimes people carelessly discard their waste by pouring it on the ground, in seemingly harmless places. Many people have discarded used oil or antifreeze, which they have drained from their automobiles, that way. Factories have, at times, similarly dumped their waste in out-of-the-way places, or even on their own property, where it would seem to harm no one. As long as it did not create an unsightly landscape, who would care? We now know that harmful materials from such carelessly discarded waste can leach into the ground and contaminate the water supply. Great quantities of runoff water from storms seeps through the ground and into underground water supplies. It eventually makes its way to rivers and lakes from which we get our water for drinking, bathing, cooking, and so forth. Much of the water we use for our personal needs has been filtered through the soil along the way to our homes, schools, and office buildings.

The purpose of this demonstration is to show how easy it is for pollutants to get through the soil and the importance of controlling the sources of those pollutants. Students will observe that "pollutants" (punch powder in this case) wash through the soil. How much gets through is affected somewhat by soil type, but no soil can filter out all of the harmful material we might dump on the ground.

Integrating

Math, language arts, social studies

Science Process Skills

Observing, inferring, classifying, measuring, predicting, communicating, comparing and contrasting, using space-time relationships, formulating hypotheses, identifying and controlling variables, experimenting, researching

How Can You Help an Ecosystem?

(Class discussion)

Materials Needed

- Group report materials from Activity 5.9
- Model of school "ecosystem" in Activity 5.10
- Newsprint
- Pencils

Procedure

1. This activity will take several days. Divide into the same groups you were in for Activity 5.9.

2. As a group, study the report you gave. Where do the problems you identified fit in the model of the school ecosystem?

3. If they are inside or close to the building, they are problems you can help solve.

4. Choose one simple problem (food waste in lunchroom, litter on school grounds, or a similar problem) and make a plan to help solve it. Discuss the plan with your teacher.

5. Contact the person in charge of the area where the problem exists and talk about your plan. Try to plan long-term solutions so the problem won't keep happening again.

6. Plan some way of reporting the results of your efforts.

7. What might happen if all people tried to solve little problems in the "ecosystems" in which they live?

Teacher Information

Following through with a plan of action is the most important segment of this series of activities. Research has shown that information has little effect on behavioral change unless it is translated into tangible action. This is especially important for students in the early and middle years.

Emphasize that it is more important to do something, rather than everything. Each individual can restore or preserve some small part of the ecosystem where he or she is.

Integrating

Language arts, social studies

Science Process Skills

Observing, communicating, using space-time relationships

How Can We Improve Our Environment?

(Teacher-conducted activity)

Materials Needed

- Tape recorder and tape with harsh noises
- Very interesting short story
- Paper
- Pencils

Procedure

1. Prepare a tape of loud music or noise of some kind.

2. Select a short but engrossing story appropriate to the age level of your students. A short video could be substituted.

3. As you reach the most interesting part of the story, turn the noise on loudly enough to drown out the narration.

4. Turn the sound off and finish the story.

5. Discuss the following:

   a. How did you feel when noise intruded on the story?

   b. Noise is a form of pollution.

   c. Noise is a health problem (ear damage can result from very loud music).

   d. Much noise pollution is unintentional. Some cannot be avoided. Think of examples of both kinds.

   e. How can personal awareness reduce noise pollution?

   f. If you want to listen to music in public, how can you do so without disturbing others?

   g. In a discussion with friends, do you occasionally talk more loudly so people will listen?

   h. Think of five people you like best. Are they noisy, average, or quiet people?

   i. Are you a listener or a talker, or do you do an equal amount of both?

j. How can you reduce your noise level? Do you need to?

k. How can you reduce the noise level around you?

l. Make an action plan of things you can do now to reduce noise pollution.

Teacher Information

This activity is the first of several to help students become aware of problems we face as we live together in a "human community."

Integrating

Language arts, social studies

Science Process Skills

Observing, inferring, classifying, communicating, using space-time relationships, formulating hypotheses, identifying and controlling variables

How Can We Involve Others?

Materials Needed

- Clean garbage cans or large wastebaskets
- Plastic drop cloths
- Paintbrushes
- Tempera paints

Procedure

1. We have seen that noise pollution and litter begin with individuals. Most people will attempt to control these problems if they become aware of them and are given help. Divide into small committees and find a clean wastebasket or garbage can.

2. Plan a picture or slogan to paint on the can to attract other people's attention. Remember, you want to attract attention and get people to use the garbage can.

3. Use bright tempera paint to decorate the can.

4. Put your can in a special place in the school to attract attention.

5. With your teacher, discuss the possibility of challenging another classroom, or even the whole school, to a wastebasket-decorating contest.

Teacher Information

Simple, brightly painted cans are best. Be sure you have the approval of your principal and custodian before undertaking this project.

This type of activity will be most effective if the focus is kept on the individual, such as by using the word "you" in the slogan.

Perhaps your PTA would be willing to offer a prize for the best garbage can (or better yet, all cans).

Integrating

Language arts, social studies, art

Science Process Skills

Observing, inferring, communicating, using space-time relationships

ACTIVITY 5.18

What Is a Wise Consumer?

(Take home and do with family and friends.)

Materials Needed

- Pictures of a modern grocery store or supermarket
- Paper
- Pencils

Procedure

1. With your teacher, plan a trip to a nearby grocery store.

2. Ask the store owner to show you some things sold in the store that could not be purchased twenty-five years ago, fifty years ago, and one hundred years ago. Find out how many products are biodegradable.

3. Make a four-column list of things available one hundred years ago, fifty years ago, twenty-five years ago, and today.

4. Look at the containers that new products come in. Ask the manager to tell you about them. Find out about sale dating.

5. When you return to your school, compare your lists. How has packaging improved our lives? How has modern food handling improved our lives? What effect have these had on ecology?

6. Would you be willing to give up the modern products to have a cleaner environment?

7. Can you think of ways you could help with this problem?

Teacher Information

A grocery store or even a neighborhood fast-food establishment or delicatessen can be a rich source for studies in many areas. Ecology, economics, merchandising, service, and courtesy are topics to be studied in most stores. Old-time general merchandise stores still exist in small communities. The suburban shopping center is simply the enlargement and modernization of the same concept. In large cities, the relationship of people to the manager of the local deli may be similar to that of the people in a small town to the owner of the general store.

332

Hands-On Earth Science Activities

Someone in your class may have a relative who owns or works in a grocery store. Make a personal visit in advance and leave a written list of specific topics you would like covered during the class visit.

Although the major topics will be packing, conservation, and food handling as related to ecology, watch for other learning opportunities for return visits.

Emphasize that the great benefits of modern packaging and handling also create additional problems in garbage disposal and littering.

Integrating

Language arts, social studies

Science Process Skills

Observing, inferring, communicating, comparing and contrasting, using space-time relationships

What Changes Have Happened Where You Live?

Materials Needed

- Two or three older people who have lived in your community for many years
- Paper
- Pencils
- Tape recorders

Procedure

1. Survey the class and identify two or three older people who have lived in your community for a long time.

2. As a class, make a list of questions you would like to ask these people about changes in the ecology of the region.

3. Contact the people and invite them to attend class and answer the questions. Be sure to ask them to bring old pictures or other items they may have to show. Emphasize that you are interested in changes in the physical environment of your community.

4. When your guests arrive, be prepared to ask specific questions about changes in ecology.

Teacher Information

Older people can be excellent sources of special information about your community. They often know of places in parks, yards of older homes, and even cemeteries where vestiges of the past still exist. Mutual, lasting bonds are often formed from these visits.

Integrating

Language arts, social studies

Science Process Skills

Observing, inferring, communicating, comparing and contrasting, using space-time relationships

Do You Conserve Your Resources Wisely?

(Total class discussion)

Materials Needed

- All clothing and other items from the school's "lost-and-found"
- Some item from home that is usable but that you have outgrown or no longer need or want
- Paper
- Pencils

Procedure

1. Look at the items in the school "lost-and-found" box. How many of the materials are still usable?
2. Why do you think they are there?
3. Can you think of a way to solve this problem?
4. Show the item you brought from home to the other class members.
5. Trade as many items as you can with other members of the class.
6. Perhaps some items left over could be used for another purpose.
7. Play the "What can you do with an old . . . ?" game. One person says, "What can you do with an old . . . ? and quickly holds up a leftover item. Everyone writes down as many things as he or she can think of in one minute. The one who has the longest list wins that item and has the chance to choose and hold up the next item. Continue this until everything is gone. At the end of class, if you really don't want the item you have won, give it to your decorated garbage can. It wants everything!
8. Return the lost-and-found items to the principal with any suggestions you have for their disposal.

For Problem Solvers

Many people have a lot of good-but-not-loved-any-more items. These things often remain unneeded and ignored for many years, while other people have need for those very things. Organize a project to help recycle unneeded articles. There are many things you can do. One possibility is to identify a central location where students can bring clean clothing and other usable items that are no longer needed, then present them to the local Salvation Army or other welfare organization. Perhaps the school could provide a place that could be used once a month, or whatever frequency seems appropriate. It might be appropriate for information to go out from the school, both advertising the project and inviting those in need to come in at a preset time and have first choice on things that would be useful to them. Use your creativity, considering the availability and need of such materials in your area, and be sure to involve the school PTA.

Teacher Information

Your school may have another solution for lost-and-found articles, or it may have been one of the problems you studied earlier when you developed the school as an ecosystem.

The purpose of this activity is to help students become aware of how much we, as consumers, waste. "Use it up, wear it out, make it do, or do without" was the slogan that many people lived by long ago. Today, in an age of plenty, it's easy for some to overlook the days before modern technology relieved much of the survival-level existence that was common in this country. In many parts of this country and in much of the world, survival-level living is still common. If you live or teach in such an area, this activity can have even more meaning.

Integrating

Language arts

Science Process Skills

Observing, inferring, classifying, measuring, predicting, communicating, comparing and contrasting, using space-time relationships, formulating hypotheses, identifying and controlling variables, experimenting, researching

How Can You Reuse Newspaper?

Materials Needed

- Newspapers
- Mixing bowls
- Wallpaper paste or liquid laundry starch
- Tables, boards, or cake pans
- Waxed paper
- Hand-operated eggbeaters
- Water
- Window screens
- Glass jars or drinking glasses

Procedure

1. Begin with a piece of newspaper about 30 cm (1 foot) square.
2. Cut or tear the newspaper into small pieces.
3. Place the pieces of paper in the mixing bowl, add a cup of water, and let it sit for a few minutes so the water will soak completely through the paper.
4. Churn the paper and water with the eggbeater until the paper is broken up into very small pieces and the mixture looks something like oatmeal.
5. Add one tablespoon of wallpaper paste or laundry starch. (If the wallpaper paste or starch is in powder form, mix it with a little water before adding it to the batch.)
6. Stir the mixture well.
7. Lay the window screen on a table, board, or inverted cake pan.
8. Spread the mixture into a thin layer on the screen.
9. Lay a sheet of waxed paper over the mixture and roll a fruit jar or a drinking glass over it to squeeze out the excess water.
10. Carefully remove the waxed paper and allow the mixture to dry. It will probably need a day or two.

Ecology

337

11. When the mixture is thoroughly dry, remove it from the screen carefully. You have made a usable product from waste material. The idea of reusing is called recycling.

12. Clean up the screen for use again.

For Problem Solvers

Organize a paper-recycling program for your school. Find out about a company in your area that buys (or at least accepts) used paper for recycling purposes. Arrange for them to pick up paper at your school periodically, or for someone to deliver the paper to them. Ask your teacher and principal to help you identify a location where all classes could deposit their used paper. The company that receives the paper might provide a collection bin.

Contact your local newspaper and tell them about your project. They might be willing to report it to the community.

Teacher Information

Much of the solid waste in the cities and towns of this nation consists of paper and paper products. Recycling of this material is an important industry and a worthy effort. Enough paper is recycled to save millions of trees each year. The paper produced by this activity is not exactly refined paper for your notebook, but it is definitely paper. Besides, it is done by the student, and the process is quite like that done on a larger scale by paper industries.

Integrating

Math, language arts, social studies, art

Science Process Skills

Observing, inferring, classifying, measuring, communicating, using space-time relationships, formulating hypotheses

Which Solids Decompose Easily?

Materials Needed

- Large, deep trays, such as suit boxes
- Plastic liner or plastic garbage bags
- Water
- Soil
- Samples of small items (solid waste) out of garbage cans
- Paper
- Pencils

Procedure

1. Line the box with the plastic.
2. Put a layer of soil about 3 to 5 cm (1 to 2 in.) deep in the bottom of the box. Spread it out so it is uniform.
3. Place your samples of solid waste around on top of the layer of soil.
4. Make a "map" on paper, showing which items you used and where they were placed on the tray.
5. Cover the items with another layer of soil about the same thickness as the first.
6. Sprinkle some water on it, enough to wet the soil.
7. Let the box sit for a period of four to six weeks. Sprinkle a little bit of water on it each day or so to keep the soil moist.
8. When the time period is up, remove the top layer of soil and check the samples.
9. Refer to your map so each item can be located easily. Record the amount of decomposition of each item.
10. Which items decomposed the most? What were they made of?
11. Which items decomposed the least? What were they made of?

Ecology

For Problem Solvers

Do the following project as a Science Investigation. Obtain a blank copy of the "Science Investigation Journaling Notes." Write your name, the date, and your question at the top. Plan your investigation through step 5 (Procedure) and have it approved by your teacher. Complete the Journaling Notes as you perform your investigation. Share your project with your group, and submit your Journaling Notes to your teacher if requested.

What type of material is most of our solid dry waste made of? What can we reuse, or even avoid using in the first place? To answer the first question, for both home and school, try this:

1. Make a list of common materials that are frequently put in the garbage, such as paper, plastic, glass, and so on.

2. Ask your school custodian which of these materials make up most of the garbage at school. List the materials in order of quantity, with the material that comprises most of the garbage at the top of the list. Estimate the number of pounds of each type of garbage discarded daily by the school. Perhaps your custodian would allow you or a member of your group to help empty the wastebaskets of the school for a day or two, so you can record types and amounts of garbage.

3. Ask each of your classmates to examine his or her garbage at home and make a similar list. Then compile all the lists into one, showing categories and estimated amounts of the most common garbage discarded at home.

4. Make a line graph or a bar graph that shows types and amounts of garbage discarded, both at school and at home.

5. Discuss your findings with your class. Use your information to estimate the amount of garbage discarded at school and at home in a week, a month, and a year. What type of material do we discard the most of? Is there something we should do to use less of it? Do we need to recycle more of our garbage? Could we use some of it for art creations, for useful containers, or can you think of other uses for it? Share your ideas and try to come up with a plan to reduce the amount of waste.

Hands-On Earth Science Activities

Teacher Information

The average solid waste in the United States has been estimated at about 5.3 pounds per person per day. Have some students use that rate to figure out the amount for your school, city, state, or nation. Much of this waste material is hauled to sanitary landfills and covered with soil. Sometimes it is crushed first. After it is covered with soil, bacteria and moisture begin their work of decomposing the material. However, some of the solids don't cooperate very well. Such materials are very difficult to completely dispose of. To keep our environment clean, materials that become garbage must either be recycled or decomposed.

This activity is to give students a way to find out which materials will decompose readily and which will not. Samples used should be small and thin. Students could use a tin can lid, a piece of aluminum foil, a toothpick, a piece of a plastic bottle, various types of paper and fabric, a rubber band, and so on. They also need to be very patient. Decomposing matter by natural means requires a lot of time. At least four to six weeks should be allowed in order for changes to be observed. For some materials, observable changes might require many years.

Integrating

Math, language arts, social studies, art

Science Process Skills

Observing, inferring, classifying, measuring, communicating, comparing and contrasting, using space-time relationships, formulating hypotheses

Ecology

How Can You Make a Water Treatment Plant?

Materials Needed

- Tin cans
- Two shallow cake pans
- Boards, slightly longer than the width of one pan
- Sand
- Small rocks
- Rubber or plastic tubing 45 cm (18 in.) long
- Metal punches
- Several books or sturdy boxes
- Muddy water

Procedure

1. Punch two or three small holes near the bottom of the can.
2. Wash the sand and the small rocks and be sure the can is clean.
3. Put sand in the can until it is about half full. Add small rocks until the can is about three-fourths full. This is the filter.
4. Place the board across the top of one of the pans and put the can on the board. The can should be placed so that the drain holes in the can are off one edge of the board for free drainage.
5. Put the other pan on a stack of books or other support so the bottom of it is slightly above the top of the can. This is the settling basin. (See Figure 5.23–1.)
6. Pour muddy water into the settling basin and let it settle for an hour or more.
7. Using the tubing as a siphon hose, siphon some of the water slowly from the settling basin to the filter and allow it the time needed to drain through the filter.
8. As the water drips out of the filter and into the pan, compare it with the water in the settling basin.

Figure 5.23-1. "Water Treatment Plant"

Settling basin

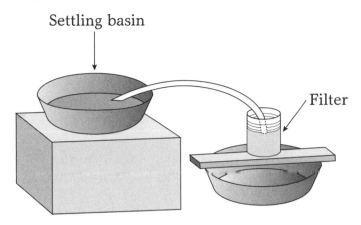

Filter

For Problem Solvers

Where does the water come from for your community? Is there a water treatment plant near you? Do some research and learn what you can about it. How does the plant work? Does it use chemicals, filters, bacteria? How much water do they process each day? How long does it take to process the water? How does the treated water get to your home and school?

How and where is wastewater from the community disposed of? If it is processed by a treatment plant, what could citizens do to make the task of the wastewater treatment plant easier and more successful? After you have studied answers to these questions, discuss them with your class. If action of individuals is needed in making the treatment process more effective, try to work up a plan to get that started. Representatives of your class could even meet with the city council or with individual city officials to seek their assistance and advice.

Teacher Information

Before beginning this activity, explain to the students that many cities use lakes and reservoirs for their culinary water supply. This water must be purified in order to make it safe for drinking and cooking. Water treatment plants are an important service to the people.

The water treatment plant constructed in this activity is a fairly effective system for filtering muddy water. If it has been constructed properly, water from the filter will be clear. Have students try filtering some salt water with it. They could test the purity of the salt water by tasting it or by evaporating a small amount of the filtered water from a jar to find out

Ecology

whether a salt residue remains in the jar. A similar amount of unfiltered salt water should be evaporated from another jar for comparison. Have students report what happens.

A field trip to a water treatment plant or a sewage plant would be timely and valuable in connection with this activity. If this is not possible, perhaps a note home suggesting such an outing for the family would result in some of the students having the experience.

Integrating

Math, reading, language arts, social studies

Science Process Skills

Observing, communicating, comparing and contrasting, using space-time relationships, formulating hypotheses, identifying and controlling variables, researching

What Have We Learned?

(Total-class activity)

Materials Needed

- Folders of materials developed during the ecology study
- Pictures, charts, and bulletin boards
- Resource persons

Procedure

1. As a class, plan an "awareness day" so you can share what you have learned with others.

2. Decide what you would like to show and how you will do it.

3. Who should be invited?

4. How can you involve and inform them?

5. To help you in your planning, consider the following ideas:

   a. Tell about the display, the notes, and the pictures you made as you studied ecology.

   b. Have a clothing (gloves, boots) exchange table.

   c. Make bumper stickers with "-ives" on them, such as "Dirt is abrasive, noise is intrusive, salt is corrosive."

   d. Display "new" things you have made out of "old" things.

   e. Create a "Lucy and Larry Litterbug" play. Record it on videotape and invite others to view it.

   f. Learn and sing some songs about ecology and a beautiful Earth.

   g. Serve school-grown foods.

   h. Make litter bags and give them to others to use.

   i. Display "prize-winning" wastebaskets and garbage cans.

   j. Invite resource people from the community to attend and display some of their materials.

   k. Show parts of a favorite video you used during your study.

   l. Think of more ideas to add to this list. Do them!

6. When this final activity is over, be sure you leave your environment neat and clean.

For Problem Solvers

Investigate "Earth Day." Find out what it is, and determine ways to extend class activities to coordinate with national Earth Day efforts.

Teacher Information

An "awareness day" will help the students organize the materials and reinforce what they have learned during the study.

Involvement of other people, parents, and classes will require the cooperation of your faculty and principal.

Integrating

Language arts, social studies, art

Science Process Skills

Observing, classifying, communicating

Can You Solve This Ecology Word Search?

Try to find the following Ecology terms in the grid below. They could appear in horizontal (left to right), vertical (up or down), or diagonal (upward or downward) position.

ecology	scavengers	decomposers
producers	consumers	primary
recycle	ecosystem	plant
energy	food web	food chain
conserve		

```
W   E   Y   F   O   O   D   C   H   A   I   N
R   E   R   T   D   Y   U   I   P   O   P   F
S   C   A   V   E   N   G   E   R   S   L   O
H   O   M   E   C   G   F   D   O   J   K   O
E   S   I   N   O   O   S   A   D   Z   E   D
C   Y   R   E   M   C   N   V   U   L   B   W
O   S   P   R   P   N   I   S   C   E   M   E
L   T   L   G   O   E   C   Y   E   A   C   B
O   E   A   Y   S   H   C   K   R   R   V   G
G   M   N   W   E   E   D   F   S   I   V   A
Y   O   T   F   R   A   S   D   E   T   I   E
E   C   O   N   S   U   M   E   R   S   N   A
```

Can You Create a New Ecology Word Search of Your Own?

Write your Ecology words in the grid below. Arrange them in the grid so they appear in horizontal (left to right), vertical (up or down), or diagonal (upward or downward) position. Fill in the blank boxes with other letters. Trade your Word Search with someone else who has created one of his or her own, and see whether you can solve the new puzzle.

_____   _____   _____

_____   _____   _____

_____   _____   _____

_____   _____   _____

_____   _____   _____

Answer Key for Ecology Word Search

```
W  E  Y  F  O  O  D  C  H  A  I  N
R  E  R  T  D  Y  U  I  P  O  P  F
S  C  A  V  E  N  G  E  R  S  L  O
H  O  M  E  C  G  F  D  O  J  K  O
E  S  I  N  O  O  S  A  D  Z  E  D
C  Y  R  E  M  C  N  V  U  L  B  W
O  S  P  R  P  N  I  S  C  E  M  E
L  T  L  G  O  E  C  Y  E  A  C  B
O  E  A  Y  S  H  C  K  R  R  V  B
G  M  N  W  E  E  D  F  S  I  V  A
Y  O  T  F  R  A  S  D  E  T  I  E
E  C  O  N  S  U  M  E  R  S  N  A
```

Date _____

Do You Recall?

Section Five: Ecology

1. Why are the various plants and animals in nature important to each other?

2. How is energy transferred in an ecosystem?

3. Why is it important that we use our natural resources wisely and keep our environment clean?

4. Why is it unwise to dump used oil and other liquid wastes on the ground?

5. What can you do to help take care of our environment?

Hands-On Earth Science Activities

Answer Key for Do You Recall?

Section Five: Ecology

Answer	Related Activities
1. Each one depends on certain others for survival.	5.1, 5.2, 5.3
2. Through the food web	5.4
3. Answers will vary.	5.11, 5.12, 5.22
4. They can get into our water supply.	5.13, 5.14
5. Answers will vary.	5.11–5.24

Above the Earth

To the Teacher

Suppose a small child at play on the beach at Kitty Hawk, North Carolina, had paused to watch the first flight of Orville and Wilbur Wright in December 1903. Less than sixty-six years later (July 20, 1969), that same individual could have watched on television as the first man walked on the moon. The incredible and fascinating story of flight above the earth is introduced in this section.

To help students understand and appreciate the progress of the human race in the 20th century, a brief background is presented as Activity 6.1. You are invited to read and discuss it with your class. Tape-record it for small-group discussions, have it read individually, or, if you prefer, choose an alternate method with your librarian or media specialist.

Learning to simulate controlled flight can be exciting and enjoyable. You may even find yourself helping to build a large cardboard mock-up of a pilot's cockpit with simulated controls. (If, as a result of these activities, you decide to fly a real airplane or space ship, we strongly recommend that you take additional lessons first.)

The following activities are offered to help you and your students learn about our remarkable progress in the quest to move into the unknown, and perhaps to challenge some of you to dream of what lies beyond.

The following activities are designed as discovery activities that students can usually perform quite independently. You are encouraged to provide students (usually in small groups) with the materials listed and a copy of the activity from the beginning through the "Procedure." The section titled "Teacher Information" is not intended for student use, but rather to assist you with discussion following the hands-on activity, as students share their observations. Discussion of conceptual information prior to completing the hands-on activity can interfere with the discovery process.

Regarding the Early Grades

With verbal instructions and slight modifications, many of these activities can be used with kindergarten, first-grade, and second-grade students. In some activities, steps that involve procedures that go beyond the level of the child can simply be omitted and yet offer the child an experience that plants the seed for a concept that will germinate and grow later on.

Teachers of the early grades will probably choose to bypass many of the "For Problem Solvers" sections. That's okay. These sections are provided for those who are especially motivated and want to go beyond the investigation provided by the activity outlined. Use the outlined activities, and enjoy worthwhile learning experiences together with your young students. Also consider, however, that many of the "For Problem Solvers" sections can be used appropriately with young children as group activities or as demonstrations, still giving students the advantage of an exposure to the experience and laying groundwork for connections that will be made at a later time.

Correlation with National Standards

The following elements of the National Standards are reflected in the activities of this section.

K–4   Content Standard A: Science as Inquiry

As a result of activities in grades K–4, all students should develop

1. Abilities necessary to do scientific inquiry
2. Understanding about scientific inquiry

Hands-On Earth Science Activities

K–4   Content Standard D: Earth and Space Science

As a result of activities in grades K–4, all students should develop understanding of

1. Properties of earth materials
2. Objects in the sky
3. Changes in earth and sky

5–8   Content Standard A: Science as Inquiry

As a result of activities in grades 5–8, all students should develop

1. Abilities necessary to do scientific inquiry
2. Understanding about scientific inquiry

5–8   Content Standard D: Earth and Space Science

As a result of activities in grades 5–8, all students should develop understanding of

1. Structure of the earth system
2. Earth's history
3. Earth in the solar system

What Is the History of Flight?

Materials Needed

- Story of flight

Procedure

Read the story below and discuss it with your classmates.

"One small step for man. One giant leap for mankind!" Neil Armstrong's famous words as he took his first step on the moon marked an end and a beginning for man's desire to fly above the earth and beyond.

From earliest times, human beings have seemed to want to follow the birds. We know there was at least one species of dinosaur that could fly (pterosaur) and an early ancestor of the modern feathered bird, called Archaeopteryx. Myths, legends, and folklore tell of our continuing interest, and sometimes passion, to fly. A famous Greek legend tells about a boy named Icarus whose father gave him wings of feathers held together with wax to help him escape from his enemies. The wings worked, but while Icarus was flying he became careless and daring and flew too close to the sun. The sun's heat melted the wax that was holding the feathers together and Icarus fell into the sea.

For many centuries, people attempted to imitate birds by using their own muscles to power larger and larger wings. Near the end of the 15th century, a famous artist and inventor, Leonardo da Vinci, drew plans and pictures of a man-powered machine for flight. There is no record that his design was ever constructed or tested.

For another three hundred years, birds, bats, insects, a few fish, and squirrels (flying) continued to be the only animals capable of rising above the earth's surface. The attempts of people to rise above the earth, using muscles as power, continued to fail time after time. People were too heavy, and their arms and legs were too weak.

Late in the 18th century, a Frenchman named Joseph Montgolfier watched burned ashes of paper rising above a fire and suddenly had an idea. Although he did not understand why hot air rises, he made a small bag of silk, built a fire under it, and watched it fly away. Later, he and his brother constructed a large balloon, built a fire under it, and it lifted a man above the earth for the first time. Soon afterward, balloons filled

with hydrogen gas were developed. The scientific principle of displacement used in "lighter than air" ballooning had been discovered by a Greek scientist, Archimedes, in about 300 B.C.

Ballooning became popular as a sport. Some practical uses were developed for balloons, but because they were so fragile and difficult to control, their use did not become widespread. People still studied birds for an answer to practical flight.

Near the beginning of the 19th century, an Englishman named George Cayley discovered the first principles that would lead to controlled flight as we know it today. By watching birds, Cayley realized they work very hard to get into the air, but once airborne, most were able to glide and fly using very little energy. Cayley became interested in how, for many birds, staying in the air required so little effort. He decided something must be holding them up. Using information about the pressure of moving air, Cayley was able to design and build the first successful glider that soared above the earth. Late in the 19th century, a German engineer named Otto Lilienthal developed methods to control glider flight, and controlled power flight became a possibility.

Before people could fly under power, they needed a simple, lightweight source of energy. Steam engines used in the 19th century were too heavy. Attempts to use them for powered flight always failed and often ended in disaster. The small, lightweight internal combustion (gasoline) engine seemed to offer a possible alternative to muscle power, which was not strong enough, and steam, which was not light enough.

At the beginning of the 20th century, American brothers Orville and Wilbur Wright began experimenting with gliders on a windy beach at Kitty Hawk, North Carolina. On December 17, 1903, the first powered flight was made. Human beings had finally learned how to control and power flight.

Since that time, progress has been rapid. Air flight was adapted to transportation, communication, and even warfare. During the 1930s and 1940s, a different source of power, rocket energy, was introduced and developed. For many centuries the Chinese, Greeks, and others had known about rocket propulsion, but it was not until the middle of the 20th century that it was seriously studied as energy for manned flight.

In 1957, the Russians put a small satellite, named Sputnik, in orbit around the earth. The first rocket-powered space flight came soon after.

For the next ten years, step-by-step, flight after flight, test after test, human beings gradually climbed the ladder to the moon. Who knows what lies beyond?

Someday, some of you may follow the countless generations of people who wanted to fly. You are the astronauts, the explorers of the future!

Teacher Information

Have your students read this story or read it to them. You may want to come back to the story as you proceed through this section.

Before beginning these activities, you might want to review the activities in Section One that deal with Bernoulli's Principle and those that deal with the rising of warm air.

Integrating

Language arts, social studies

Science Process Skills

Communicating, comparing and contrasting, using space-time relationships

What Is a Wind Tunnel?

(Teacher-supervised activity)

Materials Needed

- Variable-speed fans
- Cardboard boxes with dividers (boxes must be larger than fans)
- Rulers
- Utility knives
- Paper

Procedure

1. For the following activities, you will need a controlled source of wind. Scientists and engineers use wind tunnels to test air currents around shapes they design. Remove the top of the cardboard box and lay the box on its side.

2. Measure the diameter of the fan and cut a hole in the bottom of the box about the same size. This will control the air from the fan and conduct it through the box.

3. Put the fan behind the box and turn it on. (See Figure 6.2–1.)

4. Holding a flat piece of paper by the edges, move it in front of the box.

5. If the paper behaves the same as the one you used to test Bernoulli's Principle (see unit on the topic of "Air"), your wind tunnel is a success!

Figure 6.2-1. Wind Tunnel Model

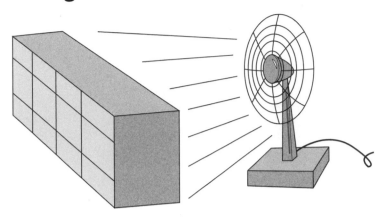

For Problem Solvers

Study about wind tunnels. What does a real wind tunnel look like? How is it used? What kind of information do scientists and engineers learn from using a wind tunnel?

Teacher Information

For the following activities, you will need to borrow several fans and make several wind tunnels. Box fans are designed to be a type of wind tunnel, but because of their size, they often produce too much air. Eight- to twelve-inch fans with variable speeds are ideal. If they oscillate, there is usually an adjustment to stop the back-and-forth movement. Boxes with many small dividers, such as those made for pint or quart jars, are better than ones designed to hold gallon containers.

Integrating

Math, reading, language arts, social studies, art

Science Process Skills

Observing, inferring, measuring, predicting, communicating, formulating hypotheses, identifying and controlling variables, experimenting, researching

How Does Shape Affect Lift?

Materials Needed

- 5-inch by 7-inch index cards
- Cellophane tape
- Pencils
- Wind tunnels
- Fans

Procedure

1. Bend two cards slightly in the middle and tape them together.
2. Put a pencil between them.
3. Hold the pencil supporting the cards in front of the wind tunnel. Turn on the fan. (See Figure 6.3–1.)
4. What happened?
5. Use other cards bent in different shapes to see which works best.
6. Arrange your designs in order, from most effective to least effective, according to their tendency to *lift* in the air stream in front of the wind tunnel. Number them from best to worst.
7. Compare and discuss your findings with your teacher and classmates.

Figure 6.3–1. Pencil and Cards in Front of Wind Tunnel

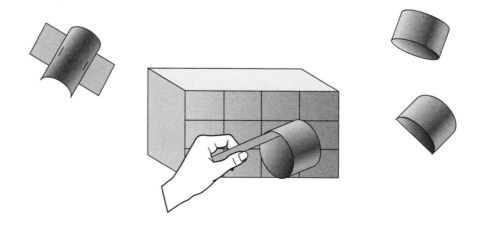

Teacher Information

This idea was introduced as Bernoulli's Principle in the unit on "Air." Cayley discovered this same idea by watching birds.

As air moves over a curved surface, it goes faster, thereby reducing the pressure. A curved surface on the top of a wing reduces the air pressure above it, resulting in lift.

Integrating

Math, art

Science Process Skills

Observing, inferring, classifying, measuring, predicting, communicating, comparing and contrasting, formulating hypotheses, identifying and controlling variables, experimenting

How Can You Build a Simple Glider?

(Take home and do with family and friends.)

Materials Needed

- Strips of oak tag 20 cm long by 8 cm wide (8 in. by 3 in.)
- Two long, thin rubber bands
- Pencils

Procedure

1. Use the patterns in Figure 6.4–1 to cut two wings from the oak tag.
2. Fold the ends of the tail up and use a rubber band to attach it near one end of the pencil.
3. Use the other rubber band to attach the wing near the opposite end of the pencil.
4. Slide the wing back and forth until the middle of the pencil will balance on the side of your index finger.
5. If your glider looks like the illustration, it is ready for the wind tunnel test.

Figure 6.4–1. Pattern for Glider

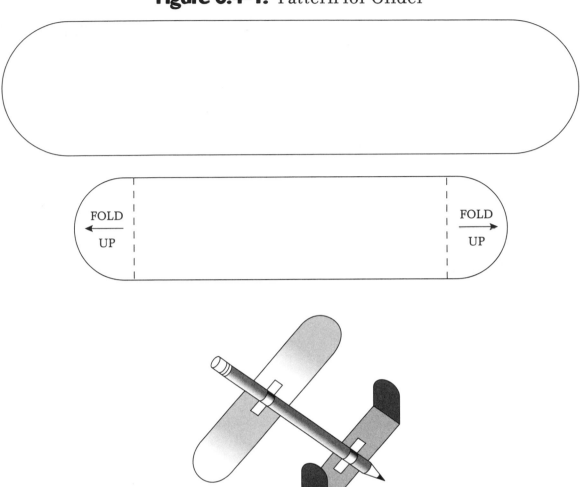

Teacher Information

You may need to help the children attach the wings to the gliders. Use hexagonal-sided pencils so the wing and tail will align easily.

Integrating

Math, art

Science Process Skills

Observing, inferring, measuring, predicting, communicating, comparing and contrasting

Will Your Airplane Soar?

(Take home and do with family and friends.)

Materials Needed

- Paper airplane
- String 60 cm (24 in.) long
- Cellophane tape
- Wind tunnel
- Fan

Procedure

1. As they are being designed, new airplanes are tested in some type of wind tunnel. Use cellophane tape to attach the ends of the string to the front and rear of your plane, as shown in Figure 6.5-1.

Figure 6.5-1. Glider with String Attached

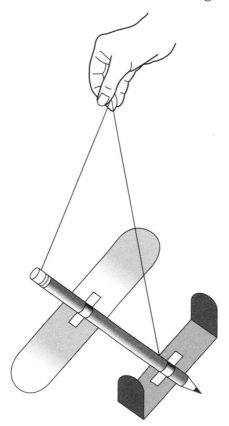

2. Hold the string so your plane is level and balanced. You may have to change the position of your hand on the string and adjust the wing until it is balanced.

3. Turn the fan on low speed and carefully move your airplane in front of the wind tunnel. What happened?

4. Twist the string to the right. Twist the string to the left. Move your hand so the nose of the plane turns up. Move your hand so the nose turns down.

5. How can you describe the behavior of your plane in the wind?

Teacher Information

If it is carefully balanced and aligned, the airplane will face the wind tunnel and maintain steady flight. Twisting the string will not turn the model because air passing the upright "rudders" on the tail section will hold it in line.

Lowering or raising the nose of the plane will cause broad, flat surfaces to be exposed to the wind, and it may spin out of control.

The purpose of this wind tunnel activity is to help children realize that gliders need more than a wing and a tail if they are to be controlled.

Integrating

Math, art

Science Process Skills

Observing, inferring, measuring, predicting, communicating, comparing and contrasting, using space-time relationships, formulating hypotheses, identifying and controlling variables, experimenting

ACTIVITY 6.6

How Can We Turn Our Gliders?

(Take home and do with family and friends.)

Materials Needed

- Wind tunnel and fan
- Glider from Activity 6.5
- Scissors
- Rulers
- Newsprint
- Pencils
- Blank copies of the "Science Investigation Journaling Notes" for all students

Procedure

1. Do the following activity using the "Science Investigation Journaling Notes." Obtain a blank copy of the form, then put your name, the date, and your question at the top. Plan your investigation through step 5 of the Journaling Notes and have it approved by your teacher. Complete the Journaling Notes as you perform your investigation. Share your project with your group, and submit your Journaling Notes to your teacher if requested.

2. Measure and carefully cut control surfaces in your glider, as shown in Figure 6.6–1. Cut along dotted lines.

Figure 6.6–1. Glider Showing Ailerons, Rudders, and Elevators

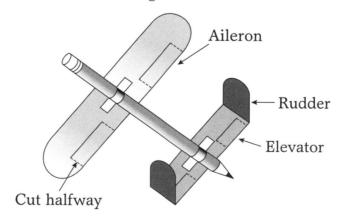

Aileron

Rudder

Elevator

Cut halfway

3. Follow the solid lines to bend the rear sections of both rudders to the left. Hold your glider in front of the wind tunnel. What happened?

4. Try step 3 again, bending your rudders to the right. On your paper, draw pictures of the glider showing right and left rudders.

5. Straighten the rudders. Bend the left aileron down along the solid line and the right one up. Hold your glider in front of the wind tunnel. What happened?

6. Reverse the ailerons and try it again. Make two pictures of your glider showing what happened when you used the ailerons.

7. Find the best combination of rudders and ailerons to make your glider turn smoothly.

Teacher Information

Rudders turn the glider left and right on a flat plane. Ailerons cause the wings to tilt or bank. With careful adjustment, the students should realize that a combination of banking with the ailerons and turning with the rudder will result in a smooth turn pattern.

Integrating

Math, art

Science Process Skills

Observing, inferring, measuring, predicting, communicating, comparing and contrasting, using space-time relationships, formulating hypotheses, identifying and controlling variables, experimenting

How Can We Make Our Gliders Go Up and Down?

(Take home and do with family and friends.)

Materials Needed

- Wind tunnel and fan
- Glider from Activity 6.5
- Scissors
- Rulers
- Newsprint
- Pencils
- Blank copies of the "Science Investigation Journaling Notes" for all students

Procedure

1. Do the following activity using the "Science Investigation Journaling Notes." Obtain a blank copy of the form, then put your name, the date, and your question at the top. Plan your investigation through step 5 of the Journaling Notes and have it approved by your teacher. Complete the Journaling Notes as you perform your investigation. Share your project with your group, and submit your Journaling Notes to your teacher if requested.

2. Be sure the ailerons and rudder are straight. Test your glider in the wind tunnel to be sure it flies level and straight.

3. Remove your glider from the wind tunnel. Bend both elevators on the tail up.

4. Hang the loop of string attached to your glider over your index finger. Carefully move the glider in front of the wind tunnel. What happened?

5. Can you predict what will happen when you bend the elevators down? Try it.

6. Draw a side view of the glider showing what happens when you turn the elevators up and down.

7. Your glider now has the basic controls found in a real airplane.

Teacher Information

Elevators use wind to push the tail up or down, thereby causing the nose of the glider to move in the opposite direction. If the tail goes down, the nose goes up (climb); tail up, nose down (descend). Too much tilt in the elevators will cause a stall (nose too high) or a dive (nose too low).

The following activities are designed to see how well children understand flight controls.

Integrating

Math, art

Science Process Skills

Observing, inferring, measuring, predicting, communicating, comparing and contrasting, using space-time relationships, formulating hypotheses, identifying and controlling variables, experimenting

What Have We Learned About Flying?

Materials Needed

- Student sketches of gliders from Activities 6.6 and 6.7
- Pencils

Procedure

1. Study the pictures of the three aircraft illustrated in Figures 6.8–1, 6.8–2, and 6.8–3. In each of the pictures, the pilot is moving a control that will make a change in the position of the airplane.

2. Use the sketches of your glider that you made in Activities 6.6 and 6.7 to identify what is happening in each figure.

3. Draw arrows on each figure showing what will happen to the aircraft.

4. Compare your answers with those of others in the class. If your arrows were correct, you are ready to try a solo flight.

Figure 6.8–1. Aileron Control Movement

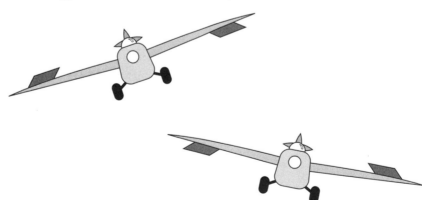

Figure 6.8-2. Rudder Control Movement

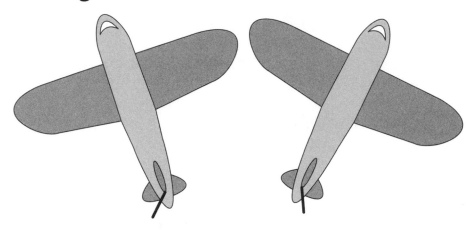

Figure 6.8-3. Elevator Control Movement

For Problem Solvers

Do you know how movements are controlled on a real airplane? Do some research and learn all you can about it. Look in your encyclopedia and other books. Try to talk to a pilot. How do the controls on a real airplane compare with the ones you have been using to control the movements of your glider? Share your information with your teacher and with your class.

Teacher Information

In Figure 6.8-1, the lowered aileron will force the wing upward. The arrows should point in the direction the aircraft is tilting. In Figure 6.8-2, the rudder forms a flat surface to push the tail in the opposite direction. Figure 6.8-3 shows the flat surface of the elevator turned down, forcing the tail up and the nose down, and vice versa. The figures show the aircraft in the middle of the maneuver. The arrows should point in the same direction as the aircraft appears to be moving.

Hands-On Earth Science Activities

Integrating

Math, art

Science Process Skills

Observing, inferring, measuring, predicting, communicating, comparing and contrasting, using space-time relationships, formulating hypotheses, identifying and controlling variables, experimenting

What Aircraft Will You Fly?

Materials Needed

- Copies of Figure 6.9–1 for all students
- Pieces of oak tag 20 cm long by 8 cm wide (8 in. by $3\frac{1}{2}$ in.)
- Pieces of oak tag 8 cm long by 5 cm wide ($3\frac{1}{2}$ in. by 2 in.)
- Pieces of oak tag 5 cm by 5 cm (2 in. by 2 in.)
- Pencils with eraser
- Staplers
- Rubber cement
- Rulers
- Scissors
- Long, thin rubber bands

Procedure

1. Shown in Figure 6.9–1 is a small picture of a larger "swept-wing supersonic" glider you can build. Look at the picture as you do the next steps.

2. Put the longest strip of oak tag across your desk. Put a dot in the center of the top, 10 cm (4 in.) from each corner.

3. From the bottom of each side, measure up 2 cm ($\frac{3}{4}$ in.) and put a dot.

4. Use your ruler to draw lines from the dots on the sides to the dot in the center. This is the leading edge of the wing of your glider.

5. From the center top, measure down 5 cm (2 in.) and put a dot. Draw a line from each bottom corner to the dot. If your outline of a wing is similar to the one shown here, cut it out. Cut ailerons in each wing 2 cm ($\frac{3}{4}$ in.) from the end, 3 cm (1 in.) long.

6. Use the larger of the other two pieces of oak tag to make the tail section. Follow the same steps as you did to make the wing. The center top will be 4 cm ($1\frac{1}{2}$ in.) from each end. Measure up 2 cm ($\frac{3}{4}$ in.) on each side and connect the dots to make the front edge. Measure down 3 cm (1 in.) from the top center to make the center of the trailing edge. From this dot, draw lines to the lower corners. Cut your tail out and cut movable tabs in it for the elevators.

7. Put the small piece of oak tag under one half of the tail. Trace it, cut it out, and make a tab in it. This will be the rudder.

8. Staple the tail to a flat side of the bare end of the pencil.

9. Use rubber cement to glue the rudder upright on top of the tail.

10. Use the rubber band to secure the wing near the eraser end of the pencil.

11. Move the wing forward or backward until the tips of the leading edges of the wing will balance on your outstretched index fingers.

12. Without moving any of the controls, try your plane in a very gentle glide. Adjust the wing position until it glides smoothly.

13. Test each of your controls, one at a time, to be sure they work properly.

14. If everything works, you are ready to demonstrate how well you can fly.

Teacher Information

Build and test a glider first before giving exact wing and tail measurements. You may prefer to increase the wing size. Exact measurements are not critical. The important factors will be balance and the ratio of wing and tail surfaces to weight. Bodies made of balsa wood or rolled oak tag weigh less but are not as sturdy and may need extra weight in the front.

If you, the students, or the parents have different "favorite" paper airplane designs, construct them. The only requirement should be that all aircraft have the three fundamental controls. Parental input should be limited to supplying interest, encouragement, and perhaps some assistance with the design, allowing the child credit for the major design and construction.

Integrating

Math, art

Science Process Skills

Observing, inferring, measuring, predicting, communicating, comparing and contrasting, using space-time relationships, formulating hypotheses, identifying and controlling variables, experimenting

Figure 6.9-1. Model for Swept-Wing Glider

Rubber band

Aileron

Pencil

Elevator · Rudder

How Well Can You Fly?

(Take home and do with family and friends.)

Materials Needed

- Gliders constructed in Activity 6.9
- String 10 m (10 yd.) long
- Large balls

Procedure

1. Now that you have the knowledge and an aircraft, let's see how well you can fly. Choose a wide, flat area either indoors or outside.
2. Put a large ball in the center of your area.
3. With one end of the string under the ball, make several spirals around the ball with the string. (See Figure 6.10–1.)
4. The spirals are your landing area, and the ball is your target.
5. Stand at least 10 meters (10 yards) away and try to land your airplane near the target. Remember, you should analyze each flight and make adjustments in your controls for the next flight.
6. Each time you hit the target, move back 5 meters (5 yards) and try again.
7. Have your teacher time you for 10 minutes.
8. At the end of the time, the pilots who are standing the greatest distance away are the "aces."

Figure 6.10–1. Illustration of Target and Landing Area

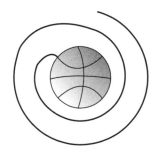

Teacher Information

This "just-for-fun" activity should help to motivate students to prepare for the skill and creativity needed for Activities 6.11 and 6.12.

Integrating

Math, art

Science Process Skills

Observing, inferring, measuring, predicting, communicating, comparing and contrasting, using space-time relationships, formulating hypotheses, identifying and controlling variables, experimenting

Can You Create an Airplane of a New Design?

Materials Needed

- Oak tag
- Construction paper
- Writing paper
- Pencils with erasers
- Staplers
- Rubber cement
- Rulers
- Scissors
- Long, thin rubber bands

Procedure

1. Now that you have constructed airplanes, tested them, and learned some ways to control the flight pattern, create your own airplane design.

2. Draw your airplane design on paper, then get the materials you need and build it.

3. Your airplane may look very different from anything you have seen. It might surprise even you to find out what it really turns out to be. Still, you will benefit from what you have learned about controlling movement in flight.

4. Work with a partner if you wish.

5. When you are finished, display your airplane with those of the rest of your class. Have each person share his or her airplane and explain what special things the airplane is designed to do.

Teacher Information

This is an opportunity for students to apply what they have learned about airplanes in a creative way. When the finished products are ready, it will be a good time to invite other classes, parents, and others to come and see what students have made. If it can be arranged for each student to stay with his or her model during display time, it would be a valuable experience for the students to explain their designs to visitors.

Integrating

Math, language arts, art

Science Process Skills

Observing, classifying, measuring, predicting, communicating, comparing and contrasting, identifying and controlling variables, experimenting

How Will You Design an Airplane for a Special Task?

Materials Needed

- Oak tag
- Construction paper
- Writing paper
- Pencils with erasers
- Stapler
- Rubber cement
- Rulers
- Scissors
- Long, thin rubber bands

Procedure

1. Prepare for a contest in airplane design.
2. First, decide what you want the airplanes to be specialized for: distance, accuracy at hitting a target, banking left, banking right, flying loops, and so on.
3. Decide whether you are going to work in teams of two, small groups, individually, or if all are to decide for themselves.
4. Draw out your design on paper.
5. Get the materials you need and construct your airplane using the design you drew.
6. When everyone is finished, test all the airplanes to see which one is best at the specialization that was selected.
7. Examine the differences carefully and find out why one particular design was best, so everyone can learn from it.
8. Repeat the activity. As a group, decide whether to target the same specialization or to choose a new one.
9. Always remember to learn from each other, as you see certain design characteristics that seem to work better than others.

Teacher Information

This is another opportunity for students to apply what they have learned about airplanes in a creative way. Emphasize the importance of being supportive with each other and learning from each other. The person who learns the most and does the best job of helping others to learn is the winner in ways that matter most of all.

A visit from a pilot (with visuals), a movie, or a field trip to an airport would be appropriate enrichment activities. The next series of investigations will help students begin a space adventure.

Integrating

Math, language arts, art

Science Process Skills

Observing, classifying, measuring, predicting, communicating, comparing and contrasting, identifying and controlling variables, experimenting

Hands-On Earth Science Activities

How Can a Ball Help You Move?

Materials Needed

- Heavy ball (such as a medicine ball) or a big rock
- Skateboard (or roller skates or in line skates)
- Masking tape

Procedure

1. Stand on the skateboard. Be sure you are on a smooth, flat surface.
2. Have a friend mark the spot (with small piece of tape) where the back rollers of your skateboard touch the floor and then have the friend stand in front of you, no closer than 2 meters (2 yards).
3. Hold the ball in both hands close to your chest. Throw it to your friend with a pushing motion.
4. Mark the position of the back rollers of your skateboard.
5. Repeat steps 3 and 4 several times.
6. What happened? What can you say about this?

For Problem Solvers

Find some objects to throw that are different weights. Be sure they are objects that you can throw and catch without hurting anyone and that the objects won't be damaged if they are dropped on the ground. Do the activity again, but this time recording the weight of the object each time, as well as the distance the skateboard moves. Compare the distance with the weight of the object thrown. Does it seem to make a difference? Graph your information.

Find an object you can throw that is a different weight from all your other objects. From the information you now have, predict how far the skateboard will move as you throw this object. Try it several times and find the average distance. Was your prediction accurate, or close?

Teacher Information

Each time the person on the skateboard throws the ball in one direction (action), he or she will move in the opposite direction (reaction). Newton stated this principle as his third law of motion: "For every action there is an equal and opposite reaction."

The student throwing the ball will not move the same distance as the ball travels due to such factors as friction and the fact that the person is bigger and heavier than the ball. However, each time the ball is thrown in one direction, the person on the skateboard will move an observable and measurable distance in the opposite direction.

Your problem solvers will do some scientific research comparing the effect of the weight of the thrown object. If no one in the group is sensitive about his or her weight, it would be interesting to use the weight of the person on the skateboard as another variable in the experiment.

Integrating

Math, language arts

Science Process Skills

Observing, inferring, measuring, predicting, communicating, comparing and contrasting, formulating hypotheses, identifying and controlling variables, experimenting

What Type of Energy Is This?

(Teacher-supervised activity)

Materials Needed

- Metal cans
- Large nails
- Hammers
- Heavy string 1 m (1 yd.) long
- Fishing swivels
- Scissors
- Sink
- Water

Procedure

1. Use the hammer and nail to punch four holes at equal distances around the can near the bottom edge. Drive the nail in at a steep angle so the holes appear semicircular. Be sure all holes point in the same direction.

2. Make three small holes around the top of the can (large enough for string).

3. Cut the string into four 25-cm (10-in.) lengths.

4. Tie one end of the string to one end of the fishing swivel. Tie the other three strands to the other end of the swivel.

5. Thread each of the three strings through a hole in the top of the can and tie them securely. (See Figure 6.14–1.)

6. Hold your can by the string over the sink at arm's length and have someone else pour water into it.

7. What happened? Do your best to explain why?

Figure 6.14-1. Can with Holes Rotating on Strings

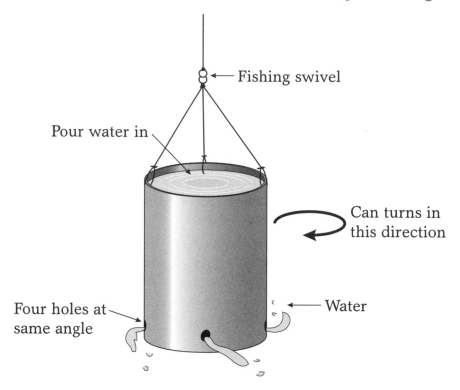

Fishing swivel

Pour water in

Can turns in this direction

Four holes at same angle

Water

Teacher Information

This principle was discovered by a Greek named Heron of Alexandria nearly 2,000 years ago. (Check the encyclopedia or the Internet.)

There are other ways of helping children discover the principle of action-reaction (for every action there is an equal and opposite reaction). One is to put an air gun (without the BB) on a roller skate. Each time the air gun is fired in one direction, the skate and gun will move in the opposite direction (recoil). A plastic medicine bottle with a snap top (not safety top) may be placed on round pencils as rollers. Put a mixture of bicarbonate of soda and vinegar in the bottle and snap on the top. CO_2 gas will form inside the bottle, pop the top off, and move the bottle along the pencil rollers in the opposite direction of the popped cap. (*Note:* This demonstration can get messy!)

Integrating

Math, language arts

Science Process Skills

Observing, inferring, measuring, predicting, communicating, comparing and contrasting

What Can a Marble Game Teach Us?

Materials Needed

- Half-inch garden hose cut in half lengthwise, 2 m (2 yd.) long (or transparent tubing)
- Marbles
- Two chairs

Procedure

1. Bend the half hose, open side up, into a nearly U-shape between two chairs. (See Figure 6.15–1.)

Figure 6.15-1. Garden Hose Between Two Chairs

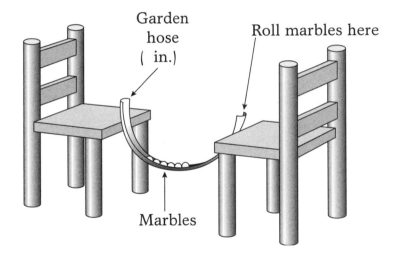

Garden hose (in.)

Roll marbles here

Marbles

2. Put six marbles in the lowest part of the hose. Be sure they move freely.
3. While observing the marbles resting in the bottom of the hose, release one marble in the groove at the top of the hose. What happened?
4. Release two marbles at exactly the same time at the top of the groove. What happened at the bottom?

5. Try releasing different numbers of marbles. What happened? Can you explain why? Can you predict what would happen if you had more marbles?

6. What will happen if you have two marbles at the bottom and release three at the top? Try it.

Teacher Information

If you can obtain small ball bearings (round wheel bearings) and plastic or rubber tubing in half-meter lengths, each student can construct this project. This is another investigation of action-reaction. When one marble is released in the groove at the top, it will roll down and strike the end marble in the row at the bottom. The marble at the opposite end of the row will move up the hose on the opposite side. If two marbles strike the row on one side, two will move away on the opposite side. If more marbles strike the row than there are marbles at rest, the nearest moving marble(s) will continue on with the ones set in motion.

Note: Lengths of foam pipe insulation can be obtained from stores that carry plumbing supplies. They are typically pre-split to accommodate installing around water pipe and can easily be cut in half lengthwise. These work well for this activity.

Integrating

Math

Science Process Skills

Observing, inferring, predicting, communicating, comparing and contrasting, identifying and controlling variables

How Can We Use Action-Reaction?

Materials Needed

- Long balloons
- Paper bags (large enough to contain blown-up balloon)
- Masking tape
- Monofilament fishing line, at least 2 m (3 ft.) longer than the classroom is wide
- Plastic drinking straws
- Paper
- Pencils

Procedure

1. Inflate a long balloon and release it. On your paper, write a description of its path of flight.

2. The balloon uses the principle of action-reaction to move. Can you explain how it works? Make a picture of an inflated balloon with air coming out. Draw arrows showing the direction of the action and of the reaction.

3. Look at the words you used to describe the path of the balloon's first flight. Try the following to correct the problems.

4. Thread the fishing line through the drinking straw and anchor the fishing line on opposite sides of your classroom, stretching it fairly tight across the room. Tape the paper bag to the straw, parallel with the fishing line.

5. Slide the bag and straw to the center of the line and put a long, inflated balloon in the open bag. You might need to inflate the balloon with the balloon already in the bag. (See Figure 6.16–1.)

6. Release the neck of the balloon. What happened?

7. Pretend your paper bag is a rocket ship and the balloon is a powerful rocket engine. What could you do to improve its flight? Test your ideas.

Figure 6.16–1. Paper Bag with Balloon in It

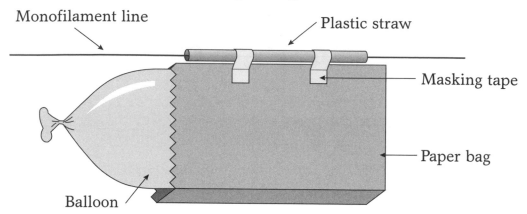

Monofilament line

Plastic straw

Masking tape

Paper bag

Balloon

Teacher Information

The balloon acts as a simple reaction (rocket) engine. When it is released by itself, its flight will be very erratic or unpredictable.

The monofilament line, straw, and paper bag provide housing, control, and direction for the thrust of the rocket engine. These are three essentials needed for space travel.

While students are experimenting to obtain greater speed and distance, you might suggest trying different-sized tubes as nozzles for the exhaust end of the rockets. Will a smaller opening (barrel of old ballpoint pen) make greater distances possible? Should the opening at the end of the balloon be larger (copper pipe)? How can you get both greater speed and greater distance (less mass, larger engine)?

Integrating

Math, language arts

Science Process Skills

Observing, inferring, predicting, communicating, comparing and contrasting

How Can You Make a Soda Straw Rocket?

(Take home and do with family and friends.)

Materials Needed

- Two-liter plastic soda bottles
- Large drinking straws
- Standard-sized drinking straws
- Modeling clay

Procedure

1. Insert the large straw into the bottle and seal around it at the mouth of the bottle with clay. (See Figure 6.17–1.)
2. Seal one end of the regular straw with a small dab of clay.
3. Insert the small straw into the large straw (sealed end out).
4. Squeeze hard on the sides of the soda bottle.
5. What happened?
6. Explain why you think it happened.

Figure 6.17–1. Two-Liter Bottle and Straws

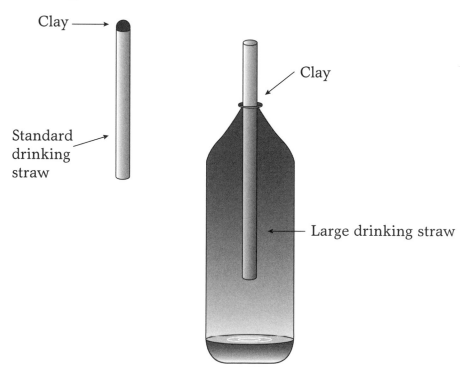

Teacher Information

This activity will be fun for all ages and will demonstrate the principle of action-reaction. It also teaches important concepts about air and what happens to air pressure when the size of the container is decreased.

Integrating

Language arts

Science Process Skills

Observing, inferring, measuring, estimating, communicating

How Do Other Forces Affect Your Rocket's Performance?

Materials Needed

- Long balloons
- Plastic drinking straws
- Monofilament line
- Masking tape

Procedure

1. Thread the monofilament line through the straw and attach it, tightly stretched, to opposite sides of your classroom.
2. Inflate a long balloon. Hold its mouth closed while using masking tape to secure it to the straw. (See Figure 6.18–1.)
3. Release the balloon. What happened?
4. Compare the performance of this balloon to that of the balloon in the paper bag in Activity 6.16. Can you think of reasons for the differences you observed?

Figure 6.18-1. Balloon on Monofilament Line

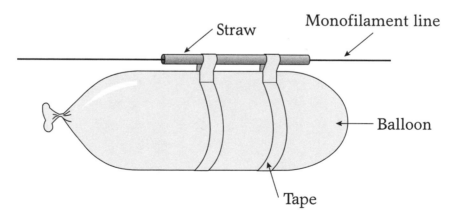

For Problem Solvers

What can you do to control the distance your balloon rocket moves along the line? Do you think the size or shape of the balloon will make a difference, or the paper bag, or how much air you put in the balloon? What about the way the system is hung on the line? Work with these and other variables that you can think of to help you control how far the rocket travels. Then mark the line with a piece of tape, showing how far you expect the rocket to go. Try it to test your prediction. Do this several times. Are you improving your skill?

Teacher Information

Without the paper bag, the balloon will move down the line at a higher rate of speed for a greater distance. Children may decide that the "weight" of the bag reduced the performance. Others may suggest that the square shape of the bag slowed it down. Some may notice that the balloon without the bag seems to get a faster start. These observations are related to the forces that are acting on the object: gravity, inertia, and friction (wind resistance). To travel into outer space, all three must be considered.

Integrating

Math

Science Process Skills

Observing, inferring, measuring, predicting, communicating, comparing and contrasting, formulating hypotheses, identifying and controlling variables, experimenting

How Does Gravity Affect Objects?

(Take home and do with family and friends.)

Materials Needed

- Objects of different sizes and weights (Ping-Pong ball, tennis ball, golf ball, marble, rock, large plastic foam ball, and so on)
- Meter stick, yardstick, or long board

Procedure

1. Place several of the objects close together on the edge of a flat table.
2. Find several classmates to be observers.
3. Use the long stick to push all the objects off the table at the same time (a rapid, even push is better than a slow, gradual one).
4. Have your observers report which object hit the floor first.
5. Try several times until you are certain of the results.
6. Find a shelf or ledge to launch the objects from a greater height. What do your observers report?

For Problem Solvers

Find some other objects to test your findings from this activity. Drop a flat sheet of paper while also dropping a marble. Do they fall at the same speed? Wad the paper up into a tight ball and try it again. Did that make any difference? Read about gravity in the encyclopedia or on the Internet. Do scientists know what causes gravity? Share your information with your teacher and with the class.

Teacher Information

If wind resistance (air friction) does not affect them, all objects fall at the same rate. Therefore, if dropped at the same instant and from the same height, they will hit the ground at the same time. The rate of fall does not depend on the size or weight of an object. This is a very difficult concept for children (and many adults) to understand. Our logic seems to say,

"Big, heavy rocks will fall faster than tiny pebbles." The story is told of Galileo's dropping large and small objects at the same time from the Leaning Tower of Pisa centuries ago. This was the principle he discovered: "Shape and mass do not affect the rate of fall."

Integrating

Math, language arts

Science Process Skills

Observing, inferring, classifying, measuring, predicting, communicating, comparing and contrasting, formulating hypotheses, identifying and controlling variables, experimenting

ACTIVITY 6.20

How Does Inertia Affect Objects?

(Teacher-supervised activity)

Materials Needed

- Plastic tumblers half full of water
- Meter sticks or yardsticks (sturdy)
- Four or five blocks 5 cm by 5 cm (2 in. by 2 in.) cut from hardened Masonite™ (or other thin slab with slick surface)

Procedure

1. Stack the square blocks on a flat, smooth surface (table). Be sure no person is close enough to be struck by the meter stick.
2. Rest your meter stick on the table behind the stack of blocks.
3. Hold the meter stick at one end and strike the bottom block with a smooth, rapid, sliding movement.
4. Repeat step 3 until no blocks are left on the table.
5. Stack the blocks again. Put a plastic tumbler half full of water on the top block.
6. Can you make the plastic tumbler with the water stand on the table without touching it or spilling any of the water?

For Problem Solvers

Find a dictionary and read the definition of the word "inertia." Using that definition, try to explain why the activity with the blocks of wood and the tumbler of water works the way it does. Why didn't the cup go flying with the block it was on? When you ride a bicycle, why does the bike continue to roll when you stop peddling? And why does the wheel skid when you try to stop quickly? What do these events have to do with inertia? What other things do you do that involve inertia? Share your ideas with your group, and together make a list of these.

Teacher Information

Be sure this investigation is done in an area where neither flying blocks nor spilled water will cause damage.

The blocks should be sanded so they are smooth to reduce friction.

As they strike the blocks, students may need to practice in developing a smooth, gliding motion with follow-through, as they would in baseball, golf, or tennis. With practice, the blocks can be removed one at a time in rapid succession. The plastic tumbler should behave as the blocks do.

Newton's law states that objects in motion remain in motion and objects at rest remain at rest unless acted upon by an outside force. If you try to stop a moving object (catch a ball) or move a stationary object (the block), its resistance to change in motion is called inertia. By using smooth blocks to reduce the friction, we can move a single block with very little disturbance to the others because the inertia of the other blocks will be greater than the friction. If you're tempted to leave the plastic tumbler empty, remember, the greater the mass, the more inertia it has. An empty tumbler is more likely to topple than a full one. Also, a short, squat tumbler will be more stable than a tall, narrow one.

Integrating

Math, language arts

Science Process Skills

Observing, inferring, predicting, communicating, comparing and contrasting

How Can You Put a Coin in a Glass Without Touching the Coin?

(Take home and do with family and friends.)

Materials Needed

- Drinking glass
- Penny
- Index card cut into a square

Procedure

1. Put the card on the top of the glass.
2. Put the coin in the middle of the card. (See Figure 6.21–1.)

Figure 6.21–1. Glass with Index Card and Coin

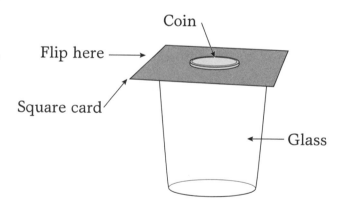

3. With your middle finger, flip the card sharply so it flies off horizontally. What happened? What can you say about this?

Teacher Information

If the card is flipped horizontally with the middle finger, the coin will fall into the glass. This demonstrates the principle of inertia. The card slips from under the coin. The inertia of the coin causes it to stay in the same place, and, having lost its support, the coin falls into the glass. Remember, one principle of inertia is that force is required to make a body at rest go into motion. When the card slips out quickly, it does not apply enough force on the coin to take the coin with it. The coin, having lost its support, is acted on by the force of gravity and drops into the glass.

You can also pull a paper out from under a glass of water if you have the paper about half off the table and pull with a sharp downward motion. Be sure the glass is dry on the bottom.

How Do Gravity and Inertia Affect Space Travel?

Materials Needed

- Short pieces of 2-inch by 2-inch lumber, about 10 cm (4 in.) long (two per person or group)
- Paper
- Pencils

Procedure

1. Stack one block on top of another. Pretend the bottom block is an automobile and the top block is the passenger. Touching the automobile part only, move it and the passenger across the table and make it crash head-on into another block. What happened? In most automobiles, there are devices designed to protect passengers in a situation like this. Can you name them? Draw the block and use arrows to show what happened.

2. Put the passenger block on top of the automobile block again. Without touching them, use a third block to crash into the rear of the stationary automobile block. What happened? Can you think of devices in most automobiles designed to protect passengers in this situation? Draw the blocks and use arrows to show what happened to the passenger.

3. Use your understanding of inertia to explain what would happen if these crashes occurred in space without safety devices. Since there is no gravity or friction in space, what would happen to the passenger? Draw the blocks and use arrows to show what happens in space.

For Problem Solvers

Consider what you have learned about gravity and inertia and apply that information to objects in space. Why does the moon continue in orbit around the earth? Why does the earth stay in orbit around the sun? Why can they shut off the engines of a space ship after it gets so far out in space and it continues traveling to the moon? And what effect does the moon have on the movement of the space ship as the ship comes nearer to it? Discuss your ideas together.

Teacher Information

This activity should help students relate inertia to familiar situations. Step 1 illustrates the importance of using seatbelts. The arrows in the first drawing should show the top block continuing forward (inertia) after the "head-on" crash and then falling to the ground (gravity). The arrows in the rear-end collision in step 2 should show the block continuing on with the passenger remaining stationary. Since the passengers cannot remain stationary in a real car, they are thrown back against the seat and, unless their heads are protected by a headrest (safety device), they receive a painful and often serious neck injury called whiplash.

In the third step, several possibilities could occur. In a head-on crash, the passenger might be thrown forward out of the automobile and, since neither gravity nor friction would stop the forward motion, continue on in a straight line forever. If a rear-end crash occurred and the passengers were not thrown out, they would be pushed against the seats with the same force as they would be on earth. If the passengers were thrown out of the automobile, the car would continue on in a straight line and the passengers would be left behind.

Integrating

Social studies

Science Process Skills

Observing, inferring, measuring, predicting, communicating, comparing and contrasting, using space-time relationships, formulating hypotheses, identifying and controlling variables

Hands-On Earth Science Activities

ACTIVITY 6.23

How Can You Compare Gravity and Inertia?

(Take home and do with family and friends.)

Materials Needed
- Two rocks of the same size
- Thin cotton thread
- Support

Procedure
1. Tie a thread around each rock and tie the thread to a support so the rocks hang freely.
2. Tie a second thread to each rock. These threads should hang freely from the rocks, as shown in Figure 6.23–1.
3. Grasp the bottom of one thread and pull down slowly.
4. What happened?
5. Now grasp the thread hanging from the second rock.
6. Pull down very sharply.
7. What happened?

Figure 6.23–1. Rocks Hanging from Threads

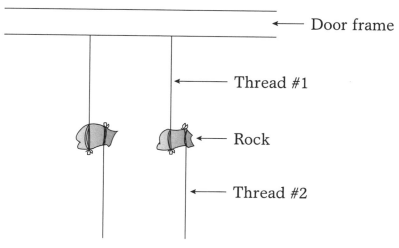

← Door frame

← Thread #1

← Rock

← Thread #2

Teacher Information

Note: The rock is suspended by one thread. Use a separate thread to hang down from the rock. The rocks need to be heavy enough to offer a substantial downward force when tied to the support.

This activity demonstrates the principle of inertia. When the thread attached to the first rock is pulled slowly, the weight (pull of gravity) on the rock will help exert pressure on the upper thread, and the thread will break above the rock. When the thread attached to the second rock is pulled sharply, the inertia of the rock (resistance to change in state of motion) will resist the sudden movement and cause the thread to break below the rock.

To control variables, the rocks and thread should be similar, or a single rock should be used for both parts of the investigation.

Hands-On Earth Science Activities

How Does Weightlessness Feel?

(Small-group activity)

Materials Needed
- Clear plastic drinking glasses
- Lightweight plastic bags
- Hard-boiled eggs
- Spring scales
- Salt
- Tablespoons
- String 20 cm (8 in.) long
- Warm water
- Paper
- Pencils

Procedure
1. Put an egg in the plastic bag.
2. Attach a 20-cm (8-in.) piece of string to the spring scale. Attach the other end to the plastic bag, being sure no air is trapped in the bag. Record the weight of the egg.
3. While it is still attached to the string and scale, lower the egg into a glass two-thirds full of warm water.
4. While the egg is submerged in the water but not touching the bottom, record its weight again.
5. Lower the egg to the bottom of the glass while it is still attached to the string and scale, but don't support its weight.
6. Add salt, one tablespoon at a time, until the egg begins to move off the bottom of the glass.
7. Predict how much the egg will weigh now. Check and record the egg's weight.
8. Compare your first and last record of the egg's weight.

9. If you have ever gone deep in the water while swimming, you may have felt like the egg. As the density of the medium (substance) in which the egg is placed increases from air, to water, to salt water, the egg will appear to weigh less. In a swimming pool, the water pressure, as you go deeper, creates the same effect by squeezing you into a slightly smaller space and thereby increasing the density of your body. Thus, at a certain depth you feel weightless. (This same thing happens to the air bubble in a Cartesian diver as you squeeze the bottle.) You may have felt this same sensation at an amusement park if you took a ride that lifted you off the seat. Astronauts are trained to move around in a weightless environment by spending time experiencing weightlessness in a deep pool. Discuss this with your teacher and other members of your class.

Teacher Information

Although weightlessness as a result of density and water pressure has different causes, the observed behavior is the same. The egg demonstration will show students that the weight of an object, as measured by a scale, is relative and can be changed in several ways. As you speed over the top to begin the second dip on a roller coaster, or similar ride, the tendency of your body to continue upward (inertia) creates the same weightless feeling for just a moment for a different reason. The pull of gravity decreases rapidly as an object moves away from the earth's surface. Astronauts experience the feeling of weightlessness as they orbit the earth or as they continue out into space.

NASA films of all space flights are available. Check with your local library or with the NASA Web site.

Integrating

Reading, language arts

Science Process Skills

Observing, inferring, measuring, predicting, communicating, comparing and contrasting, formulating hypotheses, identifying and controlling variables, experimenting

Can You Solve This Above the Earth Word Search?

Try to find the following Above the Earth terms in the grid below. They could appear in horizontal (left to right), vertical (up or down), or diagonal (upward or downward) position.

flight	lightweight	wind tunnel
soar	ailerons	rudder
elevators	fly	design
action	reaction	energy
gravity	inertia	weightless

```
F  W  L  I  R  E  A  C  T  I  O  N
L  I  G  H  T  W  E  I  G  H  T  A
I  N  L  K  J  E  L  N  H  E  F  G
G  D  N  I  D  I  E  G  E  H  N  S
H  T  O  N  A  G  V  S  S  R  E  D
T  U  I  E  F  H  A  G  O  R  G  F
Y  N  T  R  I  T  T  J  A  K  R  Y
A  N  C  T  S  L  O  D  R  F  A  G
K  E  A  I  L  E  R  O  N  S  V  H
M  L  I  A  O  S  S  K  A  D  I  B
W  E  T  D  E  S  I  G  N  Y  T  O
R  U  D  D  E  R  S  A  F  L  Y  H
```

Can You Create a New Above the Earth Word Search of Your Own?

Write your Above the Earth words in the grid below. Arrange them in the grid so they appear in horizontal (left to right), vertical (up or down), or diagonal (upward or downward) position. Fill in the blank boxes with other letters. Trade your Word Search with someone else who has created one of his or her own, and see whether you can solve the new puzzle.

_____   _____   _____

_____   _____   _____

_____   _____   _____

_____   _____   _____

Answer Key for Above the Earth Word Search

```
F  W  L  I  R  E  A  C  T  I  O  N
L  I  G  H  T  W  E  I  G  H  T  A
I  N  L  K  J  E  L  N  H  E  F  G
G  D  N  I  D  I  E  G  E  H  N  S
H  T  O  N  A  G  V  S  S  R  E  D
T  U  I  E  F  H  A  G  O  R  G  F
Y  N  T  R  I  T  T  J  A  K  R  Y
A  N  C  T  S  L  O  D  R  F  A  G
K  E  A  I  L  E  R  O  N  S  V  H
M  L  I  A  O  S  S  K  A  D  I  B
W  E  T  D  E  S  I  G  N  Y  T  O
R  U  D  D  E  R  S  A  F  L  Y  H
```

Do You Recall?

Section Six: Above the Earth

1. Why are airplane wings designed to be rounded on top and flat on the bottom?

2. If you stand on a skateboard and throw a heavy object forward, what will happen?

3. Describe an activity or an event that demonstrates the principle of action-reaction.

4. How fast do heavy objects fall compared to lighter objects?

5. Describe the effect of inertia on any object at any time.

Answer Key for Do You Recall?

Section Six: Above the Earth

Answer	Related Activities
1. This shape provides lift (Bernoulli's Principle).	6.2, 6.3
2. You will roll backward.	6.13
3. Answers will vary.	6.13–6.18
4. They fall at the same rate unless one is more air-resistant.	6.19, 6.22, 6.23, 6.24
5. Every object resists change in motion, either direction or speed.	6.20–6.23

Beyond the Earth

To the Teacher

The rapid advancement of space technology has provided an overwhelming amount of new information to astronomers in recent years. As you read this page, hundreds of satellites and controlled space vehicles are beaming messages, pictures, and other information about our neighbors in space (planets, the moon, stars). At the same time, other satellites are studying the earth and communicating new information about the weather, topography, temperature, and other features of our home planet. Astronomy and the resultant technology are on the growing edge of scientific knowledge.

Many of the numbers, distances, temperatures, and figures that we learn today will change tomorrow. If you ask students the number of planets and they say eight or ten instead of the traditional nine, think before marking them wrong. Some astronomers believe there could be planets beyond Pluto in our solar system, and some are not so sure that Pluto qualifies as a planet.

And what of intelligent life in the universe? Many astronomers believe it is just a matter of time until we are in contact. Time is related to speed, distance, and space in ways few of us can even comprehend.

In this rapidly changing field of knowledge, be wary of teaching facts as absolutes. Much information is tentative and changing.

As they begin to sense the incredible order and grandeur of the universe, your students will stand in awe and wonder. We invite you to direct the following activities toward that goal.

National Geographic (December 1969) produced exceptionally fine coverage and photographs of the first manned moon landing and exploration. Included was a small phonograph record narrated by astronaut Frank Borman, telling of the Apollo flights that led to the magnificent achievement. Neil Armstrong's first words as he stepped on the moon are recorded. This particular issue of *National Geographic* is strongly recommended, especially for students in grades 4 through 8. Through the Internet sites of NASA, *National Geographic,* and others, we can easily keep up with the latest in space exploration and technology.

The following activities are designed as discovery activities that students can usually perform quite independently. You are encouraged to provide students (usually in small groups) with the materials listed and a copy of the activity from the beginning through the "Procedure." The section titled "Teacher Information" is not intended for student use, but rather to assist you with discussion following the hands-on activity, as students share their observations. Discussion of conceptual information prior to completing the hands-on activity can interfere with the discovery process.

Regarding the Early Grades

With verbal instructions and slight modifications, many of these activities can be used with kindergarten, first-grade, and second-grade students. In some activities, steps that involve procedures that go beyond the level of the child can simply be omitted and yet offer the child an experience that plants the seed for a concept that will germinate and grow later on.

Teachers of the early grades will probably choose to bypass many of the "For Problem Solvers" sections. That's okay. These sections are provided for those who are especially motivated and want to go beyond the investigation provided by the activity outlined. Use the outlined activities, and enjoy worthwhile learning experiences together with your young students. Also consider, however, that many of the "For Problem Solvers" sections can be used appropriately with young children as group activities or as demonstrations, still giving students the advantage of an exposure to the experience, and laying groundwork for connections that will be made at a later time.

Correlation with National Standards

The following elements of the National Standards are reflected in the activities of this section.

K-4   Content Standard A: Science as Inquiry

As a result of activities in grades K-4, all students should develop

1. Abilities necessary to do scientific inquiry
2. Understanding about scientific inquiry

K-4   Content Standard D: Earth and Space Science

As a result of activities in grades K-4, all students should develop understanding of

1. Properties of earth materials
2. Objects in the sky
3. Changes in earth and sky

5-8   Content Standard A: Science as Inquiry

As a result of activities in grades 5-8, all students should develop

1. Abilities necessary to do scientific inquiry
2. Understanding about scientific inquiry

5-8   Content Standard D: Earth and Space Science

As a result of activities in grades 5-8, all students should develop understanding of

1. Structure of the earth system
2. Earth's history
3. Earth in the solar system

What Does Our Earth Look Like?

(Partners and total-group activity)

Materials Needed

- Earth globe
- Pencils
- Newsprint
- Color photographs of the earth taken from the moon

Procedure

1. Pretend you are an astronaut and have just landed on the moon. You are on the side facing the earth. Choose a partner and describe how the earth looks from your position. Record words that tell what you think you would see.

2. Examine the globe in your classroom. It is a ball-shaped map of the earth. Can you think of any ways your view from the moon might be different from your view of the globe in your classroom?

3. Your teacher has actual photographs of the earth that were taken by astronauts from the moon. Discuss with your teacher and the rest of the class ways the globe is like the photos of the earth, and ways they are different.

Teacher Information

The purpose of this activity is to introduce the globe as a fairly accurate model of the earth's surface.

In photos, clouds will often cover large portions of the earth's surface. Complete storm systems are often visible. Contrasting colors of land and water can be seen clearly. The atmosphere around the earth cannot be seen, except where clouds are present. The blue sky we see from the surface of the earth is due to scattering and absorption of different wavelengths of light as the sun's light travels through the atmosphere.

Photographs of the earth taken from space are available in encyclopedias, periodicals (especially *National Geographic*), library books, and on the Internet.

Integrating

Language arts

Science Process Skills

Observing, inferring, communicating, comparing and contrasting

ACTIVITY 7.2

How Does the Earth Move?

(Total-group activity)

Materials Needed

- Large playground ball
- Axis-mounted earth globe
- Small pieces of sticky note paper

Procedure

1. Today we are going to begin the construction of a model of the sun and some of the large objects in orbit around it. Place the playground ball on a table near the center of the room.

2. Observe the globe. Notice that it is attached to the mount at two points. These are the ends of an imaginary line running through the center of the earth, called the *axis.* We call these two points the North and South Poles.

3. Make the playground ball spin. As it spins, can you find the axis (point around which it spins)? What happens when it begins to slow down? Can you think of reasons why it slows down?

4. Spin the globe. Is its movement different from that of the ball? Explain.

5. The turning of the earth on its axis is called *rotation.* It turns completely around once every 24 hours.

6. On the globe, locate the place where you live. Put a small piece of sticky note paper on that spot.

7. Put the globe in a corner of the room and pretend you are standing on the paper trying to see the playground ball (sun) in the center of the room.

8. Slowly rotate (turn) the globe completely around. If you are standing on the globe and it is rotating, how much of the time will you be able to see the sun (playground ball)? Can you see what makes night and day where you live?

Teacher Information

The concept that the earth rotates on its axis may seem simple to the adult mind, but it is extremely important to the whole idea of movement and change in our solar system and the universe. If we rely on past experience of movement and our powers of observation, simple logic may convince us that the earth stands still and the sun moves around it. For centuries some influential philosophers and astrologers in the Western world held this belief. (See "Ptolemaic Theory" in the encyclopedia.) In the 16th century, Copernicus, Kepler, and Galileo discovered the correct principles of solar movement.

At the equator, the earth rotates at a speed of approximately 1,000 miles per hour. We do not sense any movement because everything, including our atmosphere, is moving together at a smooth pace. On the earth, we have learned to judge speed by the rush of wind, vibration, sound, abrupt changes in speed, and the rate at which we pass reference points, such as fence posts. In space, with the exception of inertia, none of the usual phenomena associated with movement are present. For this reason, astronauts traveling in orbit around the earth at over 17,000 miles an hour feel no sensation of movement. From the moon, the earth would appear to be rotating. Actually, the exact rotation time of the earth is slightly less than 24 hours. Scientists correct for this by occasionally adding one second to the official worldwide standard time kept in Greenwich, England. Many of today's clocks automatically set themselves by satellite signal, based on worldwide standard time.

The next activity develops the concepts of the earth revolving around the sun and why seasons occur.

Integrating

Language arts

Science Process Skills

Observing, inferring, communicating, comparing and contrasting, using space-time relationships, formulating hypotheses

What's the Difference Between the Rotation and the Revolution of the Earth?

(Total-group activity)

Materials Needed

- Axis-mounted earth globe
- Large playground ball
- One copy of Figure 7.3–1 for each student

Procedure

1. In addition to rotating on its axis once every 24 hours, the earth also revolves or travels around the sun, once a year ($365\frac{1}{4}$ days). Hold the globe in your hand and spin it evenly (not too fast) while you walk completely around the playground ball. You have now performed the basic movements the earth and other planets make in the solar system. It took thousands of years for people to make this basic discovery.

2. The earth is kept in the same path around the sun because of the attraction of the sun's gravity. The path an object follows as it revolves around another object is called an *orbit*. Study the drawing your teacher has given you. During a yearly trip around the sun, the earth is shown in four positions in its orbit. Notice that our planet travels in a counterclockwise direction.

3. Observe the globe and the diagram of the earth revolving around the sun. Notice that the axis upon which the earth rotates is not upright but tilted approximately 23.5 degrees. As it revolves around the sun, the north end of the earth's axis continues to point toward a relatively stationary object in the sky called the North Star.

4. The North and South American continents are shown on all four diagrams. Observe that the unchanging tilt of the earth causes the North American continent to tilt toward and away from the direct rays of the sun in its annual progress. When the continent is tipped toward the sun, the more direct rays produce more heat and cause summer. Tilting away from the direct rays causes winter. Twice a

year the angle of the rays is equal. These are the times of the *vernal equinox* (spring) and the *autumnal equinox* (autumn, or fall). The beginnings of winter and summer come at opposite points of the earth's orbit, and are called summer and winter *solstice.*

For Problem Solvers

As you do this activity, think about what causes day and night. If the earth goes around the sun once each year, why does the sun appear to go around the earth every day?

When you think you have the answer to this question, discuss your ideas with your group. Listen to their ideas and see whether you agree. As a group, present your ideas to your teacher and to the class. Demonstrate your ideas with globe models of the sun and the earth. If there are disagreements, do more research and find the right answers. Use your model to also demonstrate what causes the seasons to change.

Teacher Information

Most students will be able to understand the simple solar mechanics of rotation and revolution (steps 1 and 2).

The tilt of the earth and its effect on seasonal change requires abstract visualization and formal thinking, for which many elementary students may not be developmentally ready. The diagram may help concrete thinkers to visualize seasonal change, but many may continue to believe that the earth is closer to the sun in the summer and farther away in winter, although the opposite is true in our hemisphere.

A Note to Teachers of Young Children

The simple ideas of rotation and revolution can be developed through role playing. Have one child be the sun and stand in the center of the room. Have another be the earth and slowly walk (revolve) around the "sun" while turning around (rotating) slowly. Point out that in order to be accurate, "Earth" would need to turn around (rotate) $365\frac{1}{4}$ times each trip around the sun.

Integrating

Reading, language arts, social studies

Science Process Skills

Observing, inferring, communicating, comparing and contrasting, using space-time relationships, formulating hypotheses

Figure 7.3-1. Earth's Orbit Around the Sun

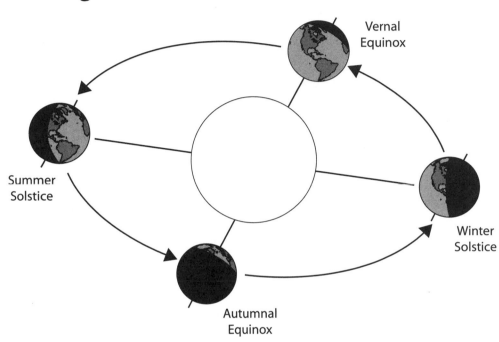

ACTIVITY 7.4

How Can We Tell Time with Soda Straws?

(Take home and do with family and friends.)

Materials Needed

- Cardboard
- Ruler
- Scissors
- Pencil or marking pen
- Five soda straws
- Clay
- Chalk
- Directional compass

Procedure

1. Using your scissors, cut the cardboard into the shape of a rectangle, about 15 cm (6 in.) long and 5 cm (2 in.) wide. Cut one end of the rectangle to a point, to make it look like an arrow.

2. Make five marks along one edge of the cardboard arrow, with equal space between them. Label these points 10:00, 11:00, 12:00, 1:00, and 2:00.

3. Now make a clay log, about 2 cm (1 in.) thick and almost as long as the arrow. Lay the clay along the other edge of the arrow so the clay does not cover the numbers. Press the clay onto the arrow, flattening it somewhat and making it stick to the arrow as seen in Figure 7.4–1. This is the base for your sundial.

Figure 7.4-1. Sundial Base

4. On a sunny day, take your sundial base outdoors and find a sunny spot on concrete or blacktop, preferably away from sidewalks in an area that isn't used a lot by people. Lay your sundial base on the ground, pointing directly west (use the compass to be sure).

5. Using your chalk, outline your sundial base on the concrete, so that you can put it in the exact same spot again later.

6. Hold one soda straw over the clay at the 10:00 position, with the soda straw pointing toward the sun. Look at the clay, not at the sun. When you can see a circle of sunlight on the clay coming through the straw, press the straw into the clay in that position. You should see no shadow from the straw. (See Figure 7.4-2.)

7. At 11:00 on the same day, place your sundial base on the ground in the exact same position as earlier. Hold the second soda straw over the clay at the 11:00 position. Place the second straw in the clay as it points to the sun, as in Figure 7.4-3. You should not see a shadow from the 11:00 straw, but you will now see a short shadow from the 10:00 straw.

Figure 7.4-2. Sundial Base with One Straw in Place

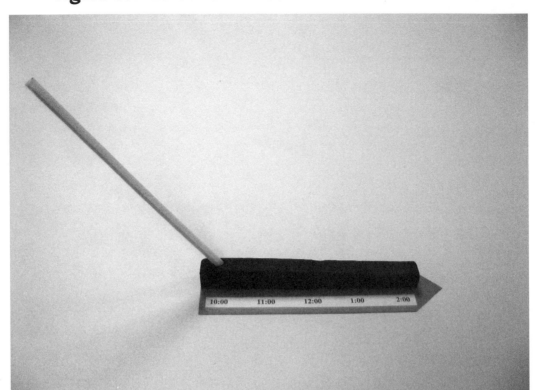

8. Repeat this process at 12:00, 1:00, and 2:00, using the other three straws. The result will look like Figure 7.4–4.

9. You now have a completed sundial, and you can use it to tell time from 10:00 to 2:00 on other days. Be sure to place your sundial in the exact same position on the ground before you read the time.

For Problem Solvers

As you use your sundial over a period of many days, you will see shadows begin to appear on one side of the straws. (Remember, the one indicating the current time had no shadow at all when you first made your sundial.) Do some research about sundials and the movement of the earth, and see if you can explain why the shadows have changed.

Use your sundial for several months, noticing the changes in the shadows of the straws. Then make another sundial using the same procedure as you used for the first one. Compare the two sundials and notice the differences in the southward leaning of the straws.

Does it really matter whether your sundial is always in the exact same spot, or does it only matter if it is pointing exactly to the west?

Hands-On Earth Science Activities

Figure 7.4-3. Sundial with Two Straws in Place

Figure 7.4-4. Completed Sundail

At what time of year do the shadows on the south side of the straws remain closest to the straws? At what time of year are they farther out on the south side of the straws? What is happening with the earth's movements to cause this to happen?

Regardless of the time of year you constructed your first soda straw sundial, make one about June 20 and one about December 20. Compare these with each other and with the first one you made.

See what you can learn about the history of sundials, the different styles that have been used, and the way people used them. Could they substitute for today's clocks?

Teacher Information

If a soda straw sundial is calibrated on the hour each hour, then the current time is the soda straw that has no shadow. If two adjacent straws each show a small shadow, the time must be somewhere between the two hours, perhaps 10:30, 12:45, or whatever.

In setting up the sundial to be used, it is important that the sundial point exactly to the west. Having an outlined spot on the ground to match up with increases the likelihood of accuracy and consistency.

In the northern hemisphere, during the month of June the sun is the most directly overhead that it will ever be, so the 12:00 straw will be standing quite straight up, with the other straws in line with it as they lean to the east or west. As the earth moves in its orbit, keeping the axis pointed toward Polaris (the North Star), the northern hemisphere tilts away from the sun and we see the sun moving farther to the south as it appears to move across the sky from east to west. The straws on your students' soda straw sundials that are constructed in December will lean noticeably toward the south.

Discuss with your students the historical applications of the sundial and how much people must have relied on them.

Integrating

Math, reading, language arts, social studies, art

Science Process Skills

Observing, inferring, classifying, measuring, predicting, communicating, comparing and contrasting, using space-time relationships, formulating hypotheses, identifying and controlling variables, experimenting, researching

What Paths Do the Earth and Similar Objects Follow?

(Individual and small-group activity)

Materials Needed

- Rubber balls attached to elastic 1 m (1 yd.) long (or paddleball toy)
- Eight- or twelve-ounce plastic foam cup per individual or group
- 45-cm by 45-cm (18-in. by 18-in.) or larger cardboard boxes for base
- 45-cm by 45-cm (18-in. by 18-in.) unlined white paper
- String 20 cm (8 in.) long
- String 60 cm (24 in.) long
- Thumbtacks or pushpins
- Sharp pencils
- Colored pencils

Procedure

1. Before the 16th century, most people in the Western world (Europe) believed the earth stood still and the sun, moon, and stars all revolved around it. Copernicus was the first man to state the idea that the sun was in the center of a system and that the earth and some other bodies revolved around it. The path of the earth around the sun was called an *orbit*. Place your paper on the cardboard box. In the center of your paper make a picture of the sun.

2. Using a thumbtack, attach one end of the 20-cm (8-in.) length of string to the center of your picture of the sun. Tie your pencil to the other end of the string.

3. Keeping the string taut at all times, use the point of your pencil to draw a circle around the sun on the paper. Draw a picture of the earth on the circle. This model is similar to the idea Copernicus had of the earth's path around the sun. A few stars, called planets (Greek word meaning "wandering star"), also moved through the sky in strange ways. Copernicus believed these "stars" were bodies similar to the earth and also moved in circles around the sun.

4. Soon after Copernicus made his ideas known, a mathematician named Johannes Kepler observed that the actual movement of the earth and other planets did not quite agree with Copernicus' theory. Using his mathematical knowledge, Kepler changed the round paths or orbits to slightly elongated orbits called *ellipses*. There are several ways you can draw an ellipse. One of the easiest is to use the mouth of a plastic foam cup. Put the cup, mouth down, on a piece of paper. With your pencil, move the point around the mouth to make a circle. Now hold the cup in its center with your thumb on one side and your fingers on the other. Gently squeeze until the mouth of the cup is no longer round. With your pencil, trace the mouth. Can you see how a circle can be elongated to form an ellipse?

5. If you have ever played with a small ball attached to a piece of elastic, you have probably accidentally or on purpose made an ellipse. Hold the end of the elastic or paddle so the ball nearly touches the floor. Slowly move your hand or the paddle around and around until the ball is moving in a circular path. Now, gradually change the motion of your hand so that the ball moves back and forth rather than in a circle. Observe the path of the ball. Describe the changes you see.

6. You can draw an ellipse over the first picture model of the sun and earth you drew on the large piece of paper (steps 2 and 3 above). Tie the ends of the 60-cm (24-in.) string together. Press two thumbtacks halfway into the paper and the cardboard box 20 cm (8 in.) apart in a line across the picture of the sun. Place the circular string loosely under the two thumbtacks. With your pencil, stretch the string taut under the thumbtacks. Keep the string taut, but allow it to make a circle. (See Figure 7.5–1.) What happened? Can you change the shape of your ellipse by moving one thumbtack? What happens if you move both thumbtacks? Kepler discovered that the planets in our solar (sun) system move in paths that are slightly elliptical. In later times, other members of our solar system, such as some comets, were found to have very elongated elliptical orbits.

Figure 7.5–1. Apparatus for Making an Elliptical Orbit

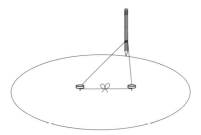

Hands-On Earth Science Activities

For Problem Solvers

Check out encyclopedias or the Internet and study about the discoveries of Copernicus, Kepler, and Galileo. Find out how they agreed or disagreed on their theories of movements within the solar system. Why were people so slow to accept the theories of these scientists? Did all scientists of the time agree with them? Looking into the sky, the sun clearly appears to go around the earth. How long do you think it would have taken you to discover that it isn't that way at all? How do you think you would have gone about the task of studying these movements hundreds of years ago? Discuss your ideas with others in your group.

Teacher Information

The theory of Copernicus, modified by Kepler and later verified by Galileo, did not electrify the scientific community in the 17th century. Galileo was convicted of heresy, partly because of his strong support of the Copernican model of the solar system. The purpose of this activity is to emphasize that objects in the solar system travel in elliptical orbits, and not round orbits, as are often pictured. You may be able to communicate this concept by using one or two, rather than all, of the activities. It is important for students to understand that orbital paths vary. The paths of the two outermost known planets, Neptune and Pluto, cross each other. Halley's Comet, which passed the earth in 1985 and 1986, is in a greatly elongated orbit that carries it beyond Pluto during its seventy-five-year journey.

Integrating

Reading, language arts, social studies

Science Process Skills

Observing, inferring, communicating, using space-time relationships, formulating hypotheses, researching

How Do Man-Made Satellites Help Us?

(Total-group activity)

Materials Needed

- Earth globe
- 1-cm ($\frac{1}{4}$-in.) ball of aluminum foil
- Bits of gummed paper
- Pencil

Procedure

1. Attach a small piece of gummed paper on the globe to mark the spot where you live and, with your pencil, make a tiny dot on the paper. If your globe is an average size, 30 to 40 cm (12 to 16 in.), you, your school, and your community could fit within the tiny dot on the paper. In fact, the dot represents the greatest portion of the earth's surface that can be seen from any given location on the earth. Can you think of ways to help you see a greater distance?

2. Since television and some other communication signals travel in a straight line, they can travel only short distances without being relayed (passed on) in some way. Hold an aluminum foil ball above the spot you marked on your globe. Have someone slowly turn the globe while you keep the foil ball directly above the mark. Notice that the foil ball is moving at a speed that matches the rotation of the earth. This is the way communication satellites work. If you were very small, standing at the marked point, would the foil ball appear to be moving? Why? Look at Figure 7.6–1. With the ball acting as a reflector, television signals could be sent to you from a great distance away, similar to the way a mirror reflects light.

3. Look at Figure 7.6–2. The orbit of this satellite is elliptical. At one point, the satellite comes very near the earth. This is called the *perigee*. The greatest distance a satellite moves away from a parent body is called the *apogee*.

Figure 7.6-1. Communication Satellites in Orbit Above the Earth

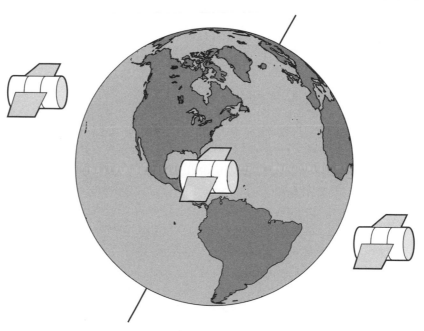

Figure 7.6-2. Satellite in Orbit Around the Earth

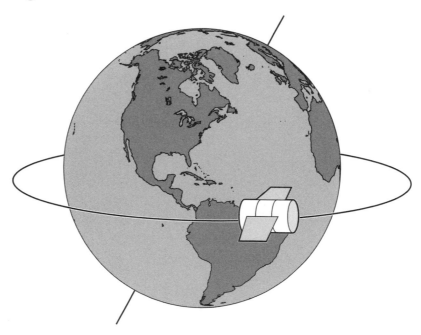

For Problem Solvers

Study about how satellites are used today. Make a list of all the ways they are used that you can find. How far above the earth are the orbits of satellites? Why are they at that altitude? Are they all the same distance from the earth's surface? Are our lives better because of satellites, or just more complicated? What do you think? Discuss your ideas with your teacher and other students.

Teacher Information

Orbits of satellites launched in space by NASA vary according to the purpose of the satellite. Some are in "stationary" orbits that are almost round and almost exactly match the speed of the earth's rotation. These communication satellites appear to "hang" stationary in the sky, and they reflect and relay television signals around the earth. Telecommunications for the entire world depend on these satellites. Some satellites are put in greatly elongated orbits in order to come very near the earth at a specific point. Satellites are also used to relay weather information, specific geographic data (including geothermal and faulting), and for military purposes.

In an elliptical orbit, the point at which a satellite is closest to its parent body is called the perigee. The point farthest from the parent body is called the apogee. There have been thousands of man-made satellites launched in orbit around the earth since 1957. Many of them are no longer useful. See the encyclopedia, the Internet, and library books for further information.

Integrating

Math, reading, language arts, social studies

Science Process Skills

Communicating, using space-time relationships, researching

Hands–On Earth Science Activities

How Is Our Moon a Natural Satellite?

(Total-group activity)

Materials Needed

- Pencils
- Paper
- One copy of the "Do You Know This About the Moon?" worksheet for each student

Procedure

1. Everyone in your class knows something about the moon. Meet in groups of four or five students. Discuss the moon and record everything your group says about the moon and what it does.

2. Come together as a whole group and take turns sharing your information about the moon. Have someone record all the information on the chalkboard.

3. Use the information on the chalkboard to answer the "Do You Know This About the Moon?" worksheet.

Teacher Information

With the exception of the earth, scientists know more about the moon than about any other object in the solar system or the universe. Your students may be familiar with many scientific facts about the moon, yet not fully understand the basic motions of the earth and the moon and their relationships to the sun. The purpose of the following activities is to establish a concept of the relationships involved as objects move in a solar system. More detailed answers to the worksheet may be found in your encyclopedia. Tides (question 9) are not developed in these activities. If students can observe or experience tides in your region of the country, see your encyclopedia or library books for specific activities and information.

Integrating

Language arts

Science Process Skills

Communicating

Do You Know This About the Moon?

1. How large is the moon compared with the earth?

_____

2. What is the average distance from the earth to the moon?

_____

3. How long does it take the moon to revolve around the earth?

_____

4. Since the moon always keeps the same side facing the earth, does it rotate on its own axis?

_____

5. What are phases of the moon?

_____

6. What causes phases of the moon?

_____

7. Why is the moon often visible in the daytime?

_____

8. What causes the shapes we call the "man in the moon"?

_____

9. How does the moon's gravity affect the earth?

_____

10. If you weigh 60 pounds on the earth, how much would you weigh on the moon?

_____

Answers to "Do You Know This About the Moon?" Worksheet

1. The moon has a diameter of about 2,150 miles, approximately one-fourth the diameter of the earth.

2. 238,900 miles

3. About 28 days

4. Yes, once for each revolution

5. Apparent changes in shape of the moon

6. Changes in the portion of the lighted side of the moon that is visible from the earth

7. The moon is visible from the earth just as much during our day as during our night. It shows up more brightly at night because of its contrast with the night sky.

8. Configurations of the moon's surface—craters, volcanic flows, and mountain ranges

9. Causes tides, possibly contributes to some earthquakes

10. About 10 pounds. The pull of the moon's gravity is roughly one-sixth that of the earth's gravity.

What Is the Appearance of the Surface of the Moon?

(Small-group, teacher-directed activity in darkened room)

Materials Needed

- One large, plastic foam ball
- Magnifying glass
- Brown poster paint
- Plastic table cover
- Lamp with exposed light bulb
- Meter stick (yardstick), large screwdriver, or similar dull objects

Procedure

1. In a darkened room, bring a plastic foam ball to within one meter of the light bulb. Use the magnifying glass to examine the surface of the plastic foam ball (globe). Under magnification, you will notice that the surface is rough and has many dents in it. Notice that the indentations cast tiny shadows. The surface of your plastic foam ball is similar to the moon's surface, except the moon has more irregularities. Scientists believe the craters or dents and mountains on the moon were caused by volcanic flows (dark color) and countless numbers of collisions with large solid objects from space, mostly meteors.

2. Carefully use the end of a meter stick, a large screwdriver, or a similar dull object to make several additional meteor "strikes" on the moon model. (Remember, most meteors will not come straight in but will strike from different angles.) Pour brown paint (representing lava) in some of the craters (do this over the plastic table cover).

3. Place your plastic foam ball near the light again. Observe it from two or three meters (yards) away. Can you see why there appears to be "a man in the moon"?

4. Discuss your ideas with your teacher and your group.

Teacher Information

The atmosphere of our earth protects us from most small meteors, usually causing them to burn up before reaching the ground. Large meteors have struck the earth in the past and will probably do so in the future. Many scientists believe that most large species of dinosaurs were killed within a short span of time by dust caused when a large meteor strike blocked the sun for several months (or years) and killed most of the vegetation upon which the dinosaurs depended for food.

Because it does not have the advantage of an atmosphere, the moon has been more heavily bombarded with meteors. Many scientists believe the moon once had a hot liquid core, but as it cooled, volcanic activity ceased and molten materials no longer flowed onto the surface. Plate tectonics also ceased, and the moon's surface has become increasingly scarred by meteor damage (estimated time: 3 to $4\frac{1}{2}$ billion years; very heavy meteor bombardment in early years, followed by massive dark lava flows before cooling).

Integrating

Math, language arts

Science Process Skills

Communicating, using space-time relationships, formulating hypotheses

How Does the Moon Give Off Light?

Materials Needed

- Earth globes
- White baseball-sized balls
- Flashlights

Procedure

1. Use a large globe of the earth.
2. Darken the room.
3. Hold the ball approximately 50 cm (20 in.) above and behind the globe.
4. Shine a flashlight on the globe and ball, as shown in Figure 7.9–1.
5. Can you find "moonlight" reflected onto the dark side of the earth globe?
6. What can you say about this?

Figure 7.9–1. Globe, Ball, and Flashlight

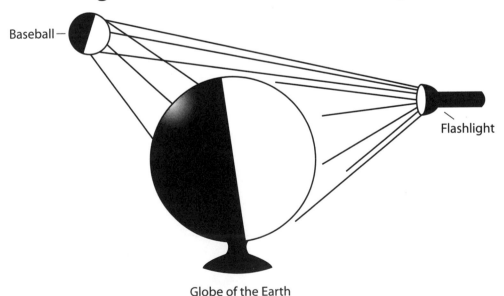

Baseball —

Flashlight

Globe of the Earth

Hands-On Earth Science Activities

Teacher Information

Some light will strike the ball and be reflected onto the dark side of the globe. This is a way of introducing the idea of night and day and moonlight. If the white ball is about one-fourth the diameter of the globe, they will be in approximately the correct size ratio to each other.

The earth is visible from distances in space for the same reason the moon is visible from the earth, because the sun's light reflects from its surface. If you were on the moon, you would see the earth go through phases, just as we see the moon go through phases, and for the same reason. And on a "full earth" night, you would find the moon's surface to be somewhat lighted by "earthlight," just as we experience moonlight during a full moon. Perhaps you have noticed that sometimes, during a crescent moon phase, a faint outline of the rest of the moon can be seen. This is because of earthlight.

Integrating

Language arts

Science Process Skills

Observing, inferring, communicating, using space-time relationships

How Does the Moon Travel Around the Earth?

(Total-group activity)

Materials Needed

- Earth globe
- Plastic foam ball with "Seen from Earth" written on one side
- Round toothpicks
- Small piece of gummed paper

Procedure

1. Locate on the globe the place where you live and put a tiny piece of gummed paper on that spot.

2. The foam ball represents our moon. The moon revolves around the earth once in approximately twenty-eight days. The same side of the moon (in this case the labeled side) always faces the earth. Have another student hold the moon and walk slowly around the earth (globe) while keeping the labeled side facing the earth.

3. Rotate the earth globe twenty-eight times while the moon goes around it once.

4. As the moon goes around the earth, pretend you are standing on the tiny piece of paper. Notice that part of the time you would not be able to see the moon.

5. From the model, you can easily see that the earth rotates and that the moon revolves around the earth. Does the moon also rotate? How can you tell?

Teacher Information

The moon rotates once each time it revolves (its period of rotation equals its period of revolution), thereby always keeping the same side facing the earth. When the model of the moon is held by a toothpick at its axis, it must be manually rotated to keep the same side facing the earth.

To give some idea of scale, the ideal-sized plastic foam ball would have approximately one-fourth the diameter of the earth globe (scale size is not essential to this activity).

Integrating

Language arts

Science Process Skills

Observing, inferring, communicating, using space-time relationships, formulating hypotheses

What Are Phases of the Moon?

(Teacher-supervised activity using pairs)

Materials Needed

- Lamp with exposed low-watt bulb (15 to 25 watts)
- Large plastic foam ball
- Meter stick or yardstick
- String 50 cm (20 in.) long
- Masking tape
- Pencil
- Paper
- Chair

Procedure

1. Tape one end of the string to the plastic foam ball and the other end to the meter stick.

2. Have your partner sit on a chair. Stand behind your partner and hold the meter stick horizontally at arm's length so the plastic foam ball is hanging in front of your partner at about his or her eye level. (See Figure 7.11–1.)

3. Slowly move the meter stick in a counterclockwise direction. Have your partner turn in the chair and observe the ball (moon) while it makes a complete circle. With room lights on, this is the way the moon would appear to you from the earth if light came from all directions or if the moon produced its own light, as the sun does.

4. Place the lamp on a chair approximately 2 meters (2 yards) behind and to the right of your partner.

5. Turn the lamp on and turn the room lights off.

6. Move the ball around with the meter stick until your partner says it appears brightest. This position should be almost directly opposite the light source.

7. Slowly move the ball one-fourth of a revolution, similar to the movement you made in step 3. Stop. Observe the ball carefully. How much is now brightly lighted? Which side(s)?

Figure 7.11-1. Partners Showing Phases of the Moon

8. Continue to move the ball slowly through one complete revolution. Stop and carefully observe at intervals of one-fourth of a revolution.

9. Trade places with your partner and perform a second revolution. Draw four circles on a sheet of paper and use your pencil to shade the circles so they resemble what you observed.

10. Try stopping between each of the original four stops and drawing four additional circles, one between each of the original four. Shade them to show what you see.

11. After everyone has completed the activity, discuss it and compare your diagrams with those of the rest of your group.

Teacher Information

Phases of the moon are difficult to portray in a realistic manner. In most schools, it is impossible to find a completely dark room where no light is reflected. The low-watt lamp will provide a soft light with less reflected glare. However, under almost all conditions, the students will be able to see the part of the ball that is in shadow. Students should understand that only the bright part of the ball represents the light the moon reflects. (If the room cannot be darkened at all, try using an overhead projector to provide the needed contrast.)

Eight named phases of the moon are shown in Figure 7.11–2.

Figure 7.11–2. Eight Phases of the Moon

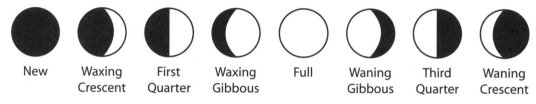

| New | Waxing Crescent | First Quarter | Waxing Gibbous | Full | Waning Gibbous | Third Quarter | Waning Crescent |

If shadows interfere as the ball representing the moon is revolved around the student sitting on the chair, elevate the ball above the shadow.

Note: Each student can experience the phases independently by inserting a tongue depressor into a plastic foam ball and using the stick as a handle. The handle keeps the hand out of the way for viewing.

Integrating

Math, language arts, social studies

Science Process Skills

Observing, inferring, communicating, comparing and contrasting, using space-time relationships, formulating hypotheses

How Can We Make a More Accurate Moon Model?

(Take home and do with family and friends.)

Materials Needed

- Hollow plastic ball
- Plastic foam ball slightly smaller than the hollow ball
- Hacksaw (*Caution:* Use with adult supervision.)
- Black permanent marking pen with wide tip
- Lamp

Procedure

1. Using the hacksaw, cut the hollow ball in half.
2. Check the other ball for fit by placing it inside one of the halves of the hollow ball. It should just nest inside.
3. Draw a line around the circumference of the foam ball.
4. On one half of the foam ball, write the words "Seen from Earth." This will be your moon model.
5. With the black marker, color the outside of one of the halves of the hollow ball. This will be your moon's shadow.
6. Nest the moon model inside the shadow.
7. Turn on the lamp. This is your sun.
8. Letting your head be the earth, hold the moon at arm's length. Turn the moon so that the words "Seen from Earth" face you, the earth. Place the shadow on the moon so it is opposite the sun.
9. Move the moon around yourself very slowly, to show the moon orbiting the earth. Be sure that the side of the moon that says "Seen from Earth" faces you all the time, and that the shadow remains opposite the sun.
10. As you turn around slowly, watching the moon, say the name of the moon's phases as it appears to progress from new moon, to crescent, first quarter, gibbous, full, gibbous, third quarter, crescent, and back to new moon.
11. Use your moon-and-shadow model to teach someone else about the moon's movements and phases.

For Problem Solvers

Carry this activity further by showing the earth's movements as the moon orbits the earth. How long does it take for the moon to travel around the earth? How long does it take for the moon to advance from new moon to new moon? Find the answers to these two questions and find out why the two answers are different and teach your friends and family. They will learn new information, and they will probably be excited about it.

Did you ever hear about a "blue moon"? How about a "harvest moon"? Although these terms are used frequently, many people don't know what they mean, or if they really mean anything at all. You could have some interesting conversations at the dinner table, or with your friends. Do you think your teacher knows what these phrases mean? Try it, and have some fun with it.

Teacher Information

A common practice is to show the moon with one dark side. This is a deceiving and confusing model, and it develops misconceptions. If you think of the light side as the side facing the earth, and the dark side as the shadow, the shadow is shown facing the sun during each new moon. Shadows can't do that. Such a model also perpetuates the misconception that the moon has a dark side. The model used in this activity allows students to keep the correct side of the moon facing the earth and the moon's shadow opposite the sun.

It takes a little longer for the moon to progress from new moon to new moon than for it to revolve 360 degrees around the earth. In the four weeks required for the moon to progress 360 degrees around the earth, the earth shifts about 30 degrees in its orbit, so the moon must go a little farther to return to the same relative position with the earth and sun.

Note: The hollow balls used in playpens of fast-food restaurants work well for this activity and can often be found at large toy stores. These can be cut with scissors or a utility knife. *Caution:* A hacksaw or utility knife must be used only by an adult.

A "blue moon" is the second full moon in a month, which is how the expression "once in a blue moon" came about because it's a very long period of time. A "harvest moon" is the full moon nearest the time of the September equinox.

Integrating

Math, language arts

Science Process Skills

Observing, inferring, measuring, communicating, comparing and contrasting, using space-time relationships, formulating hypotheses, researching

Hands-On Earth Science Activities

How Can You Safely View a Solar Eclipse?

Materials Needed

- Two index cards or pieces of heavy paper
- Straight pins

Procedure

1. Never look directly at the sun.
2. Make a pinhole in one card. Don't make the hole larger than a pinhole.
3. Stand with your back to the sun.
4. Hold the pinhole card in one hand and the other card in the other hand.
5. Let sunlight pass through the pinhole card and shine onto the other card. (See Figure 7.13–1.)
6. The tiny spot of light that you see on the lower card is more than a spot of light. It is an image of the sun. During a solar eclipse, you will see part of the spot of light blocked out as the moon passes in front of the sun.
7. Use this method to watch a solar eclipse. *Warning:* Never look directly at the sun, even with dark sunglasses. Sunglasses do not protect your eyes from damage if you look at the sun.

Figure 7.13–1. Cards in Position for Viewing a Solar Eclipse

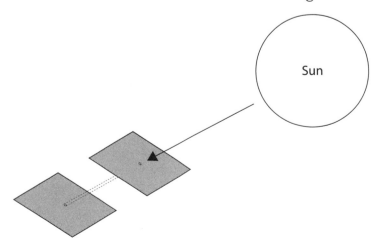

For Problem Solvers

People have not always known what causes solar eclipses and lunar eclipses, and at times throughout history these events have created a lot of fear. Do some research and find out what some of the early theories and beliefs were. Are there any superstitions about eclipses today? Share your information with others who are interested in these beliefs.

Teacher Information

Many experts claim that looking at the sun even for a moment will cause some damage to the retina, and a few seconds can cause major, permanent damage. This activity describes a way to view a solar eclipse safely. Invite students to do other things to project small spots of sunlight onto a white paper or sidewalk. If you cross the fingers of one hand with the fingers of the other hand (fingers slightly open), several eclipses can be projected onto the ground. Also, as sunlight filters through the leaves of a deciduous tree, many round spots of light are projected onto the ground. These are not just spots of light; each one is an image of the sun. Place a large sheet of white paper under the tree during a solar eclipse and you will see a mass of solar eclipses on the paper.

There are ways to safely view the solar eclipse directly; unfortunately, using sunglasses isn't one of them—not even dark sunglasses. If you have a planetarium nearby, ask them about inexpensive glasses that are designed especially for viewing solar eclipses.

Integrating

Reading, language arts, social studies

Science Process Skills

Observing, inferring, communicating, using space-time relationships, formulating hypotheses, researching

What Is a Solar System?

Materials Needed

- One copy of Figure 7.14–1 for each student
- Paper
- Pencils

Procedure

1. Look at the drawing in Figure 7.14–1. This is a picture of our sun and some of the objects that move around it. The strong gravitational attraction of the sun and the weaker pull of the smaller objects keep them in orbit around the sun.

2. Count the planets shown in the drawing. Scientists have identified nine planets and a ring of millions of solid particles called the asteroid belt that revolve around the sun.

3. On your paper write the names of the four planets closest to the sun. These are sometimes called the rocky planets because they are made of solid materials. The earth is a rocky planet.

4. Write the names of the next two planets. These are sometimes called the giant planets.

5. Write the names of the last three planets. These are often called the icy planets because they are so far from the sun their temperatures are very, very cold. Some scientists believe there are other planets even farther out in the solar system. Perhaps, as you are reading this material, another planet may be discovered!

6. Compare your information with that of others in your group. Talk about what you know about the planets and what you would like to know. Do you think you could be an astronaut someday? Would you like to be? Do others in your group have such interests?

Teacher Information

The diagram of the solar system is not presented in scale. Because of the immense contrast in size and distance, as is shown in the diagram, the orbits of most planets are on a similar plane in relation to the sun. The orbit of Pluto is at a different angle.

The force of gravity alone would pull planets into the sun and they would be consumed by it. Gravitational forces are balanced by inertia, which is the tendency of a body in motion to continue moving in the same direction and at the same speed unless some force causes it to change direction or speed (Newton's first law of motion). Without gravity, on the other hand, the planets would move out into space away from the sun. The planets are moving at tremendous speeds, with nothing to slow them down. Due to their forward motion, balanced by the gravitational attraction between them and the sun, the planets remain in orbit around the sun. The same forces are at work, of course, as moons orbit planets.

No attempt has been made to mention or name the many moons or rings in orbit around the planets. Within the past few years, the number of planets known to have rings and the number of known moons has increased. Journals, such as *National Geographic,* and Internet sites, such as NASA, are excellent sources for current information.

Integrating

Math, reading, language arts, social studies, art

Science Process Skills

Observing, inferring, measuring, estimating, communicating, comparing and contrasting, using space-time relationships

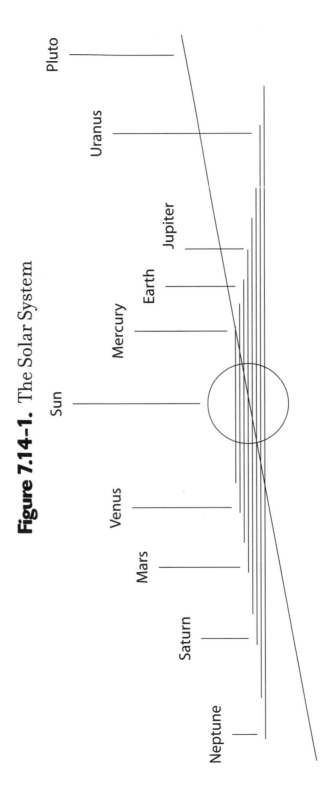

Figure 7.14-1. The Solar System

How Can You Study a Planet?

(Groups of five or six students)

Materials Needed

- Worksheets for all students
- Library books, magazines, encyclopedias, newspaper articles
- Pencils
- Paper

Procedure

1. The information we know about our solar system and other bodies in the sky is increasing rapidly. Choose a planet you would like to study and join other students to form a group.

2. Use the books and other reference materials (including the Internet) to find out as much as you can about your planet. Start your study by researching and answering the questions on the worksheet your teacher will give you.

3. Plan a way to share your findings with the rest of the class.

Teacher Information

The earth should not be included in the planets studied. Knowledge of the earth will increase, since it is used as a base or standard with which other planets are compared. Not all planets need to be studied in depth.

Major goals of the activity will be met if students gain some idea of the vast differences found among the planets and the growing and changing nature of the information we have about them. It is not recommended that students be required to memorize factual information about the solar system or the universe. Very general concepts that lead to some understanding of the awesome nature of the universe should be the goal. Current issues of science journals, *National Geographic,* and Internet sites (including NASA) are excellent sources of current information on the known planets. A vast amount of information is available from NASA and other Internet sites.

Integrating

Reading, language arts

Science Process Skills

Communicating, comparing and contrasting, researching

How Can You Study a Planet? Worksheet

1. Where did your planet get its name?

2. How was it discovered?

3. How big is it?

4. How far is it from the sun?

5. How long is a day on your planet? How long is a year?

6. What is the average temperature on your planet?

7. Do you think you could live on your planet? Why or why not?

8. Pretend you are on a spaceship flying near your planet.
   Draw a picture of what you see on a separate sheet of paper.

9. Tell why your planet is unique and not like any others.

How Large Is the Solar System?

(Group activity)

Materials Needed

- Ping-Pong balls
- Grains of sand (average size)
- Meter sticks or yardsticks

Procedure

1. The pictures and diagrams you have been using do not show the real sizes and distances in the solar system. It is difficult to construct a scale model that will fit in your classroom. First, pretend the Ping-Pong ball is the sun. Compare it with one grain of sand. If you pretend the grain of sand is the earth, the earth and sun are in approximate scale to each other. About one million Earths could fit inside the sun. More than one hundred Earths could be lined up bumper to bumper across the diameter of the sun.

2. Put the Ping-Pong ball in the center of the room. Measure $3\frac{1}{2}$ meters (almost 4 yards) from the ball and place the grain of sand at that point. The sun (represented by the Ping-Pong ball) and the earth (represented by the grain of sand) are now in approximate scale, both in size and distance.

3. Pluto in this scale model would be another grain of sand about one-fourth the size of the earth, but you would not be able to see it without a very strong telescope because it would be nearly 100 meters (about 100 yards) away from the sun (Ping-Pong ball).

4. Think of a football field. It is measured in yards. The field is 100 yards long with white lines running across it at five-yard intervals. Roughly, if you put the Ping-Pong ball (sun) on one goal line, the grain of sand representing the earth would be located near the five-yard line. Pluto, the smaller grain of sand, would be located on the far goal line 100 yards away.

Hands-On Earth Science Activities

Teacher Information

The scale measurements used in this activity are broad estimates. The differences in size and distance are almost incomprehensible for most young people and adults. Concrete activities such as this may help to give at least a tiny glimpse of the vastness of our solar system and universe.

Integrating

Math, language arts

Science Process Skills

Observing, inferring, measuring, communicating, comparing and contrasting, using space-time relationships, formulating hypotheses, identifying and controlling variables

How Can You Make a Distance Scale Solar System in Your School?

(Total-group activity)

Materials Needed

- Nine strips of oak tag 2 cm by 4 cm (1 in. by 2 in.) per small group
- Different-sized buttons and juice, soup, and soft-drink cans
- Different-colored paper (not black)
- Meter sticks or yardsticks
- Black marking pens
- Masking tape
- Balls of heavy string
- Long hallway (or auditorium)
- Yellow circles with 30-cm (12-in.) diameter

Procedure

1. Tape the yellow circle to one end of the hall (or auditorium). Label it "Sun." In this model, the sizes of the sun and planets will not be in scale.

2. Use different-sized buttons as patterns to draw circles on colored paper to represent the smaller planets: Mercury, Venus, Earth, Mars, and Pluto.

3. Use cans of different sizes as patterns for Jupiter, Saturn, Uranus, and Neptune. Remember Jupiter and Saturn are much larger than the others.

4. Write the name of a planet on each of the nine strips of oak tag.

5. Tape the planet and its name in order from the sun along the wall of the hall (or auditorium) of your school. Use your meter stick to measure the following distances from the sun:

   a. Mercury: 39 centimeters

   b. Venus: 72 centimeters

   c. Earth: 1.00 meter

   d. Mars: 1.52 meters

e. Jupiter: 5.20 meters

f. Saturn: 9.52 meters

g. Uranus: 19.60 meters

h. Neptune: 29.99 meters

i. Pluto: 39.37 meters

The distances were computed by using a measure called an astronomical unit (AU). The distance from the earth to the sun, 149,600,000 kilometers (93,000,000 miles), is one AU. For this activity, the distance of one meter has been assigned to represent one AU.

6. Your planets are now in rough-scale distance from the sun. Close your eyes and try to imagine how far they really are in space.

Teacher Information

If you use pictures of the planets drawn by the students, steps 2 and 3 should be omitted. The scales and distances used in Activities 7.16 and 7.17 are only rough estimates intended to give a feeling of comparative size and distance.

If you do not have a long hallway or auditorium, go outdoors and measure and tape the planets to a long piece of string.

Integrating

Math, language arts

Science Process Skills

Observing, inferring, measuring, communicating, using space-time relationships, formulating hypotheses, identifying and controlling variables

How Can We Learn More About the Solar System and Space?

(Enrichment activity)

Materials Needed

- A copy of the worksheet for each student
- Library books, magazines, newspaper articles, and encyclopedias
- Internet access
- Drawing paper and lined paper
- Paints, crayons, and other art supplies and media
- Photos and videos of recent space explorations

Procedure

In your classroom there are books, magazines, newspaper articles, and other materials to help you learn more about the solar system and space. Find out as much as you can about one or more of the questions on your worksheet and prepare a report for the class using your paper and art supplies.

Teacher Information

Major areas of importance not developed in this section include the effect of tides on water, land, and atmosphere; the profound effect of Jupiter's strong gravitational field; the effect of variations in the sun's atmosphere; theories as to the origin of the solar system and universe; and the probability of the existence of other solar systems—with a real possibility of some form of life beyond the earth. These topics may suggest other areas of study or discussion for motivated students.

Integrating

Reading, language arts

Science Process Skills

Communicating, using space-time relationships, formulating hypotheses, researching

Name _____   Date _____

 # How Can We Learn More? Worksheet

1. What are comets?

2. What are meteors?

3. Do meteors ever strike the earth?

4. What causes meteor showers?

5. How big is the planet Jupiter?

6. How does Jupiter affect other objects in the solar system (both now and in the past)?

7. If you had to try to live on another planet or moon in the solar system, which would you choose, and why?

8. If you wanted to become an astronaut, when, how, and where would you begin?

9. Some animals such as coyotes and wolves are known to howl during a full moon. See whether you can find stories or legends about ways the full moon is thought to affect people.

10. Choose a special interest of your own, not listed above, and make a study of it.

🪑 Can You Solve This Beyond the Earth Word Search?

Try to find the following Beyond the Earth terms in the grid below. They could appear in horizontal (left to right), vertical (up or down), or diagonal (upward or downward) position.

space	orbit	Earth
moon	sun	solar system
rotation	revolution	star
sundial	Galileo	elliptical
satellite	perigee	meteor

```
A  S  N  S  P  A  C  E  G  C  E  T
T  U  N  O  R  B  I  T  A  B  M  U
S  V  Y  L  H  R  L  E  L  Y  P  O
U  B  S  A  T  E  L  L  I  T  E  L
N  O  I  R  O  V  N  L  L  I  R  N
D  L  E  S  U  O  Y  I  E  P  I  O
I  M  F  Y  H  L  S  P  O  R  G  I
A  J  E  S  B  U  T  T  E  T  E  T
L  T  C  T  R  T  A  I  A  D  E  A
U  L  T  E  E  I  R  C  R  E  O  T
K  A  H  M  O  O  N  A  T  S  K  O
W  F  E  G  T  N  R  L  H  B  N  R
```

Name _____ Date _____

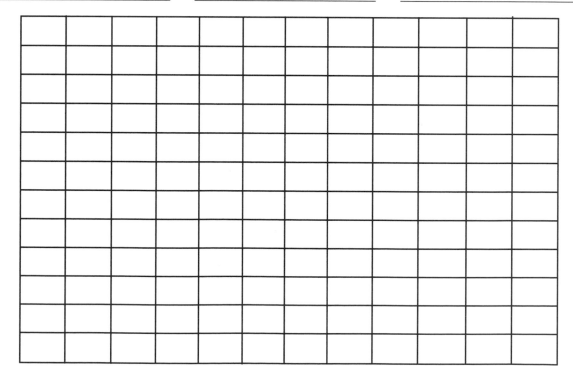

Can You Create a New Beyond the Earth Word Search of Your Own?

Write your Beyond the Earth words in the grid below. Arrange them in the grid so they appear in horizontal (left to right), vertical (up or down), or diagonal (upward or downward) position. Fill in the blank boxes with other letters. Trade your Word Search with someone else who has created one of his or her own, and see whether you can solve the new puzzle.

_____ _____ _____

_____ _____ _____

_____ _____ _____

_____ _____ _____

Answer Key for Beyond the Earth Word Search

```
A  S  N  S  P  A  C  E  G  C  E  T
T  U  N  O  R  B  I  T  A  B  M  U
S  V  Y  L  H  R  L  E  L  Y  P  O
U  B  S  A  T  E  L  L  I  T  E  L
N  O  I  R  O  V  N  L  L  I  R  N
D  L  E  S  U  O  Y  I  E  P  I  O
I  M  F  Y  H  L  S  P  O  R  G  I
A  J  E  S  B  U  T  T  E  T  E  T
L  T  C  T  R  T  A  I  A  D  E  A
U  L  T  E  E  I  R  C  R  E  O  T
K  A  H  M  O  O  N  A  T  S  K  O
W  F  E  G  T  N  R  L  H  B  N  R
```

Do You Recall?

Section Seven: Beyond the Earth

1. Describe the movement of the earth as it rotates.

2. Describe the movement of the earth as it revolves.

3. Explain why we are able to determine time of day with a sundial.

4. How have satellites increased the accuracy of weather reports and forecasts?

5. How does the moon give off light?

6. Why do we see the moon go through phases?

7. What causes a solar eclipse?

Answer Key for Do You Recall?

Section Seven: Beyond the Earth

Answer	**Related Activities**
1. Turns on its axis	7.2–7.5
2. Travels in orbit around the sun	7.2–7.5
3. The earth moves in a consistent pattern across the sky. (Wording will vary.)	7.4
4. Weather patterns across the globe can be seen. (Wording will vary.)	7.6
5. The moon only reflects light from the sun.	7.9
6. We see varying portions of the moon's lighted side, according to the relative positions of the earth, moon, and sun. (Wording will vary.)	7.10, 7.11
7. The moon passes between the earth and the sun, casting its shadow on a small part of the earth.	7.13

Hands-On Earth Science Activities

Hands-On Life Science Activities For Grades K–6, Second Edition

Marvin N. Tolman, Ed.D.

Paper/300 pages   ISBN: 0-7879-7865-5

www.josseybass.com

The perfect complement to any elementary school science program, these activity books foster discovery and enhance the development of valuable learning skills through direct experience. The updated editions include an expanded "Teacher Information" section for many of the activities, enhanced user friendliness, inquiry-based models, and cooperative learning projects for the classroom. Projects use materials easily found around the classroom or home, link activities to national science standards, and include other new material. Many of the activities could become, or give rise to, science fair projects.

The study of life science at the elementary school level is best conducted through an exploration of the following topical areas: plants and seeds, animals, growing and changing animal life cycles, animal adaptation, body systems, the five senses, and health and nutrition. This book consists of more than 150 easy-to-use, hands-on activities in the following areas of sciences:

- Living Through Adaptation
- Animals
- Growing and Changing: Animal Life Cycles
- Plants and Seeds
- Body Systems
- The Five Senses
- Health and Nutrition

Current trends encourage teachers to use an activity-based program, supplemented by the use of textbooks and many other reference materials. Activities, such as those in this series, that foster hands-on discovery and enhance the development of valuable learning skills through direct experience are key to the exploration of new subject matter and to the goal of attaining mastery.

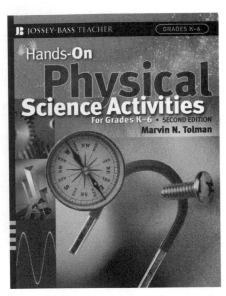

Hands-On Physical Science Activities For Grades K–6, Second Edition

Marvin N. Tolman, Ed.D.

Paper/300 pages   ISBN: 0-7879-7867-1

www.josseybass.com

The perfect complement to any elementary school science program, these activity books foster discovery and enhance the development of valuable learning skills through direct experience. The updated editions include an expanded "Teacher Information" section for many of the activities, enhanced user friendliness, inquiry-based models, and cooperative learning projects for the classroom. Projects use materials easily found around the classroom or home, link activities to national science standards, and include other new material. Many of the activities could become, or give rise to, science fair projects.

The study of physical science at the elementary school level is best conducted through an exploration of the following topical areas: the nature of matter, energy, light, sound, simple machines, magnetism, static electricity, and electromagnetism. This book consists of more than 175 easy-to-use, hands-on activities in the following areas of sciences:

- Nature of Matter
- Energy
- Light
- Sound
- Simple Machines
- Magnetism
- Static Electricity
- Current Electricity

Current trends encourage teachers to use an activity-based program, supplemented by the use of textbooks and many other reference materials. Activities, such as those in this series, that foster hands-on discovery and enhance the development of valuable learning skills through direct experience are key to the exploration of new subject matter and to the goal of attaining mastery.

Dr. Art's Guide to Science: Connecting Atoms, Galaxies, and Everything in Between

Art Sussman, Ph.D.

Cloth/250 pages   ISBN: 0-7879-8326-8

www.josseybass.com

Dr. Art's Guide to Science teaches major science ideas that are relevant to people's lives in ways that are very enjoyable. It expands the approach successfully used in his popular and award-winning previous book, *Dr. Art's Guide to Planet Earth.* As in that book, *Dr. Art's Guide to Science* uses a "systems thinking" framework to connect major ideas in the physical, life, and earth sciences. This book also helps the reader recognize, develop, and apply skills in using literacy strategies to enjoy and learn by reading science nonfiction.

Here's What's Inside:

- Why Science
- Two Plus Two Equals Hip-Hop
- What's The Matter?
- Energy And Dr. Art's 50th Anniversary Ball
- Forces Be With Us
- Putting The You In Universe
- Home Sweet Home
- Energy On Earth
- Life On Earth
- How Life Works
- The Famous E Word
- The Day The Dinosaurs Died
- Where Are We Going?

Art Sussman, Ph.D. is a science educator, and the author of the award-winning book, *Dr. Art's Guide to Planet Earth.* He presents "Dr. Art's Planet Earth Show" at education conferences and science centers nationally.

Science Essentials, Elementary Level: Lessons and Activities for Test Preparation

Mark J. Handwerker, Ph.D.

Paper/320 pages   ISBN: 0-7879-7576-1

www.josseybass.com

Science Essentials, Elementary Level gives classroom teachers and science specialists a dynamic and progressive way to meet curriculum standards and competencies. Science Essentials are also available from Jossey-Bass publishers at the middle school and high school levels.

You'll find the lessons and activities at each level actively engage students in learning about the natural and technological world in which we live by encouraging them to use their senses and intuitive abilities on the road to discovery. They were developed and tested by professional science teachers who sought to give students enjoyable learning experiences while preparing them for district and statewide proficiency exams.

For easy use, the lessons and activities at the elementary school level are printed on a big 8 1/2" x 11" lay-flat format that folds flat for photocopying of over 150 student activity sheets, and are organized into four sections:

    I.   Methods and Measurement Lessons & Activities

    II.   Physical Science Lessons & Activities

   III.   Life Science Lessons & Activities

   IV.   Earth Science Lessons & Activities

Mark J. Handwerker, Ph.D., has taught science in the Los Angeles and Temecula Valley Unified School Districts. As a mentor and instructional support teacher, he has also trained scores of new teachers in the "art" of teaching science. Dr. Handwerker is the author/editor of articles in several scientific fields and the coauthor of an earth science textbook currently in use.

Science Puzzlers!
150 Ready-to-Use Activities to Make Learning Fun, Grades 4–8

Robert G. Hoehn

Paper/255 pages   ISBN: 0-7879-6660-6

www.josseybass.com

For the upper elementary and middle school teacher, this unique resource offers 150 science puzzle activities ranging from word scrambles, word searches and categorizing, to variations on crosswords and mini-problem solvers to help you add challenge and humor to instruction while keeping lessons moving at a steady pace.

With puzzles like these, you can present science in a light-hearted manner, give a break from the daily routine, and provide an intrinsic motivator. Students feel good when they solve a puzzle.

Life Science

- The Cell • Genetics • Evolution • Plants • Invertebrates • Vertebrates
- Human Skeleton • Human Body Systems • Health and Human Diseases

Physical Science

- Energy • Sound • Light • Electricity/Magnetism • Matter • Atomic Structure
- Chemistry • Heat • Force and Motion • Potpourri

Earth Science

- Minerals • Rocks • Weathering and Erosion • Earth Features • Fossils • Meteorology
- Oceanography • Nonrenewable Energy Sources • Renewable Energy Sources

Robert G. Hoehn (B.A., San Jose State University) has taught earth science, physical science, and biology in the Roseville Joint Union High School District of California high schools since 1963 and uses wit and humor daily as an educational tool. Author of numerous publications, including *What's Up in Science* (Jossey-Bass, 2004), he counts seven National Summer Science grants from the National Science Foundation among his many accomplishments.